CHICAGO

FODOR'S TRAVEL GUIDES

are compiled, researched, and edited by an international team of travel writers, field correspondents, and editors. The series, which now almost covers the globe, was founded by Eugene Fodor in 1936.

OFFICES
New York & London

FODOR'S CHICAGO:

Editor: Andrew E. Beresky
Area Editors: Alfred S. Borcover; Shirley Rose Higgins
Illustrations: Ted Burwell; Michael Kaplan; Sandra Lang
Maps and Plans: Pictograph

FODOR'S

CHICAGO
1986

FODOR'S TRAVEL GUIDES
New York & London

The following Fodor's Guides are current; most are also available in a British
edition published by Hodder & Stoughton.

Country and Area Guides

Australia, New Zealand
& The South Pacific
Austria
Bahamas
Belgium & Luxembourg
Bermuda
Brazil
Canada
Canada's Maritime
  Provinces
Caribbean
Central America
Eastern Europe
Egypt
Europe
France
Germany
Great Britain
Greece
Holland
India, Nepal &
  Sri Lanka
Ireland
Israel
Italy
Japan
Jordan & The Holy Land
Kenya
Korea
Mexico
North Africa
People's Republic of
  China
Portugal
Scandanavia
Scotland
South America
Southeast Asia

Soviet Union
Spain
Switzerland
Turkey
Yugoslavia

City Guides

Amsterdam
Beijing, Guangzhou,
  Shanghai
Boston
Chicago
Dallas–Fort Worth
Greater Miami & The
  Gold Coast
Hong Kong
Houston
Lisbon
London
Los Angeles
Madrid
Mexico City &
  Acapulco
Munich
New Orleans
New York City
Paris
Philadelphia
Rome
San Diego
San Francisco
Stockholm, Copenhagen,
  Oslo, Helsinki &
  Reykjavik
Sydney
Tokyo
Toronto
Vienna
Washington, D.C.

U.S.A. Guides

Alaska
Arizona
California
Cape Cod
Colorado
Far West
Florida
Hawaii
New England
New Mexico
Pacific North Coast
South
Texas
U.S.A.

Budget Travel

American Cities (30)
Britain
Canada
Caribbean
Europe
France
Germany
Hawaii
Italy
Japan
London
Mexico
Spain

Fun Guides

Acapulco
Bahamas
London
Montreal
Puerto Rico
San Francisco
St. Martin/Sint Maarten
Waikiki

CONTENTS

CONTENTS

FOREWORD

Whether you want to take an architectural tour of Chicago or experience some of its famous nightlife in between business appointments, you will find practical information and useful background reading in *Fodor's Chicago*.

Chicagoans are justifiably proud of their city and *Fodor's Chicago* has been written to help you understand why. We have attempted to describe and explain the city of Chicago to you, and to help you decide what, once you're there, you want to do and where you want to go. The book is intended to be your tool for making some order out of a chaos of possibilities. We have therefore concentrated on giving you the broadest *range* of choices they city offers, and within that range to present *selections* that will be safe, solid, and of value to you. The descriptions we provide are just enough for you to make intelligent choices from among our selections, based on your own tastes and pocketbook.

The selections and comments in *Fodor's Chicago* are based on the editors' and contributors' personal experiences. We feel that our first responsibility is to inform and protect you, the reader. Errors are bound to creep into any travel guide, however. We go to press each winter, and much change can and will occur in Chicago even while we are on press and during the succeeding 12 months or so when this edition is on sale. We cannot, therefore, be responsible for the sudden closing of a restaurant, a change in a museum's days or hours, a shift of chefs (for the worse), and so forth. We sincerely welcome letters from readers on these changes, or from those whose opinions differ from ours, and we are ready to revise our entries for next year's edition when the facts warrant it.

Send your letters to the editors at **Fodor's Travel Guides, 2 Park Avenue, New York, NY 10016.** Continental readers may prefer to write to Fodor's Travel Guides, 9-10 Market Pl., London WiN 7AG, England.

FACTS AT YOUR FINGERTIPS

LANGUAGE/30

For the Business or Vacationing International Traveler

In 27 languages! A basic language course on 2 cassettes and a phrase book ... Only $14.95 ea. + shipping

Nothing flatters people more than to hear visitors try to speak their language and LANGUAGE/30, used by thousands of satisfied travelers, gets you speaking the basics quickly and easily. Each LANGUAGE/30 course offers:

- approximately 1½ hours of guided practice in greetings, asking questions and general conversation
- special section on social customs and etiquette

Order yours today. Languages available: (New) POLISH

ARABIC	GREEK	KOREAN	SERBO-CROATIAN
CHINESE	HEBREW	NORWEGIAN	SPANISH
DANISH	HINDI	PERSIAN	SWAHILI
DUTCH	INDONESIAN	POLISH	SWEDISH
FINNISH	ITALIAN	PORTUGUESE	TAGALOG
FRENCH	TURKISH	VIETNAMESE	THAI
GERMAN	JAPANESE	RUSSIAN	

To order send $14.95 per course + shipping $2.00 1st course, $1 ea. add. course. In Canada $3 1st course, $2.00 ea. add. course. NY and CA residents add state sales tax. Outside USA and Canada $14.95 (U.S.) + air mail shipping: $8 for 1st course, $5 ea. add. course. MasterCard, VISA and Am. Express card users give brand, account number (all digits), expiration date and signature.
SEND TO: FODOR'S, Dept. LC 760, 2 Park Ave., NY 10016-5677, USA.

FACTS AT YOUR FINGERTIPS

 WHEN TO GO. Guidelines once dictated by school schedules and rigidly set vacation times are no longer true in this changing world. When you go is pretty much determined by what you want to do when you get there.

City-bound types really have their choice—Chicago with its wealth of museums, entertainment, and excellent shopping possibilities is a special delight just before Christmas, when State Street stores welcome Santa with eye-opening window displays and tempting gifts. January with its bountiful discount sales offers unexpected fringe benefits. There is so much going on in the city at any time that it is up to travelers to decide whether they prefer a summer sightseeing boat trip on the lake or a winter view of that snowy shore from the comfort of a cozy rooftop dining room.

Yes, it can get brisk in this region in midwinter and Chicago has recently been buried under several newsmaking blizzards. So do bring the woolies. Tempera-

1

tures in the teens are not uncommon, but neither are those in the 30s. Weather patterns seem to be changing and there have been a number of very mild winters. Windchill factors often tend to make it all sound rather more ominous than it is. There is no disputing it can be quite raw and damp in winter, then equally humid in summer when temperatures climb into the 90s during hot spells. But there is plenty of glorious weather too and there are so many worthwhile indoor attractions that weather need not be a factor.

A word about that wind and the lake effect. Lake Michigan has a marvelous cooling effect in summer and a moderating effect in winter. Areas on the shore can be many degrees cooler in summer and many degrees warmer in winter than places farther inland. It may come as a surprise to learn that in terms of wind velocity Chicago ranks seventeenth among major American cities.

There are a few interesting stories on how Chicago got nicknamed "The Windy City," and none of them has anything to do with the weather. It seems that way back in one of those whoop-and-holler elections the city seems to prefer, one candidate generated so much hot air during the campaign that eastern papers began to label Chicago the Windy City. The term stuck and is now part of the vernacular. However, there are admittedly places downtown on a brisk day where the combination of open plazas, tall buildings, and wind currents will make you inclined to believe otherwise.

 PACKING. *What to take, what to wear.* Where you are staying and what you plan to do will determine the kind of clothes you need. Obviously a super deluxe hotel, dinner at posh restaurants, and evenings at the theater call for a dressier wardrobe than staying at a motel, frequenting museums and moderate-priced restaurants. Women may be interested to know that one sees more skirts and dresses among Chicago's fashionable set these days. Also keep in mind the city's changeable climate and always be prepared by bringing something to get through a weather emergency, whatever the season. Make a packing list for each member of the family. Then check off items as you pack them. It will save time, and reduce confusion. If you fly, remember that despite official claims to the contrary, airport security X rays do in fact damage your film in about 17 percent of the cases. Have them inspected separately or pack them in special protective bags.

All members of the family should have a sturdy pair of shoes with nonslip soles. Keep them handy in the back of the car. Carry rain gear in a separate bag in the back of the car (so no one will have to get out and hunt for it in a downpour en route).

Men will want a jacket for dining out; include a dress shirt and tie for the most formal occasions.

CLIMATE. There are almost always breezes off the Lake. This is more desirable in the summer—and remember that downtown Chicago has a beachfront—than in the winter, when gales can knock you off your feet. Below is a table of weather by month, but "rainfall" in wintertime (mid-November to mid-March) will most likely mean snow, and more snow, which is measured as melted down.

Daily Average Temperature (F)

Month	Temp	Month	Temp
January	25	July	74
February	27	August	73
March	36	September	66
April	48	October	55
May	58	November	40
June	68	December	29

TIPS FOR BRITISH VISITORS. Passports. You will need a valid passport and a U.S. Visa (which can only be put in a passport of the 10-year kind). You can obtain the visa either through your travel agent or directly from the *United States Embassy,* Visa and Immigration Department, 5 Grosvenor St., London W1 (tel. 01–499–3443).

No vaccinations are required for entry into the U.S.

Customs. If you are 21 or over, you can take into the U.S.: 200 cigarettes, 50 cigars, or 3 lbs. of tobacco; 1 U.S. quart of alcohol; duty-free gifts to a value of $100. Be careful not even to try to take in meat or meat products, seeds, plants, fruits, etc. And avoid narcotics like the plague.

Insurance. We heartily recommend that you insure yourself to cover health and motoring mishaps with *Europ Assistance,* 252 High St., Croydon CR0 1NF (tel. 01–680–1234). Their excellent service is all the more valuable when you consider the possible costs of health care in the U.S.

Air Fares. We suggest that you explore the current scene for budget flight possibilities, including *People Express* and *Virgin Atlantic Airways.* People Express in particular is worth considering as they have connecting flights from the arrival airport in New Jersey to Chicago for much less expense than regular commercial fares. Be warned, however, that these cut-rate flights are fiendishly hard to come by, so be sure to book well in advance. Check, also, on APEX and other money-saving fares, as quite frankly, only business travelers who don't have to watch the price of their tickets fly full price these days—and find themselves sitting right beside an APEX passenger!

Information. For more information on Chicago, you can contact, in **England:** *The London Convention Bureau,* 26 Grosvenor Gardens, London SW1 WOD; in **France:** *The Paris Convention Bureau,* 127 Champs Elysées, Paris 75008.

WHAT WILL IT COST? This is a crucial question and one of the most difficult to answer. Even within Chicago there are some startling price differentials. A fairly well-located family-oriented motel could be as low as $60 double, with children free. One of the older but well-maintained big name hotels pretty much in the center of things might charge you $60 a night for a single and $70 for a double. Yet just down the street, gilt-edged prestige establishments on Michigan Avenue could easily cost twice that. Breakfast in one of those posh establishments might run to $10, while the budget conscious could eat in a coffee shop around the corner for $2.50. It is not uncommon to see a coffeeshop or fast-food-chain breakfast "to go" being carried across the lobby of one of those hotels.

For the above reasons, any talk of cost can be only a broad estimate. Two people who watch their spending carefully can travel in Chicago for $110 to $125 a day (not counting gasoline or other transportation costs, but considering lodging, meals, at least one museum admission, and even an evening drink).

The budget-minded traveler can also find bargain accommodations at Bed & Breakfast establishments covered in the Practical Information section. Many colleges and universities offer inexpensive accommodations to tourists during the summer vacations (some year-round) at single room rates of $7.00 to $16.00 per night, doubles from $6.00 to $10.00 per person, with meals around $3.50. A directory of 200 such opportunities all over the U.S. is *Mort's Guide to Low-Cost Vacations and Lodgings on College Campuses, USA–Canada,* from CMG Publishing Co., P.O. Box 630, Princeton, NJ 08540 ($5.00 postpaid). Included are such surprises as Barat College in Lake Forest, Evanston's National College of Education (both just outside Chicago), and Chicago's Roosevelt College.

A word of explanation. A 2-hour sightseeing bus tour of Chicago costs $9.00 per person, a 3-hour tour costs $14.50 per person. Although many of the major museums have a $2.00 admission charge per person, they also have days when admission is free.

If you are budgeting your trip, don't forget to set aside a realistic amount for the possible rental of sports equipment, entrance fees to amusement and historical sites, etc. Allow for tolls for superhighways, extra film for cameras, and souvenirs.

After lodging, your next biggest expense will be food, and here it is possible to cut costs if you are willing to eat just one major restaurant meal a day. Lunch can vary between economical fast-food chains and some outdoor picnics as weather permits. Settling down at a park or rest area can add a more relaxing dimension to any trip and is especially good for those traveling with restless youngsters. Many travelers find it far more enjoyable to be out lunching at a picnic table surrounded by beautiful scenery than crowded into a restaurant at midday. Those so inclined will find it helpful to put together a picnic kit and be ready to enjoy the bountiful Midwest crop of melons, farm-grown tomatoes, fresh berries, and other seasonal favorites.

Typical Chicago Expenses for Two People

Room at *moderate* hotel or motel	$65 to $80
Breakfast, including tip	$10.00
Lunch at *inexpensive* restaurant, including tip	$15.00
Dinner at *moderate* restaurant, including tip	$30.00
Sightseeing bus tour	$18.00
An evening drink	6.00
Admission to museum or historic site	4
	Total $148 - $163

HOTELS AND MOTELS. *General Hints.* Don't take pot luck for lodgings. You'll waste a lot of time hunting for a place and often won't be happy with what you finally get. If you don't have reservations, begin looking early in the afternoon. If you have reservations, but expect to arrive later than 5:00 or 6:00 P.M., advise the hotel or motel in advance. Some places will not, unless advised, hold reservations after 6:00 P.M. And if you hope to get a room at the hotel's *minimum* rate, be sure to reserve ahead or arrive very early.

Hotel and motel chains. In addition to the hundreds of excellent motels and hotels throughout the country, there are also many that belong to national or regional chains. A major advantage of the chains is the ease of making reservations en route, or at one fell swoop in advance. If you are a guest at a member hotel or motel, the management will be delighted to secure you a sure booking at one of his affiliated hotels for the coming evening—at no cost to you. Chains also usually have toll-free WATS (800) lines to assist you in making reservations on your own. This, of course, saves you time, worry and money. The insistence on uniform standards of comfort, cleanliness, and amenities is more common in motel than in hotel chains. (Easy to understand when you realize that most hotel chains are formed by simply buying up older, established hotels, while most motel chains have control of their units from start to finish.) Some travelers, however, prefer independent motels and hotels because they are more likely to reflect the genuine character of the surrounding area.

Since the single biggest expense of your whole trip is lodging, you may well be discouraged and angry at the prices of some hotel and motel rooms, particularly when you know you are paying for things you neither need nor want, such as a heated swimming pool, wall-to-wall carpeting, a huge color TV set, two huge double beds for only two people, meeting rooms, a cocktail lounge, etc.

Prices in the budget chains are fairly uniform, but this is not the case in chains such as Ramada, Quality, Holiday Inn, Howard Johnson's, and TraveLodge. Their prices vary widely by location and season. Thus, in Illinois alone, two adults in one bed may pay $55.00 in a Springfield Holiday Inn and $90.00 at one in Chicago. Among the national nonbudget motel chains, the upper price range is occupied by Hilton, Marriott, and Sheraton; the middle range includes Holiday Inns, Howard Johnson, Quality Inns, and TraveLodge; and the least expensive are usually Best Western and Ramada. In the budget category, Days Inns are in Chicago.

HOTEL AND MOTEL CATEGORIES

Hotels and motels in the Fodor's guidebooks to the U.S.A. are divided into five categories (*Super Deluxe, Deluxe, Expensive, Moderate,* and *Inexpensive*), arranged by price, and taking into consideration the degree of comfort you can expect to enjoy, the amount of service you can anticipate, and the atmosphere that will surround you in the establishment of your choice.

Limitations of space make it impossible to include every establishment. We have, therefore, listed those that we recommend as the best within each price range. Our ratings are flexible and subject to change.

Senior citizens may in some cases receive special discounts on lodgings. The *Days Inn* chain offers various discounts to anyone 55 or older. *Holiday Inns* give a discount to members of the NRTA (write to National Retired Teachers Association, Membership Division, 401 Grand Ave., Ojai, CA 93023). *Howard Johnson's Motor Lodges, Marriott, Quality Inns, Ramada Inns,* and *Sheraton* have all offered varying discounts to members of the AARP, the NRTA, the National Association of Retired Persons, the Catholic Golden Age of the United Societies of U.S.A., and the Old Age Security Pensioners of Canada. However, the amounts and availability of these discounts vary, so check their latest status. *The National Council of Senior Citizens,* 925 15th St. NW, Washington, D.C. 20005, works especially to develop low-cost travel possibilities for its members.

DINING OUT. For evening dining, the best advice is to make reservations whenever possible. Most hotels have set dining hours.

Some restaurants are relatively fussy about customers' dress, particularly in the evening. For women, pants and pants suits are now almost universally acceptable. For men, the tie and jacket remains the standard, but turtleneck sweaters are becoming more and more common. Shorts are almost always frowned on for both men and women. Standards of dress are becoming progressively more relaxed, so a neatly dressed customer will usually experience no problem. If in doubt about accepted dress at a particular establishment, call ahead.

If you're traveling with children, you may want to find out if a restaurant has a children's menu and commensurate prices (many do).

When figuring the tip on your check, base it on the total charges for the meal, not on the grand total. Don't tip on tax.

RESTAURANT CATEGORIES

The restaurants mentioned in this volume that are located in large metropolitan areas are categorized by type of cuisine: French, Chinese, Armenian, etc., with restaurants of a general nature listed as American-International. Restaurants are further divided into price categories as follows: *Super Deluxe, Deluxe, Expensive, Moderate,* and *Inexpensive.* As a general rule, expect restaurants in Chicago to be higher in price than what you may be used to, although many restaurants that feature foreign cuisine are surprisingly inexpensive. We should also point out that limitations of space make it impossible to include every establishment. We have, therefore, listed those we recommend as the best within each price range.

Prices do not include alcoholic beverages, cover or table charges, tip, or extravagant house specialties.

Chains: There are now several chains of restaurants, some regional, some nationwide, that offer reliable eating at budget prices. Look for them as you travel and check local telephone directories in towns and cities where you stop. Chains that operate in the Chicago area are: *Arthur Treacher's Fish and Chips* (low prices, Tuesday-night special); *Big Mac* (sit-down restaurants along with drive-in facilities); *Bob Evans Farm Restaurants* (good dollar value); *Burger King; Holiday Inns* (many have all-you-can-eat buffets and special days; nationwide); *Long John Silver* (nautical theme, specializes in seafood); *Marc's Big Boy* (burgers, but lots of other specials); *Mr. Steak* (children's portions, Senior Citizen discounts; entire Midwest); *Pizza Hut* (try their salads, too; nationwide); *Poppin' Fresh Pies* (regular menu, noted for variety of pies); *Ponderosa Steak House* (excellent all-you-can-eat salad bar, lots of specials); *Red Barn Restaurants* (all Midwestern states); *Red Lobster Inns of America; Sambo's* (nationwide); *White Castle* (good for budget breakfast, moderate meals). Even *McDonald's,* the granddaddy of them all, is changing its image. They range from highway drive-ins to two rather posh locations on Chicago's Michigan Avenue. One is in Water Tower Place, the other on the avenue.

TIPPING. Tipping is supposed to be a personal thing, your way of expressing your appreciation of someone who has taken pleasure and pride in giving you attentive, efficient, and personal service. Because standards of personal service in the United States are highly uneven, you should, when you get genuinely good service, feel secure in rewarding it, and when you feel that the service you got was slovenly, indifferent, or surly, don't hesitate to show this by the size, or withholding, of your tip. Remember that in many places the help are paid very little and depend on tips for the better part of their income. This is supposed to give them incentive to serve you well. These days, the going rate for tipping on restaurant service is 15% on the amount before taxes or 20% if service has been exceptional. Tipping at counters is not universal, but many people leave 25¢ on anything up to $1.00 and 15% on anything over that. Even if you check in with only one bag in a top hotel, it is assumed you will give the bellboy $1.00. If you have two bags, you can still give him the $1.00. However, if you load him down with all manner of bags, hatboxes, cameras, coats, etc., you would add something extra. For one-night stays in most *hotels* and *motels,*

you leave nothing. But if you stay longer, at the end of your stay leave the maid $1.00–$1.25 per day, or $1.00 per person per week for multiple occupancy.

For the many other services you may encounter in a big hotel, figure roughly as follows: doorman, $1.00 for taxi handling, 50¢ for help with baggage; bellhop, 50¢–$1 per bag, more if you load him down with extras; parking attendant, 50¢; bartender, 15%; room service, 10–15% of that bill; laundry or valet service, 15%; pool attendant, 50¢ per day; snackbar waiter at pool, beach, or golf club, 50¢ per person for food and 15% of the beverage check; locker attendant, 50¢ per person per day, or $2.50 per week; golf caddies, $6.00–$8.50 per bag; barbers, 15%; shoeshine attendants, 25¢; hairdressers, masseurs, and masseuses, 20%; manicurists, $1.00.

Transportation: Give 15% of the taxi fare. Limousine service, 20%. Car rental agencies, nothing. Bus porters are tipped 50¢ per bag, drivers nothing. On charters and package tours, conductors and drivers usually get $5.00–$10.00 per day from the group as a whole, but be sure to ask whether this has already been figured into the package cost. On short local sighseeing runs, the driver-guide may get 50¢ per person, more if you think he has been especially helpful or personable. Airport bus drivers, nothing. Tipping at curbside checkin is unofficial, but at least $1.00 is the usual tip in Chicago. On the plane, no tipping.

Railroads suggest you leave 10–15% per meal for dining car waiters, but the steward who seats you is not tipped. Sleeping-car porters get about $1.00 per night. The 25¢ or 35¢ you pay a railway station baggage porter is not a tip but the set fee that he must hand in at the end of the day along with the ticket stubs he has used. Therefore his tip is anything you give him above that, 50¢–$1.00 per bag, depending on how heavy your luggage is.

BUSINESS HOURS AND LOCAL TIME. Illinois is on central time. Central Standard Time is six hours earlier than Greenwich Time, one hour earlier than Eastern Standard Time, and two hours later than Pacific Time.

Most businesses keep about the same hours as do those in your own community. However, you will find that some stores stay open later than the usual 5:00, 5:30 or 6:00 P.M. closing, although hours have fluctuated considerably during the recent recession when shopkeepers cut back on hours to reduce overhead. It is the custom for many shops in suburban areas to close on Wednesday afternoon during the summer.

Clocks "spring ahead" the last Sunday in April when Standard Time changes to Daylight Saving Time, and "fall back" the last Sunday in October.

HOLIDAYS. Most businesses, banks and many restaurants will be closed the following holidays (the dates are for 1986): New Year's Day, January 1; Washington's Birthday (observance), February 17; Easter Sunday, March 30; Memorial Day (observance), May 26; Independence Day, July 4; Labor Day, September 1; Thanksgiving Day, November 27; and Christmas Day, December 25.

In addition, banks and some businesses may be closed on Martin Luther King's Birthday, January 20; Lincoln's Birthday, February 12; Good Friday (from noon), March 28; Columbus Day (observance), October 14; Election Day (partially), November 4; Veterans Day, November 11.

HINTS TO HANDICAPPED TRAVELERS. One of the newest, and largest, groups to enter the travel scene is the handicapped, literally millions of people who are in fact physically able to travel and who do so enthusiastically when they know that they can move about in safety and comfort. Generally their tours parallel those of the non-handicapped traveler, but move at a more leisurely pace, and all the logistics are carefully checked out in advance. Important sources of information in this field are: 1) the book, *Access to the World: A Travel Guide for the Handicapped* by Louise Weiss, published by Chatham Square Press, Inc., 401 Broadway, New York, NY 10013. 2) the *Travel Information Center,* Moss Rehabilitation Hospital, 12th Street and Tabor Road, Philadelphia, PA 19141. 3) *Easter Seal Society for Crippled Children and Adults,* Director of Education and Information Service, 2023 West Ogden Avenue, Chicago IL 60612. And for a list of tour operators who arrange travel for the handicapped, write to: *Society for the Advancement of Travel for the Handicapped,* 26 Court Street, Brooklyn, NY 11242.

In addition, two publications that give valuable information about motels, hotels, and restaurants (rating them, telling about steps, table heights, door widths, etc.) are: *Where Turning Wheels Stop,* published by Paralyzed Veterans of America, 3636 16th Street, Washington, DC 20010, and *The Wheelchair Traveler,* by Douglass R. Annand, Ball Hill Road, Milford, NH 03055.

SECURITY. To its great embarrassment, Chicago seems to be remembered worldwide for its infamous gangsters. And so-called gangland slayings still continue to generate national news. Yes, bodies do still turn up stuffed in trunks with some regularity, but these are strictly very professional, interorganizational killings and certainly not something a tourist has to worry about. But, like most major cities, Chicago does have a crime problem and the wise traveler takes the same precautions reasonable anywhere. Except for the Magnificent Mile along Michigan Blvd., it is wise to be cautious about roaming around on foot at night. Don't stroll through parks after dark, keep your hotel door securely locked, don't carelessly leave valuables in your room, and ask at the desk about the safety of that particular neighborhood. Districts can go from ultra posh to poverty in blocks, and it's safe to walk in one direction, but not another. Use common sense in all things, particularly at night when muggers and purse snatchers lurk in even the best neighborhoods.

INTRODUCTION

The Ultimate American City

by
ALFRED S. BORCOVER

Alfred S. Borcover is travel editor of the Chicago Tribune *and a past president of the Society of American Travel Writers.*

Chicago is the heartland of America and the ultimate American city. Almost any Chicagoan will tell you that. Not because Chicagoans are chauvinistic, mind you, but just because it is so. What you see is what you get in this matter-of-fact city.

Wherever you look, from the glorious lakefront to the sprawling neighborhoods, from the soaring skyscrapers to the screeching elevated trains, you see the fabric of America and the forces that built this city

10

of 3 million that is the ultimate melting pot. Beyond it lies the all-American dream, the suburbs with another 4 million.

You name it and Chicago has it or has been an integral part of it. Architecture. The skyscraper took its form here. Atomic energy. The first sustained nuclear chain reaction was achieved here. Art. Just wander through the Art Institute of Chicago, the Museum of Contemporary Art, or view the city's collection of plaza art. Music. The Chicago Symphony is world renowned. Business. Education. Finance. Ballet. Opera. Industry. Theater. Publishing. It's all here. Chicago has given the world great writers, Nobel laureates, social reformers, and a saint, as well as a goodly share of sinners.

Chicago owes much of its greatness to its crossroads position. Jets roar in and out of Chicago's O'Hare International Airport by the minute, making it the world's busiest. On Lake Michigan, ships still carry ore to the steel mills in nearby Gary and East Chicago and imports from distant lands via the St. Lawrence Seaway to Chicago. And Chicago in turn sends machinery and grain from the Midwest to destinations around the world. As it has been for decades, Chicago also remains the nation's rail hub, not only for freight but for Amtrak passenger service to the East and West coasts and the South.

Chicago, always on the move, changes as quickly as its fickle weather. Some old buildings disappear, for example, and new ones sprout, making Chicago a collection of architectural styles. Few things stay the same, although old perceptions of the city linger. They are difficult to dispel. In 1916 Carl Sandburg succinctly captured Chicago when he wrote about "Hog Butcher for the World . . . City of the Big Shoulders." But the stockyards and the hogs are long gone. The shoulders are still big, but not in the sense of pure brawn that Chicago used to display. Later, Nelson Algren wrote "Chicago: City on the Make." The city still hustles, but in a more refined way.

Class Takes Over

Chicago acknowledges its global greatness, but it is unpretentious about it. It doesn't display the lofty airs of a New York or Paris, just a resoluteness to be Chicago and succeed with its own style, from crass to world-class.

In appearance, class wills out at Chicago's unmatched lakefront, 29 miles of verdant parkland backed by spectacular high-rise condominiums and apartments as well as the downtown skyline. Not just a stretch of green, the lakefront embraces yacht and sailboat harbors, tennis courts, a golf course, bicycle and jogging trails, beaches, picnic facilities, the Lincoln Park Zoo, even a chess pavilion. During the summer, the lakefront serves as a metropolitan resort. During the winter, the lake, white with ice floes, takes on an Arctic mood. Throughout the year Lake Michigan acts as a thermostat that can cool the lakeshore in the summer and warm it in the winter. It also adds to the air the moisture for monumental snowstorms.

Class takes other forms along Michigan Avenue's Magnificent Mile and the Loop, the city's two main commercial areas. The glamorous stretch of North Michigan Avenue between the Chicago River and Oak Street Beach is lined with such landmarks as the 100-story John Hancock Center, Water Tower Place, Olympia Centre, Tribune Tower, the Wrigley Building, and the old Water Tower, a survivor of the Great Chicago Fire of 1871. Interspersed between the new One Magnificent Mile shopping and residential tower and the river are great hotels, superb stores, fine restaurants, innovative architecture, luxury condominiums—all expressions of an elegant standard of living.

Chicago's Loop, the central downtown with a slightly less affluent shopping appeal, nevertheless is dotted with new dramatic glass and steel skyscrapers and plazas decorated with outdoor sculpture by Pablo Picasso, Marc Chagall, Alexander Calder, and Joan Miró. The modern towers include the Civic Center, the First Chicago complex, State of Illinois Building, Xerox, and the Federal Center, all guarded by the 110-story Sears Tower, tallest building in the world. Shoppers flock to State Street, that great street, now a pedestrian mall. Chicago's financial hub throbs on La Salle Street in the brokerage houses, the big banks, the Midwest Stock Exchange, and the Board of Trade.

The old steel elevated train structure that frames the five-by-seven-block Loop is anything but delicate no matter how many coats of paint it wears. Even the bridges that span the Chicago River wear their rivets like badges of honor. It's all part of the Loop's masculine environment. The plazas, however, with splashing fountains, shady trees, and seasonal flowers add human touches to a city where form usually follows function. None of this diminishes the fact that Chicago always seems to say, "I'm tough and don't forget it."

Ethnic Pockets

As if to prove the point, a mile beyond Chicago's pretty face lie declining areas and the projects such as Cabrini-Green, where the people are poor and the gangs prevail. Farther west the skyline flattens out, punctuated only by smokestacks, water tanks atop buildings, and church steeples. Tucked in between are the shot-and-a-beer neighborhoods, rows of bungalows, three-flats, and gingersnap brick homes. That view to the west seems to go on and on as the endless prairie unfolds.

As one observer described Chicago, "It's the town with a Queen Anne front and a Mary Ann back."

The neighborhoods, the city's ethnic pockets, keep changing, but you can identify many by the signs and grocery store merchandise. Chicago's hearty Midwest stock is derived from the early waves of Poles, Germans, Irish, Italians, Greeks, Scandinavians, Bohemians, Lithuanians, Ukrainians, and Czechs and joined by blacks, Hispanics, and Orientals. And thus there are several Greektowns, enclaves of Italians around the University of Illinois-Chicago Campus, Latinos in Pilsen, Scandinavians in Andersonville, Irish in Bridgeport, and blacks on the south and west sides. Even a Chinatown. Add to this the University of Chicago crowd in Hyde Park, lakefront liberals in Lincoln Park and Streeterville, and a mix of everything in New Town and Rogers Park.

While Chicagoans cling to their neighborhoods, they, along with visitors share a common playground—that marvelous lakefront with its diverse activities, athletic as well as cultural. On a summer evening, downtown Grant Park attracts tennis players, softball teams, cyclists, and joggers while the Grant Park Symphony lures its own audience to the James C. Petrillo Music Shell. On a flawless July night, 750,000 people jammed the park for a triple-header: *A Taste of Chicago* (a week-long food celebration with some 80 restaurants serving their specialties), a free concert, and spectacular fireworks set off to Tchaikovksy's "1812 Overture."

A gentle breeze off the lake drifted across the eight-lane OuterDrive and through the park's tree line, caressing the listeners fanned out from the bandshell in the vast expanse of green. Another cultural treasure, the modern wing of the Art Institute and the adjoining Goodman Theater, formed a pleasant wall across the street to the west of Grant Park. Farther west along Michigan Avenue stood a mix of grandiose architectural styles from decades ago.

The sterile 80-story Standard Oil Building and the glass facade and sloped roof of the 41-story Associates Center monopolized the view to the north, along with the 41-story Prudential Building, the city's tallest in the mid-1950s.

Evident at the concert was a mix of young picnickers, elderly groups on an outing, politicians, the stylishly affluent, and down-at-the-heels residents representing Chicago's rich ethnic mix. Every walk of Chicago life was enjoying the cultural evening and the dramatic setting, both products of a city driven by achievement.

Over 150 Years of Greatness

In 1983, Chicago celebrated its 150th birthday, a youngster as major cities go. Chicago has managed to thrive and survive on adversity from its earliest swampy days. It rebuilt with abandon and verve after the Great Chicago Fire of 1871 left most of the city in rubble. By 1893 Chicago was hosting the Columbian Exposition, a great world's fair. Today, the glorious building that houses the Museum of Science and Industry stands as a lasting reminder that Chicago did things in big ways, even then.

It was the farsightedness of city fathers that made the lake a treasure. In the late 1800s, the Chicago River carried the city's waste into Lake Michigan, polluting the water supply and creating typhoid epidemics. Engineers devised an ingenious scheme to reverse the flow of the river, which, in turn, preserved the lake for the people.

While engineers were reversing the course of the Chicago River, a remarkable feat, Chicago's architects were producing buildings that reached for and scraped the sky. William Le Baron Jenney started the style, and the greats that followed are legend—Louis Sullivan, Dankmar Adler, Frank Lloyd Wright, Ludwig Mies van der Rohe, Bertrand Goldberg, Harry Weese, Helmut Jahn, and Bruce Graham. And let's not forget Daniel Burnham, whose grand design shaped much of today's Chicago.

Over the years, Chicago also has provided the environment for Jane Addams, Carl Sandburg, Nelson Algren, Saul Bellow, Studs Turkel, and such institutions as the Art Institute, Lyric Opera, and the Chicago Symphony, oft described as the finest orchestra in the world. With equal fervor, Chicagoans support their sports teams, once perennial losers, but now contenders as baseball, basketball, football, hockey, and soccer teams have done about faces.

For several years Chicago moved tentatively toward a 1992 World's Fair, but soaring costs, dwindling civic support, and city and state politics scuttled the effort. Chicago continues to struggle to overcome its past and come to grips with its contradictions. Those who seek to make Chicago a world-class city have lost sight of the fact that it is. Politically, the city has been groping for leadership since the death in 1976 of Richard J. Daley, the mayor who ruled Chicago for 21 years. A snowstorm did in Mayor Michael Bilandic and Mayor Jane Byrne did in Mayor Jane Byrne. Today, Harold Washington, Chicago's first black mayor, still struggles to reform a classic political city that sometimes is and sometimes is not ready for reform.

A *New York Times Magazine* article summed up Chicago's extremes:

"Chicago is a blunt, quid-pro-quo, punch-in-the-nose city that could in all its tumult harbor Al Capone and Mother Cabrini, the first American saint; Eugene Debs, the Socialist, and Milton Friedman, the conservative economist; the first sustained chain reaction, which launched the nuclear age, and a nuclear-freeze advocate named Joseph Cardinal Bernadin, the city's archbishop."

The beat goes on and on in the city that some people love to hate, but most simply forgive and love. Every day in Chicago is a new chapter, a new day of drama.

EXPLORING CHICAGO

Touring that Toddlin' Town

by
MICHAEL J. CONNELLY

Michael Connelly was editor of Consumers Digest *magazine and formerly Editorial Director of Signature Publications. Among his many published articles are "Chicago, A Most American City" and "In Search of Abe Lincoln" in addition to a 32-page guide to the United States.*

Your first look at Chicago is likely to be from the window of a jet liner headed for the world's busiest airport—O'Hare International. If you fly in from the east, you'll be over water for a while—Lake Michigan. Then, off to the south, you'll suddenly see the impressive skyline of the city. If you fly in from the south or the west, you will see some

16

of the downtown area from the plane's east side. The tallest building you'll be able to spot—even at night—is Sears Tower. Other tall ones are the Standard Oil (of Indiana) building and John Hancock Center, both super-skyscrapers.

Chicago's Layout

After landing, two main areas of interest to the visitor are the Loop and the Near North Side. The Loop is roughly the area bounded by Michigan Avenue on the east, Wacker Drive on the north and west, and Congress on the south. Purists contend that the Loop's borders are smaller than that, but in practical terms, this larger area is what most Chicagoans have in mind when they refer to "the Loop."

What is designated as the Near North side is the area immediately north of the Chicago River, bounded by Lake Shore Drive on the east, North Avenue on the north, and La Salle Street on the west. This and the Loop are where most hotel visitors stay, whether they're well off or on a tight budget.

Michigan Avenue, since it takes you through sections, is a good artery to use as a guide. Beginning at Oak Street on the north (the Drake Hotel and the towering "Magnificent Mile" buildings are located here), you'll encounter these major east-west streets, successively, south to Congress: Chicago Avenue (at the Water Tower), Ohio Street (the Marriott Hotel is nearby), Wacker Drive (immediately south of the Chicago River), Randolph, Madison, Adams (the Art Institute is here), and Congress.

The major streets west of Michigan to look for are Wabash, State (State and Madison form the numerical center of the city), Rush (north of the River only), Dearborn, Clark, La Salle (in the Loop, the city's financial center), Wells, Franklin, and Wacker Drive. (Names of the presidents denote many of the east-west streets in the Loop: Washington, Madison, Monroe, Adams, Jackson, and Van Buren. Lincoln, practically a native son of Chicago, was used for a northwest street that runs on a diagonal beginning around 1800 north and extending into the suburbs.)

If you arrive by car, you're likely to see only the backside of the city along the expressways unless you drive along Lake Shore Drive. To do so, if you're driving in from the east or south, take the Indiana Tollway and Chicago Skyway, to the Indianapolis Boulevard (Route 41) exit and follow the Route 41 signs until you're on Lake Shore Drive. The Drive takes you past Jackson Park and the Museum of Science and Industry, Hyde Park, Soldier Field, the Field Museum of Natural History, John G. Shedd Aquarium, and, off to the right, Adler

Planetarium. Turn left at Balbo, just north of the Field Museum, to Michigan Avenue.

To enjoy the lakefront views from the north, take I-94 (the Illinois Tollway) to the Edens Expressway exit and the Edens to Lake Avenue via Skokie Blvd. Then drive directly east to Sheridan Road. From there, stay on Sheridan south through Wilmette and Evanston and into Chicago, where you pick up Lake Shore Drive at Hollywood Avenue, about three miles south of the Evanston-Chicago border at Howard Street. You then drive through Lincoln Park, the city's largest preserve and home of the Lincoln Park Zoo. Exit from Lake Shore Drive at North Michigan Avenue, just before the sharp left turn that takes you around the Gold Coast and into heavy traffic.

Incidentally, driving on Lake Shore Drive at twilight is one of the great joys of the city; the soft light of the setting sun casts golden beams onto the buildings that form Chicago's greatest asset—its lakefront skyline.

Lake Michigan

Lake Michigan and the city's skyline combine to make Chicago a most attractive place to visit. Photographers delight in standing a few feet north and west of Adler Planetarium to snap pictures of the view that encompasses Monroe Harbor and the skyline extending north as far as the Chicago River. From this location you can easily distinquish most of the city's major skyscrapers: Sears Tower, Standard Oil Building, and three distinctive lakefront apartment buildings: Outer Drive East, Harbor Point, and near Navy Pier, beautiful Lake Point Tower. In summer, the harbor is dotted with luxurious sailboats (in July, it's the starting point of the famous, but grueling, Chicago to Mackinac Boat Race).

Lake Michigan, as one of the Great Lakes, serves Chicago as an outlet to the Atlantic Ocean via the Saint Lawrence Seaway. Lake waters actually flow northward with Chicago at 500 feet above sea level—one of the highest points in the waterway. At one time, Navy Pier was the city's principal commerical dock, but the larger ships in transatlantic commerce required the major port developed at Lake Calumet, some 15 miles south of the Loop. This inland port also serves barge traffic, which transships grain and other local products south through a river waterway that connects Chicago with the Mississippi River.

Lakefront tours are available on the *Wendella, Mercury,* and *Sunliner* sightseeing boats, docked on the Chicago River at Michigan Avenue. The cruise usually includes a short ride downriver, past the twin "corn cob" towers of Marina City, the imposing Merchandise Mart (at one time the world's largest office building), and the backside of the Civic Opera House. During the rush hour, these boats carry commuters between Madison Avenue at the river and lower Michigan Avenue in a matter of seven minutes.

The boats also take you through the locking system immediately south of Navy Pier. These locks date from the early 1930s, when the flow of the river was reversed, draining (often-polluted) water downstream rather than into the lake.

The city's dependence on the lake for its water supply is abundantly apparent on the cruise: as you leave the locks, you see the Carter Harrison water crib, where some of the lake water enters the city's vast water-processing system. The raw lake water is piped directly to the water-filtration plant, a bit west of Navy Pier, where it is treated and then transshipped to various pumping stations, such as the old one at Chicago and Michigan.

Lake Michigan, of course, is one of the city's great attractions. Generally, the lake has a very positive effect on the climate—keeping lakeside neighborhoods, including the Loop and Near North areas, cooler in summer and warmer in winter. Best times for walking are May, June, September, and October. The very worst is January and early February, when even the lake effect can't guarantee temperatures above zero degrees Fahrenheit.

Chicago's Pulse

Chicago has a rhythm, what the French call *joi de vivre,* which you can miss completely unless you visit the city on a business day. The Loop and Magnificent Mile (North Michigan Avenue) come alive on summer business days with outpourings of al fresco music, dance, and other mini-entertainments at such locations as the First National Bank Plaza, the Daley Center (adjoining City Hall), and the plazas along Michigan Avenue north of the Chicago River. Programs vary, and it's great fun to mimic Chicagoans by eating a box lunch amid the strains of rock, jazz, or classical music—all free.

The city is far more than the relatively small Loop and Near North sections. Chicago has evolved over the years from a series of neighborhoods that at one time were mostly little towns on their own. As the city grew, from the 1880s on, it gradually took over any number of villages and towns to become what it is today—a major, still highly industrial community of some 3,005,000 residents surrounded by a conglomeration of suburbs in Illinois and northwestern Indiana (encompassing an additional 3.5 million residents). Countless thousands of the suburbanites commute to the city by car and train.

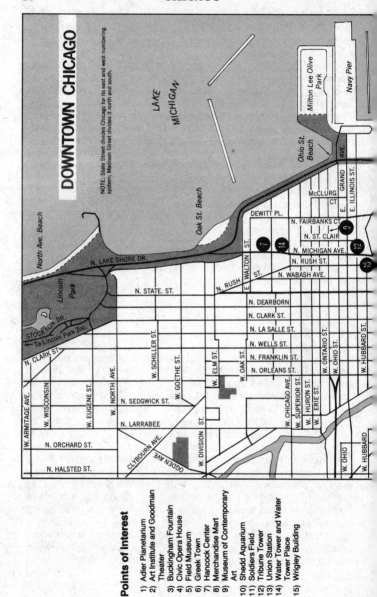

DOWNTOWN CHICAGO

NOTE: State Street divides Chicago for its east and west numbering system. Madison Street divides it north and south.

Points of Interest

1) Adler Planetarium
2) Art Institute and Goodman Theater
3) Buckingham Fountain
4) Civic Opera House
5) Field Museum
6) Greek Town
7) Hancock Center
8) Merchandise Mart
9) Museum of Contemporary Art
10) Shedd Aquarium
11) Soldiers Field
12) Tribune Tower
13) Union Station
14) Water Tower and Water Tower Place
15) Wrigley Building

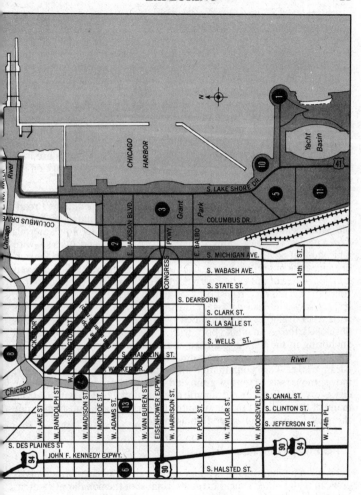

Chicago is one of the nation's major financial centers, with its own stock exchange, several commodities exchanges, a Federal Reserve bank, and two of the nation's leading banks, the Continental and First National Bank of Chicago. The city has long been a center of graphics and printing; scores of popular magazines—including the *New Yorker* —are printed here, as are three of the nation's major mail-order catalogs: Sears, Montgomery Ward, and Spiegel.

Steel was once the foundation of the industrial belt that borders the city's South Side, but some major plants have closed, causing major unemployment problems in that area. Chicago no longer claims the title, "Hog Butcher for the World," coined by poet Carl Sandburg, once a newspaper reporter here. The old (smelly) stockyards are long gone, leaving in their wake a budding, high-tech industrial park on the South Side.

Being a steel center and centrally located, Chicago at one time was the nation's largest railroad center. It was here that the famous Broadway Limited, linking Chicago with Manhattan, terminated, as did the old Santa Fe Super Chief, running its way from Chicago to glamorous Los Angeles. Amtrak trains still link these cities—and others—with Chicago, but air travel, via O'Hare International Airport, has far outdistanced the old railroad passenger trains. The city remains, however, a major center of rail cargo, with Santa Fe still a major operator of rail transport here. Truck transportation is also important. The Dan Ryan Expressway, the leading artery on the South Side, nearly overflows with truck traffic every day, much of it interstate. And Chicago has developed, too, as an inland port, with ships from throughout the world anchoring in the Port of Chicago at Lake Calumet, especially during the summer months when the Saint Lawrence Seaway route is open to ocean traffic. This combination of water, rail, and truck transport moves thousands of tons of grain and industrial products through the city every year. There's a dramatic alignment of Chicago with Detroit; many of the products that go into the modern car are built in machine shops of Chicago and other Illinois cities.

Planning Your Tour

Develop a plan to cover as many of the city's diverse attractions as you can with limited time. Fortunately, most of the popular attractions are within walking distance of each other—or at least a short bus or cab ride. Some more distant ones, though, like the Museum of Science and Industry, require some planning. Most visitors begin with the Art Institute of Chicago. It's centrally located, at Adams and Michigan, and you can see the highlights of the permanent and temporary exhibits in a matter of two or three hours.

Then move on to the three Grant Park museums: Field Museum of Natural History, John G. Shedd Aquarium, and the Adler Planetarium, all within walking distance of each other. If you really like to walk, you can trek from the Art Institute through Grant Park directly to the museums, stopping at Buckingham Fountain for a pleasant rest along the way.

On a business day, you may prefer to head directly into the Loop for a peek at Chicago at work. The important places here would be State Street, the observation deck of the Sears Tower for a great overview, the Chicago Board of Trade at Jackson and La Salle, the Rookery on La Salle, the Federal Plaza at Adams and Dearborn, First National Bank Plaza at Dearborn and Monroe, and Daley Plaza—site of the famed Picasso sculpture—at Dearborn and Washington. Be sure to allow time for Michigan Avenue and the "Magnificent Mile," highlighted by Water Tower Place, one of the nation's great vertical shopping centers. These are but a few of the highlights that you should see in a brief visit to the city by the lake.

One thing you'll notice immediately—just in case you had any fears —is that Chicago is not overrun by gangsters and thugs. The Loop and Near North areas, especially, are made up primarily of office workers, well-tailored business executives, city workers, police officers (some on horseback), and an occasional "blue collar" construction worker engaged in building another skyscraper. When asked what they enjoy most about Chicago, visitors from abroad usually say, "The people; they're so friendly." And, generally, that's true. If you have a question or need directions, don't hesitate to stop a total stranger on the street and ask; you may get a long-winded answer, but an answer—and a friendly one—you will receive.

Like other cities, Chicago has a certain rhythm. Traffic during rush hours can be excruciating, so you're advised to avoid driving between 7:30 and 9 A.M. and 4:30 and 6 P.M. on any business day. Rain or snow can stifle traffic too, and for some reason, Fridays in the Loop are always up for grabs, as merchants make their last-minute deposits and many office workers get ready for the weekend. Otherwise, though, traffic moves comfortably, and the pace of pedestrians is relatively slow and easygoing. On a weekend, you practically have the Loop off State Street to yourself.

When you're in Chicago on a Sunday or holiday, take advantage of the CTA (Chicago Transit Authority) super transfer. For $1.40 you can ride on any bus or El train throughout the city. Another 60 cents puts you on the Culture buses, which serve the city's museums and other attractions during the summer from approximately 11:00 A.M. to 5:15 P.M. The Culture bus routes are labeled North, South, and West, and they do get visitors around to the city's major attractions. For

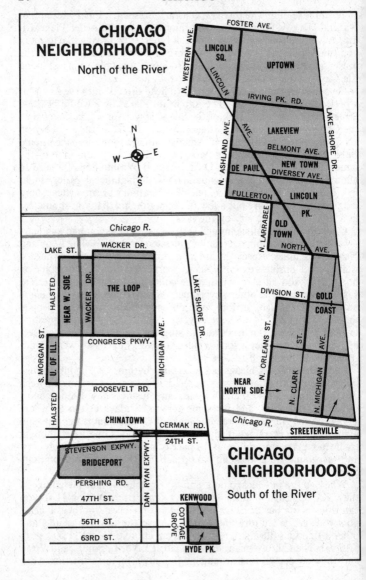

Chicago Neighborhoods

North of the River

Streeterville, built mostly on landfill, now houses everything from TV stations to great hotels and exclusive condominium apartments. Also located here are the medical-professional campus of Northwestern University and the extremely popular Water Tower Place.

Near North is Chicago's renaissance area, gradually undergoing renewal with numerous art galleries at Erie and Wells welcoming visitors. By day the area bustles with office workers. Rush and Division Streets (east of Clark) are focal points of nightlife for singles and conventioneers. North Michigan Avenue is best known as the Magnificient Mile because of its concentration of exclusive stores, hotels, and galleries catering to a classy clientele.

Gold Coast is a three-block-wide strip of high-rise buildings that commands some of the steepest rents and best lake views in the city. The area includes the Astor Street Historic District featuring some great old homes.

Old Town, actually Wells Street north to Lincoln Avenue, is undergoing a revival as a nightlife center—although most Chicagoans prefer New Town. Some good shops are here for daytime browsing and area restaurants are competitive in this city where dining is considered one of life's greatest pleasures. Side streets north of North Avenue and west of Wells are remarkable for daytime walking tours of restored 19th-century homes.

Lincoln Park is old Chicago at its finest, featuring fine old buildings. The strip along the park itself is particularly beautiful.

De Paul area west of Lincoln Park is quiet and neighborly. Renovations during the 1970s and 1980s have improved the small older homes on these tree-lined streets.

New Town, primarily Broadway and Clark Street north of Diversey to Belmont, features antique shops, informal bars, and—some say—an occasional Off-Loop theater. Young Chicagoans love this area—especially its nightlife.

Lakeview is home to Wrigley Field where the Chicago Cubs play. The Belmont-Lincoln Avenue shopping area still retains vestiges of old German-American shops and restaurants.

Uptown remains one of Chicago's poorest neighborhoods although it remains hidden behind a façade of lakefront high-rises. It houses a pocket of subsistence level residents—Appalachians, Indians, and Hispanics, primarily, and there is little here for tourists.

South of the River

Jackson Park, Hyde Park, and **Kenwood** are often referred to as the South Side. This whole area is dominated by the Museum of Science and Industry in Jackson Park—one of the city's leading attractions—and the University of Chicago in Hyde Park. Visits to this area are recommended for daytime only.

Bridgeport was home to the late Mayor Richard J. Daley and remains a bastion of Chicago's old-style machine politics based on ethnic interests. The area once housed the Union Stockyards but remains a holdout of Polish, Irish, Lithuanian, and other ethnic groups. Comiskey Park—where the Chicago White Sox play ball—is located here.

The University of Illinois is a combination of low- and high-rise architecture in which many classroom buildings are interconnected by overhead walkways. It is located just south of what was once Chicago's Greek Town.

Near West Side is best-known for good restaurants in Greek Town.

Chinatown is a four-block area with an Asian accent. Replete with fine restaurants and interesting shops.

The Loop is extremely lively any business day and is the city's financial heart—as well as its government center. The shopping areas along State Street and Wabash Avenue are fun on Saturday, as well as on weekdays. Theaters are scattered throughout the city and nightlife has shifted north of Chicago River—so consider the Loop as primarily a daytime attraction.

instance, if you take the South Culture Bus, you can visit most of the major museums in a day's time: Field Museum, Shedd Aquarium, Adler Planetarium, and in Jackson Park (58th and Lake Shore Drive), the Museum of Science and Industry. Buses operate between the Art Institute and these points at approximately half-hour intervals. The West Culture Bus takes you (from the Art Institute) by the Sears Tower, Merchandise Mart, and into some older, ethnic neighborhoods, while the North route spans Michigan Avenue, Old Town, Lincoln Park, Navy Pier, and Grant Park.

On a weekday, you can easily ride CTA transportation too. Just dial the CTA information number, 836–7000, and ask for the route number of the bus or El that will take take you to your destination.

Commuter trains are also available. The old Illinois Central electric trains that depart from below Randolph at Michigan can take you to most South-side destinations such as Hyde Park and the Museum of Science and Industry. Commuter trains from Union Station, at Adams and Canal (just west of the Chicago River) serve the western suburbs and many northern ones, while the Chicago and North Western line will take you directly to Arlington Park Racetrack northwest of the city. All of the commuter trains are now operated by the RTA (Regional Transportation Authority).

Taxis in Chicago are costly. Figure on spending at least $15 or $20 (depending on traffic flow) for a one-way fare from the Loop to O'Hare International Airport. Rides of any distance at all within the city generally cost from $3 to $8 and up, plus tip. When you're in the Loop or Near North areas, don't bother to phone for a cab: just hail one that's passing along the street, or pick one up at your hotel. Limousine services are also available (inquire at your hotel), and if you stay at the Ritz Carlton, you can engage that hotel's Rolls Royce to arrive at your destination in the grand style.

Touring the Loop

There are few places better than the Art Institute of Chicago at Adams and Michigan Avenue to begin a walking tour of the city. The building is one of the few ever allowed to be erected in Grant Park. With recent additions, it now occupies almost two full city blocks, from Monroe Street on the north to Jackson Boulevard on the south. Among its most distinguished paintings are Rembrandt's *Young Girl at an Open Half-door,* Renoir's *On the Terrace,* Grant Wood's *American Gothic,* the famous painting of a somber farm father and daughter with pitchfork, and Seurat's *Sunday Afternoon on the Island of La Grande Jatte.*

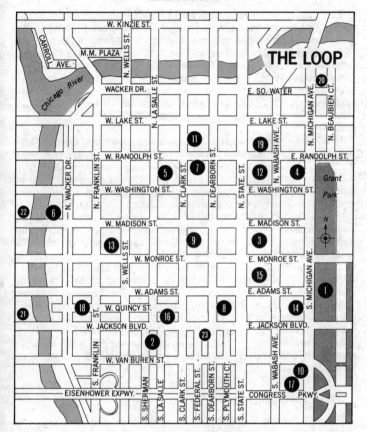

Points of Interest

1) Art Institute
2) Board of Trade
3) Carson Pine Scott and Co
4) Chicago Public Library Cultural Center
5) City Hall—Cook County Building
6) Civic Opera
7) Daley Plaza
8) Federal Plaza
9) First Nat'l Bank Plaza
10) Fine Arts Bldg.
11) Greyhound Stn.
12) Marshall Field's
13) Chicago Mercantile Exchange
14) Orchestra Hall
15) Palmer House Hotel
16) Rookery and Continental Illinois Nat'l Bank
17) Roosevelt University
18) Sears Tower
19) Trailways Stn.
20) Illinois Center
21) Union Station
22) Northwestern Station (RTA)
23) ArchiCenter

These and countless other art works from the nineteenth and twentieth centuries have been accumulating in Chicago since 1871, when the great Chicago Fire wiped out the old Chicago Academy of Design. The replacement Chicago Academy of Fine Arts, incorporated in 1878, was renamed the Art Institute of Chicago in 1892, when the main building you see today at Michigan and Adams was occupied. The last major addition, extending the structure eastward to Columbus Drive, was completed in 1977. The institute is one of the nation's leading art schools, with annual enrollment of some 1,800 students, many from abroad.

In addition to the galleries of French Impressionists, Oriental artworks, and the stunning Chicago Stock Exchange Room (salvaged when the old Chicago Stock Exchange building was demolished), the Art Institute contains the renowned collection of miniature Thorne Rooms, a fine children's museum, an excellent gift shop, a film center, and a lovely courtyard for summertime dining.

Orchestra Hall, at 220 South Michigan, diagonally across Michigan Avenue from the Art Institute, is diminutive only in size. Within its walls you can hear great music, with the Chicago Symphony Orchestra reaching extraordinary heights under the baton of music director Sir Georg Solti. From September through May, you can count on some musical event at Orchestra Hall, with seating at Friday afternoon matinees of the Symphony usually available. The Sunday afternoon Allied Arts Series, featuring solo performances by world-famous musicians and singers, is highly popular. Orchestra Hall, itself, has been carefully restored to its original 1904 Georgian design. Intermission cocktails are available in the elegant second-floor ballroom. Call the theater or check local newspapers for program information and schedules.

South Michigan Avenue

From Orchestra Hall walk south to the Fine Arts Building, 410 South Michigan, one of those vestiges from the past that is a true cultural find. You can have a fine violin repaired (or purchase one) on the tenth floor, or find a comparable quality woodwind on the seventh. The building, itself, is an official city landmark dating from the nineteenth century. It was built for a carriage business in the 1880s, and converted to the Chicago equivalent of Carnegie Hall in 1898. The Romanesque entrance displays the motto: "All passes—ART alone endures." Inside is an ornate marble-and-wood interior that has witnessed much of the city's cultural history. The Fine Arts Theaters now feature a wide variety of films, including foreign films and documentaries. Frank Lloyd Wright had offices here, as did sculptor Lorado Taft, whose works abound in Washington Park on the city's South Side. Other early tenants were Harriet Monroe's *Poetry* magazine (which introduced such writers as Carl Sandburg, T. S. Eliot, and Ezra Pound) and *The Dial* and *Saturday Evening Post.*

Just south Roosevelt University and the Auditorium Theater, at the corner of Michigan and Congress, are both housed in one of Chicago's architectural jewels. Designed by Dankmar Adler and Louis Sullivan in 1889, the structure was originally a grand hotel and theater. The entrance to Roosevelt University still showcases the splendor of the old hotel's lobby. Even more outstanding is the fully restored Auditorium Theater, with entrance around the corner on Congress. The golden, turn-of-the-century lights cast a warm glow over the theater lobby and interior. It was, at the time it opened, one of the largest and most acoustically perfect indoor theaters of its kind, and even today you can practically hear a pin drop on stage from the upper reaches of the top balcony. Virtually every one of the 4000 seats in theater has an unobstructed view of the stage. Call the theater or check the local listings if you want to see any of its fine concerts or dance programs. Tours are also available.

State Street That Great Street

Walk west along Congress Street, and you'll come to State Street. State Street is undergoing change, due, no doubt, in part to the overwhelming developments across the river along North Michigan Avenue. While the latter has seen the rise of Water Tower Place and other great centers of shopping, hotels, and modern condominium apartments, State Street has actually gone downhill to some extent. The Sears Roebuck store, a mainstay at the south end of State, has closed, as has the great old Goldblatts store (soon to become a permanent site of the main Chicago Public Library).

Still, at least two of State's great buildings survive and prosper. One, Marshall Field's Department Store, occupies the entire block bounded by State, Washington, Wabash, and Randolph. Starting from the day after Thanksgiving through late December, children still ogle some of the city's finest holiday decorations displayed in the store windows— usually themed and highly animated. Inside, at Christmastime, the store takes on a Dickens-like aura—its high, magnificent ceilings reflecting the glitter of thousands of baubles dangling from huge trees, as a department store Santa hears endless requests for those expensive toys advertised on TV. The store at any time of year maintains some 450 separate departments, ranging from fine furs to a bargain basement with direct access to the north-south Howard-Jackson subway of the CTA.

A block south of Field's at Madison you encounter the great and grand Carson Pirie Scott & Co., housed since 1904 in a Louis Sullivan-designed building, which is now both a city and national landmark. Windows and a grand rotunda here are accented by Sullivan's iron ornamentation (good photo possibilities). The store, itself, has more of an international flair than does Field's. Here you're likely to find the latest in fashion from France and Italy, as well as unusual pieces of furniture and gourmet cooking items from Scandinavia. A favorite stop in the store is the east-wing site of what used to be the Men's Grill and is now a large, wood-paneled room where the luncheon buffet is a true bargain.

You can continue to amble north at will along the relatively new State Street Mall. It is not completely closed to traffic, so be wary of buses and police patrol cars. If you're ready for a night of theater, look for the Hot Tix Booth on the west side of State. Or, if you feel like stopping a while, another grand luncheon spot, the Berghoff, is just west of State on Adams. This nineteenth-century-style German restaurant and stand-up bar has scrumptious food and great beers, served from lunchtime through the moderately early dinner hour. No reservations, though, so be prepared to wait a bit. The room at the east end of the restaurant is extremely popular among Chicagoans because of its great steins of rich German beer and made-on-the-spot sandwiches of beef, corned beef, thuringer, cheese, and ham. The place is strictly stand-up—nary a stool to be seen.

State and Wabash

In many ways the area of Wabash Avenue (parallel to State one block east) between Congress and Wacker is as good for shopping as is State Street. Field's and Carson's both have entrances off Wabash, but the street is known for smaller, one-of-a-kind stores. Rose Records, at 214 South Wabash, houses a great and comfortably priced collection of records and tapes. You'll also find the city's main Kroch's and Brentano's Bookstore here, a great place for browsing through racks of best sellers, paperbacks (in the basement), and beguiling gifts and magazines.

The old Field's Men's Store at Wabash and Washington has been absorbed into the main building, but Wabash still features two major men's clothiers: Brooks Brothers, just east of Wabash on Madison, and Capper & Capper, at Wabash and Madison. The first and largest Chicago outlet of Eddie Bauer sporting goods and equipment is on the east side of Wabash just south of Randolph. Here, too, you'll find the famous Blackhawk Restaurant, one of the few remaining first-class restaurants in this end of town. But you can pass these up and still get good food at moderate prices in two old favorites: the Loop Hole, just east of Wabash on Randolph (lunch with wine for under $5.00), and Mort's Delicatessen on the east side of Wabash between Randolph and Lake.

Daley Center and Plaza and City Hall

Head west from Wabash on either Randolph or Washington. Every big city has something of a geographical heart, the place most of the residents think of as the center of town, or the place where the action is. Well, Richard J. Daley Center and Plaza seems to fit both criteria. It's an entire city block bounded by Washington, Dearborn, Randolph, and Clark.

Daley Plaza, of course, memorializes the late and renowned mayor Richard J. Daley, who personified the homespun character of Chicago. He was born, reared, and lived out his life in Bridgeport, a humble South Side district. The mayor, like many leading Chicago politicians, was entirely Irish, and rabid about the city and its people, most of whom were delighted with his somewhat autocratic rule of the "City that Works." The Daley era (1955–1976) brought to the city not only the Picasso, which adorns the plaza that bears his name, but countless skyscrapers that literally transformed the skyline. Since his death, the construction of skyscrapers has continued unabated under three mayors.

Mayor Daley (and successor mayors) presided over the workings of the city and the local Democratic Organization from a fifth-floor sanctuary on the Clark Street side of the City-County Building, immediately west of Daley Plaza.

Mayors Row, a restaurant on Dearborn, between Randolph and Washington, just east of the Plaza, shows pictures of Daley and Chicago's other old-time mayors, including the colorful (but not necessarily revered) "Big Bill" Thompson, the last Republican mayor. Others, since the twenties, have included Anton Cermak, who was killed in Florida by an assassin's bullet intended for Franklin Delano Roosevelt.

Among Daley's other achievements are the new Chicago Campus of the University of Illinois, immediately south and west of the Loop.

The tall building that overlooks the Daley Plaza is a county courthouse, one the first buildings that used cor-ten, an unpainted, self-eroding steel, which in its aging years looks pretty good. The Picasso statue in the southeast quadrant of Daley Plaza is made of the same metal. Most artistic authorities believe the Chicago Picasso depicts the head of a woman.

The eternal flame on the Washington Street side of the Plaza memorializes the late President John F. Kennedy, whose 1960 victory over Richard M. Nixon was decided, they say, by a controversial vote count under Daley's direction right here in downtown Chicago.

Almost directly across Washington from the flame is Joan Miró's *Chicago,* a feminine figure with pitchfork, one of the many sculptures adorning downtown plazas and building interiors. If you happen to be in the city on a cold or rainy business day, you can get to the Plaza entirely underground; just go down to the subway station at State and Randolph and walk west, first to the courthouse; if you turn south you'll emerge in the lobby of the Brunswick Building on the south side of Washington at Dearborn. It's a pleasant walk where you'll encounter a variety of city workers and lawyers, as well as city exhibits. At the Brunswick Building, you'll find underground shops and a restaurant.

If you go west to the huge neoclassical City Hall–Cook County Building from the Plaza, enter off Clark Street and walk through to the City Council Chambers on the La Salle Street side.

In the spring of 1983, the city elected its first black mayor, Harold G. Washington, a former congressman. The election, one of the bitterest political battles in the city's history, resulted in a major split between the old-time Democratic machine, as personified in its white chairman, Eddie Vrdolyak, and the mayor, who seemed determined to carry out campaign pledges of political and administrative reform. Despite the tumult, the city continues to work. Meetings of the city council on the second floor, often fiery these days, are open to the public. There is no regular schedule, but if you're in the town on a business day, the visitors' gallery could present an interesting insight into the workings of big city government.

La Salle Street—The Financial District

Several blocks south of the City Hall–Cook County Building you'll find yourself amidst the frantic pace of Chicago's financial center, where all of the exchanges operate. The Chicago Board of Trade towers over the foot of La Salle Street at 141 West Jackson Boulevard like a benevolent mother. The statue of Ceres, goddess of grain, looks down from atop the 45th floor. The Chicago Board of Trade opened for business in 1848, but was housed elsewhere until the current Art Deco building was opened in June, 1930. In 1982 a large addition designed in the Art Deco style was completed in order to accommodate a second trading floor. Together, the old and new buildings occupy an entire city block. Now visitors to the fifth-floor gallery can look south to see traders in grain, and north to see the old but refurbished trading floor, where big-dollar futures contracts in financial instruments are traded. Witnessing the close of trading (shortly after 1 P.M. on any business day) makes the Board of Trade alone worth a visit to Chicago. Traders in more than ten different trading pits wind up the day in a hand-waving shouting match as they try to take best advantage of closing prices to buy or sell their remaining futures contracts. One of the south Loop's most popular restaurants, the Sign of the Trader, is open here for lunch, and the basement cafeteria, just below the Jackson Boulevard entrance, isn't bad either. Visitors are also welcome in the new quarters of the Chicago/Mercantile Exchange (established in 1874) at South Wacker Drive and Monroe. Trading there lasts till 3:00 P.M.

West of the Board of Trade, along Jackson, you come to Union Station, one of the city's two remaining major railroad stations and the center of all Amtrak travel into and out of Chicago. Union Station's magnificent interior has recently been renovated. Pedestrian commuter traffic here and in the nearby Northwestern Station (north along Canal Street) from 7:30 A.M. to 8:30 A.M. and 4:30 P.M. to 5:30 P.M. is a no-nonsense affair, as suburbanites by the thousand move quickly and efficiently to and from their jobs in the Loop or Near North.

South Loop Area

Backtracking east again on Jackson to La Salle, you'll come to the Continental Illinois National Bank (1924) and adjoining Rookery (1886) across from the Board of Trade. Go inside the bank and be sure to take the escalator to the second banking floor to view the block-long panorama of tall columns supporting a magnificent ceiling. Dating from 1886, The Rookery (209 South La Salle) is rugged on the outside but delightfully warm and welcoming on the inside, the result of a design by Frank Lloyd Wright when it was remodeled in 1905.

Walk north across Adams to the stunning La Salle National Bank Building, an Art Deco structure dating from the 1930s. On business days, you can enjoy a good, reasonable lunch in the basement cafeteria and grill at the building's east side. Then cross Clark Street to the Commonwealth Edison Building and continue east to the 1894 Marquette Building (140 South Dearborn), where you'll see bronze reliefs at the entrance of an otherwise forbidding-looking building. Inside, the lobby mosaics depicting expeditions by explorers Marquette and Jolliet are well worth viewing.

As you leave the Marquette Building, look south to the Mies van der Rohe-designed Federal Center and Plaza. At this pristine federal office-building complex you'll delight in the great and colorful Calder sculpture entitled *Flamingo,* a striking orange-painted structure that seems like it would soar to the heavens were it unstuck from its concrete foundation. For modern history buffs, the Dirksen Federal Courthouse across the street was the site of the notorious "Chicago Seven" trial of radical "Yippies" in the late 1960s, presided over the by late Julius

Hoffman. The single-story building at Clark and Adams, incidentally, is a convenient post office.

As you turn north on Dearborn from Adams, you soon encounter the 1980 Xerox Center at Dearborn and Monroe, one of the bold works by Chicago architect Helmut Joah Jahn. Its curving facade is a striking contrast to the older, more traditional Inland Steel Building of stainless steel with glass columns, diagonally across Dearborn on Monroe. Directly across Monroe from the Xerox Center is First Illinois Plaza, a lower-level center of lively music and box lunches in summer (wintertime events are held in a small, comfortable auditorium). Look up at the First National Bank building with its unique, sweeping design. And, as you walk north along Dearborn, look for the mosaic sculpture on the east side of the plaza, *The Four Seasons,* by Marc Chagall. A nice touch of color, especially in summer when the plaza is lively and people-watching is at its best.

Head west on Monroe to Wacker Drive.

Sears Tower and North Wacker Drive

Only the Pentagon claims to have more office space than the Sears Tower, but it's the building's height that is most impressive. Rising 1,454 feet above Wacker Drive at the southwest corner of the Loop, Sears Tower long ranked as the world's tallest building. A Canadian edifice has now won that distinction. But the Sears building still outranks every other superstructure in Chicago, including the Standard Oil Building (1,136 feet) and the John Hancock Center (1,127 feet).

There is of course an entire floor, the 103rd, devoted to an observation deck, and it's here that visitors by the hundred flock daily, except when the dramatic views are blocked by clouds.

The best way to visit the tower is from the entrance on Wacker Drive, between Adams and Jackson. Climb the steps to the mammoth second-floor lobby, where you'll see the Alexander Calder mobile mural *Universe,* set in motion in October, 1974, and still moving.

To get to the observation floor, descend on an escalator to the lower level, pay a moderate entrance fee, and enter the express elevator, which whisks you up to the observation floor at a rate of 1800 feet per minute—you travel those 100-plus floors in less than one complete minute. Here on a clear day, you can look east to the eastern most shores of Lake Michigan, north to Milwaukee and Wisconsin, south to the factories of northwestern Indiana, and west to the vast expanse of residential area that is Chicago and her western suburbs. The best views, though, are of the immediate downtown areas. You can easiliy pick out many of the buildings such as the distinctive First National Bank Building, Marina City, the Art Institute, the Board of Trade, the

Field Museum of Natural History, Adler Planetarium, McCormick Place, Meigs Field, the Standard Oil of Indiana Building, and the Hancock Center. One of the best times to see the sights from the tower is about an hour before sunset (there's still enough light to see a great distance, and you can also watch the sun go down).

As you leave Sears Tower, walk north along Wacker Drive past the lineup of stunning new office buildings (including the unique U.S. Gypsum building at Monroe and Wacker) to the Civic Opera House, home of Chicago's well-endowed Lyric Opera, which attracts such stars as Luciano Pavarotti and Renata Scotto. (The opera season begins in late September and runs through mid-December.)

The Opera House is only a small portion of the block-long structure: the Civic Theater is located in the northern section, and in addition there are scores of offices and a cozy, ground-level bar and grill. Just north of the Opera House on the west side of Wacker you'll pass the old Morton Salt Building ("When It Rains, It Pours").

On any business day, walk east along Randolph to the Illinois Bell Telephone headquarters building at 225 West Randolph to see old-time telephones on display in a telephone museum. There are also new telephones on display, as well as exhibits and films explaining modern communications technology, from microwave transmission through the earth satellite systems.

Bigger, of course, isn't always better, but in the case of Chicago's Merchandise Mart, bigger has meant better for the city's home furnishings and apparel industries. At one time, not too long ago, Chicago was the hub of the nation's wholesale furniture trade; the city even had a separate Furniture Mart (still an imposing building along the lakefront, but converted to exclusive condominiums). Back in the 1920s, a Marshall Field executive dreamed up the idea of building a huge structure to house the store's wholesale operations along with those of other major retailers. The biggest building of its kind in the world emerged on a two-block area bounded on the south by the Chicago River, on the west by Orleans, the north by Kinzie, and the east by Wells Street. The Great Depression of the 1930s and a certain amount of mismanagement led to near disaster until the building was purchased in 1945 by the late Joseph Kennedy, father of John F. Kennedy. Since then, the Merchandise Mart has been converted into a lavish showcase for interior decorators, furniture wholesalers, and related businesses; two floors are devoted to the radio and TV Studios of the National Broadcasting Company.

More recently, the adjoining Apparel Center has risen to become a major enterprise for the Midwestern wholesale clothing industry, with over 4,000 lines of women's children's, and mens-and-boys wear in permanent showrooms. Another sign of the times: a 527-room Holiday

Inn occupies the Apparel Center's top floors and features a good bar, attractive atrium, and exposition center.

Greek Town and Chicago Circle

About a mile or so west of the Loop, along Halsted between Monroe and Van Buren, you can see most of what's left of Chicago's original Greek Town, once a concentration of immigrants from Greece, who have since moved north to the Lawrence and Western area. There remain any number of small shops—butchers and bakers mostly—and some really interesting restaurants where dining is something of an adventure. The cuisine is invariably interesting and moderately priced, and the interiors of such spots as the Parthenon, between Van Buren and Jackson, are well-appointed but decidedly informal, with shirt-sleeved executives and students lingering over long lunches of a Chicago favorite, gyros and Roditos.

Farther south on Halsted beyond the Eisenhower Expressway, you come to the University of Illinois Chicago Circle campus which dates from 1965. It's a pleasant place to visit, even when school is out, as you amble through a labyrinth of buildings enjoying an interesting combination of low- and high-rise architecture. The administration tower is larger at the top than on the bottom, and most of the classroom buildings are interconnected by overhead walkways, which literally keep the students off the streets.

Actually the University of Illinois in Chicago comprises more than 25,000 students on two campuses. The liberal arts and engineering campus, formerly known as Chicago Circle, is the new one. The older Medical Center to the west, is part of a major medical, teaching, and hospital complex of some sixty health-care institutions. They include Cook County Hospital, St. Luke's Rush-Presbyterian Hospital, and the $60 million University of Illinois Hospital, which opened in 1981.

A historically significant building in the area is Jane Addams' Hull House (800 South Halsted), a landmark memorializing the social-service pioneer Jane Addams, who established the first settlement house in Chicago. Her efforts, combined with those of other reformers, led to such pioneer welfare laws as tenement-house regulations, an eight-hour work law for women, workmen's compensation, and insurance for all workers. She was a staunch advocate of women's rights and co-winner of the Nobel peace prize in 1931. The old Hull House is an exhibit now, and the building diagonally across the street is a modern parking garage for students—but vestiges of the old "settlement" style neighborhoods remain to the west along Taylor Street.

You can still find some great Italian neighborhood eateries on Taylor. One favorite is Florence restaurant at 1030 West Taylor, an informal place frequented by medical students; the linguini is mouthwatering, as is made-to-order chocolate rum torte.

If you're in a shopping mood, walk south on Halsted from Taylor to Roosevelt Road and turn east across the Dan Ryan Expressway to the little-known Jeffro Plaza shopping center at 555 West Roosevelt. Look especially for the Conte di Savoia international food market and be prepared to spend a half hour taking in the sights and smells of this unusual shop with its open kegs of parmesan and oregano plus sausages and huge rounds of cheese. There are gourmet condiments and cookware, too—a great place, even though it's a bit off the beaten path.

On the other side of Roosevelt, at Jefferson, look for Manny's, a modern version of a cafeteria-style Jewish deli, where the food quality is high, portions are large, and the price for a lunch, say of Kreplac soup and a corned beef sandwich for example, is under $5.00.

Maxwell Street at 2000 South on Halsted in the not so distant past was a galaxy of surprises, with a memorable cigar store Indian, which stood in the middle of swarms of shoppers who haggled endlessly, European-style, over the price of a pair of shoes, a girl's dress, or a set of that prickly, long-handled wool underwear that little boys of the time hated with a passion. Now, though, Maxwell Street shows signs of age. Head back northeast to Jackson and return to Grant Park.

Grant Park West to Chinatown

In Grant Park immediately east of the Art Institute, between Monroe and Jackson, you'll come to the James C. Petrillo Bandshell, site of free summer concerts by the Grant Park Symphony Orchestra. The concerts, presented each Wednesday, Friday, Saturday, and Sunday evening between late June and the end of August, feature popular as well as classical music. Around Labor Day, the area becomes even livelier when a free festival draws some of the jazz world's greatest musicians. A limited number of seats are available for early arrivals (concerts usually begin around 7:30 or 8:00 in the evening) so check local newspapers for dates.

If you were lucky enough to hear the concert, walk south to the Clarence Buckingham Fountain for the hour-long, computer-programmed light-and-color water display. Children especially are fascinated as the lights turn the huge sprays of water from deep red to blue, yellow and green, and all shades in between. The huge, rococo-style fountain dates to 1927.

The Field Museum of Natural History is the first of three major museums located at the south side of Grant Park, the others being the Shedd Aquarium and the Adler Planetarium. Of the three the Field is the largest—in fact, it's one of the largest marble buildings in the world—and is likely to impress you the most. It's been doing that for me since my childhood, leaving lifelong impressions of lifelike cave dwellers and stuffed African bull elephants. Recently the museum has mounted major exhibits of national stature, making it even more popular with both Chicagoans and visitors. The gift shop is small but unique, with many items imported from the exotic lands depicted in the anthropological exhibits of the museum. From here it's only a short walk under Lake Shore Drive to a museum of living beings, the Shedd Aquarium.

John G. Shedd, president and chairman of Marshall Field and Company in the 1920s, bequeathed $3 million to establish the aquarium, but died before construction began in 1927. The octagonal building was completed in 1929, and all the galleries were fully stocked with fish by 1931. Located between the Field Museum and Adler Planetarium, the Shedd Aquarium houses 5,000 aquatic animals in 200 exhibition tanks. Species range from exotic tropical saltwater fish to freshwater ones taken from adjoining Lake Michigan. Favorites (only to look at) include the sharks, moray eels, penguins, and huge sea turtles that seemingly could break through their glass enclosures.

A leisurely stroll east of the aquarium brings you to the Adler Planetarium, the structure built because Max Adler, a wealthy Sears, Roebuck Company executive, wanted to bring the first artificial "sky" to the United States from Germany and have it installed in a planetarium in his hometown. Sky shows now are given on a Mark VI Zeiss planetarium projector, successor to the original Zeiss unit that intrigued Adler. Each show depicts the stars, nearby planets, and distant galaxies as seen from Chicago, and after an evening show, visitors are invited to view the actual sky through the Doane Observatory telescope. Moderate admission is charged for the sky show, but the other exhibits are free. These cover astronomy, space exploration, telescopes, (including one used to discover the planet Uranus), navigation, and antique scientific instruments. There's even a moon rock returned to Earth by the *Apollo 15* mission crew.

Soldier Field, just south of the Field Museum, is a huge lakefront stadium that is home to the Chicago Bears and the city's professional soccer team, the Chicago Sting. It's a mammoth place, singularly suited to mammoth extravaganzas such as the American Legion's annual Fourth of July pyrotechnic displays.

McCormick Place, the commanding lakeside structure, at Cermak (22nd Street) and Lake Shore Drive, is Chicago's leading exhibition center, attracting up to 100,000 conventioners for a single show. It is surprisingly ill situated in relation to Chicago's restaurant and hotel center. Most trade shows are closed to the public, but one important exception is the annual Chicago Auto Show, held in late February. The

Arie Crown Theatre in McCormick Place presents road tours of Broadway plays, concerts, dance programs, and other special events.

West of Lake Shore Drive along Cermak is McCormick Center Hotel, a tall, isolated hotel catering mostly to convention clientele. Immediately west of the hotel, you'll come to Donnelley Hall, a city exhibition center that once housed the huge four-color presses that printed *Life* magazine. The R. R. Donnelley Plant, due north of here, still prints scores of national magazines and catalogs in two gigantic buildings.

As you leave Donnelley Hall and head west toward Chinatown, continue north a few blocks to 18th Street and Prairie, site of the Prairie Avenue Historic District and lifework of the Chicago Architecture Foundation. Prairie Avenue was known as Chicago's "Gold Coast" when tycoons started building mansions along it after the great fire of 1871. By the turn of the century, however, it had become unfashionable, and the area started to go to seed and then became a warehouse district. Today, only a handful of houses remain, most carefully restored. Here you can tour fortress-like Glessner House, built in 1886–87 for John Jacob Glessner, a vice-president of International Harvester. See, too, the interior of the brightly restored Greek Revival Widow Clarke house, built in 1836 (at another site and moved to this one in 1977), the oldest surviving residence in Chicago. Other distinctive buildings are the 1891 Kimball mansion (Kimball pianos) and the 1870s Joseph Kohn house.

From there, it's a convenient bus ride west along Cermak to Clark and Chinatown. Chinatown was first centered around Clark and Van Buren Streets but settled into the area around Cermak Road and Wentworth Avenue around the 1920s. Like New York City's Chinatown, Chicago's abuts a Little Italy, making this an area rich in mix of ethnic culture. There are some very interesting shops to browse around in Chinatown—and don't be surprised to hear mostly Chinese spoken. Some of the residents do not speak English at all. Plan to have lunch or dinner here—the food in selected restaurants can be extraordinary and quite reasonable. A personal favorite is the Three Happiness, on the north side of Cermak.

Backtrack east to Michigan Avenue and head north.

The Cultural Center—North Michigan Avenue

Chicago is not always kind to its historic buildings. The old Stock Exchange Building, long a landmark (but not an official one) on La Salle Street, fell to the wrecker's ball years ago, with only its Trading Room salvaged for posterity as a special exhibit in a new wing of the Art Institute. But in the case of the Main Library at Michigan and

Randolph, the city has held its own, converting the old Italian Renaissance building into the charming Chicago Public Library Cultural Center, which should be included on any walking tour of the Loop.

The building dates from 1897, when it became the first permanent quarters of the city's library system. (The library system itself dates from the Chicago Lyceum of 1834, but all of that 30,000-volume collection was destroyed in the Fire of 1871; much of the new collection derived from a British donation of several thousand volumes.) Renovated over three years (1974 to 1977), the Cultural Center has become a focal point of special fine arts events—concerts, films, and art exhibits —as well as a general interest reading room for thousands of Chicagoans.

Most visitors are attracted mainly by the building's fascinating interior. Here you see majestic, stained-glass domes, one at each end of the block-long (and half-block wide) building. One of the domes (nearest the Randolph Street entrance) tops the Grand Army of the Republic Museum, a permanent collection of Civil War memorabilia, with special emphasis on the Union Forces from Illinois. Abraham Lincoln of Illinois was president during that bloody war, while Ulysses S. Grant, who had lived at Galena in western Illinois, served as a leading general.

Even more impressive, though, is the southern end of the building, where in Preston Bradley Hall you see a stunning, Tiffany-designed stained-glass dome. The room's supporting arches are adorned with mosaic scrolls and rosettes bearing the symbols of sixteenth-century master printers. The first floor circulation desk at the Washington Street entrance provides visitors with current information on special events at the Cultural Center and other places around town.

Michigan Avenue and the Near North

As you work your way north along Michigan Avenue from the Cultural Center at Randolph past the international bank and tourism offices and an occasional McDonald's, you have to be impressed with the diversity of architecture, mostly new. The city's architectural renaissance dates from the 1950s. Its first lakefront high-rise observation tower was in the Prudential Building on Randolph just east of Michigan. Now it is dwarfed by the huge Standard Oil (of Indiana) Building, immediately to the east, and an even newer architecturally striking skyscraper at Randolph and Michigan, directly across Randolph from the Cultural Center.

The Chicago renaissance is partly due to the amazing growth of new and restored hotels. Some, like the Bismarck (Randolph at La Salle in the Loop), remain characteristically old and wood paneled, while oth-

The Near North Side

Points of Interest

1) Chicago Academy of Sciences
2) City Hall
3) Daley Center
4) John Hancock Center
5) Magnificent Mile
6) Marina City
7) Merchandise Mart
8) Museum of Contemporary Art
9) North Rush St. Night-Life Area
10) Old Town Night Life Area
11) Olympia Center
12) Prudential Bldg.
13) Tribune Tower
14) Water Tower (Information Center)
15) Water Tower Place
16) Wrigley Bldg.
17) Chicago Historical Society

ers, like the Hyatt Regency, on Wacker east of Michigan, are open and airy. The Hyatt, made up of two huge buildings, adjoins the modern office-shopping complex called One Illinois Center. You can almost get lost in the labyrinth of shops, bars, and restaurants in the combination hotel and office complex, but what a way to lose yourself! Both structures—and others to the south—are built on air rights looming over the old Illinois Central Railroad right-of-way. (As an historical footnote, Abraham Lincoln once served as a legal counsel for the Illinois Central Railroad.) By the year 2000, it is said, Illinois Center, the complex north of Michigan between East Lake Street and Wacker, will extend its labyrinth of shops and offices all the way to Lake Shore Drive.

Other hotels worthy of a visit, either for afternoon tea or cocktails, or just a look: The Palmer House, State and Monroe; the Marriott, Michigan and Ohio, a little glitzy but some nice shops here; the Sheraton Plaza on Huron just east of Michigan; and the Whitehall and Tremont, two among several small, intimate hotels in the city, both located a half-block west of Michigan north of Chicago Avenue. Still others are the Ambassadors East and West, at Goethe and State Street Parkway, north of Division, and the exclusive Park Hyatt, which is visited mostly for dinner. It's just west of the Old Water Tower at Chicago and Michigan with the main entrance off Chicago.

North along Michigan and Wacker look for the plaque commemorating the Fort Dearborn Massacre (Michigan Avenue Bridge), one of those ugly historic events that school children are taught along with details of the great Chicago fire in 1871, which destroyed the face of the old city in and around the Loop. Like any number of Midwestern cities, Chicago traces its roots to the late seventeenth-century French explorations by Louis Jolliet and Father Jacques Marquette, but the first permanent establishment was the U.S.-controlled Fort Dearborn, set up on the banks of the Chicago River and Lake Michigan in 1804. The Fort Dearborn massacre occurred in 1812 about two miles south of the Fort while the settlers were in full retreat. The fort was reestablished and remained functional until 1837. Cook County was organized in 1831 with the village of Chicago as the county seat of justice. The city was incorporated on September 12, 1833.

Pioneer Court, immediately across the river, honors many leaders of early Chicago, especially Cyrus McCormick, inventor of the reaper, which was to transform the Midwestern frontier into a veritable breadbasket for the world. In fact, the Equitable Building, which borders the north side of the river on the east side of Michigan, is corporate headquarters of International Harvester Company, a successor to the old McCormick Reaper Works, which was situated on the north side of the river, east of Michigan Avenue.

The McCormick family in the 1920s affiliated themselves with the Pattersons to form one of the nation's major communications empires, controlling the *Chicago Tribune* and the *New York Daily News*. Today the Tribune Company also owns Chicago-based WGN radio and super-television station (on Addison Avenue) and the National League Chicago Cubs baseball team.

Robert R. McCormick was instrumental in the construction of the Gothic Tribune Tower, immediately north of Pioneer Court. The news-paper maintains a good public-information center on the ground level and provides conducted tours. (Most of the papers, however, are printed at a newer plant some distance northwest of here.)

Another Chicago family, the Wrigleys, of chewing gum fame, gave their name to the distinctive Wrigley Building (built 1921–24 and actually two buildings in one) on the west side of Michigan. Although now partially hidden from Lake Shore Drive by newer structures, the Wrigley Building remains especially attractive at night, when its near-white terra-cotta walls are beautifully lighted by floodlights beaming from the south bank of the Chicago River. In the rear of the north wing is the Wrigley Building Restaurant, one of those lesser-known spots where you can dine quietly and comfortably without spending a for-tune.

The south wing of the Continental Hotel, on the east side of Michi-gan immediately north of the Tribune Tower, was completed in 1928 as the Moorish-style Medinah Club of Chicago. The second floor din-ing room and other areas still reflect that colorful design: the hotel's north wing is conventionally modern, but its basement houses Kon Tiki Ports, a popular multinational restaurant with emphasis on Polynesian and Oriental cuisine. The luncheon buffet is a gastronome's delight, but to do it justice plan to skip breakfast and dinner.

As you walk north along Michigan Avenue to Grand, you'll notice an occasional stairway in the sidewalk leading to lower Michigan Ave-nue. This phenomenon grew out of plans to create a series of streets under the Loop that would keep upper levels free of traffic.

Those plans never materialized, but examples of what might have been are to be seen below Michigan between Grand on the north and Randolph on the south (and also below Wacker Drive from Michigan all the way around the Loop to the Eisenhower Expressway). If you're interested, walk on either side of the Chicago River (in the daytime) and cross the lower Michigan Avenue Bridge, actually a two-tiered structure serving both levels of the avenue. You can board one of the sightseeing boats at the river or walk north to East Hubbard Street, where you'll spot Billy Goat Tavern, a favorite hangout for printers and other newspaper folk. It's a short-order cafe and bar where a grilled club-steak sandwich is considered to be an elaborate dish. But fun.

Around the corner, on Rush Street, you'll find Riccardo's, a regular restaurant where the bar has some dramatic Art Deco murals as a backdrop. Although the ambience is Italian, Greeks run the place. The sidewalk café at Riccardo's is especially congenial late in the afternoon of a warm summer's day. The relaxed atmosphere of the Corona Café at Rush and Illinois also is popular with Chicagoans. Wabash, just north of the Chicago River, is home to two major institutions, the *Chicago Sun-Times* on the east side of the street and the Chicago headquarters of IBM on the west. The *Sun-Times* is open year-round, and you can see a nice array of photography in the first-floor gallery. Just walk on through, or time permitting, tour the plant, which at one time also housed the now-defunct *Chicago Daily News.*

Moving north along Wabash, a bilevel street at this point, look down on Hubbard and take the westside steps to Andy's (11 East), especially around 5:00 on a week night. Chances are you'll encounter some of Chicago's popular jazz being played informally behind a huge and usually crowded bar. There's a modest cover charge but it's worth it. The music ends around 7:30 P.M., giving the musicians time for gigs at places where the cover charge isn't quite so modest.

Back on Michigan Avenue, turn east toward the Lake on Ontario for a block and a half to the Museum of Contemporary Art. Founded in 1967 in a building that once housed a bakery, the museum has established itself as a popular attraction in a city that traditionally has nurtured commerce and industry more than culture. Since 1979, when the museum added an adjoining remodeled townhouse, the Museum of Contemporary Art has occupied over 16,000 square feet in seven large, bright galleries. Here you are likely to find the unknown as well as the established artist of the avant garde, including such well-known twentieth-century names as Bacon, Braque, Calder, de Kooning, Magritte, and Picasso. The museum also delights in bringing forth the new names in film and video artistry. From here continue east past the local outlet of CBS at McClurg Court to Lake Shore Drive. The Holiday Inn at Ontario and the lake has a pleasant rooftop restaurant with great views of the lake and a popular first-floor jazz domain called Rick's Café Americain, decorated like the cafe in the film "Casablanca."

Chicago's past as a bustling lake port is best represented by the 3,000-foot long Navy Pier at the foot of Grand Avenue east of Lake Shore Drive. It was built in 1916 to receive ships plying the waters of Lake Michigan. Over the years commercial shipping has moved south to the huge Lake Calumet facilities of the Port of Chicago, leaving the city-owned Pier available to host all sorts of ethnic and cultural events. One favorite is the annual two-day International Folk Fair held in October, when Chicago's diverse ethnic groups—Irish, Poles, Orientals, blacks, Hispanics, Eastern Europeans, ad infinitum—gather in booths of bric-a-brac. The conglomeration of exotic foods fills the air with appetizing smells. A staple of the fair is ethnic music and costumed folk dancing—a great way to capture in one brief hour or so the cultural mix of the "melting pot" that continues to be Chicago.

Outside the Pier, in the summer months, you'll find any number of water attractions. A general favorite is the U.S.S. *Silversides,* a still waterborne World War II submarine that served in the Pacific. The many Japanese flags painted on its conning tower signify the number of Japanese ships it destroyed in wartime and attest its military prowess.

As you wander the Pier Area near Lake Shore Drive, don't overlook Lake Point Tower, between Illinois and Grand, one of the city's most stunning skyscraper apartments. Its especially attractive late in the day when the western sides of the building literally glow in the fading light of the setting sun.

The Magnificent Mile

Returning east to Michigan Avenue and heading north toward Ontario until you come to Erie Street, you will pass a number of classy but not necessarily well-known shops and an occasional art gallery. Here Saks Fifth Avenue maintains its main Chicago-area outlet, a multilevel store that has just about everything you'd find at the original in New York City. In a sense, this is the beginning of what is known as Chicago's "Magnificent Mile," a Chamber of Commerce phrase for a series of exclusive stores that cater to the well-to-do and those who aspire to become so. Along this stretch of Michigan there's an Elizabeth Arden, of course, along with Tiffany's, Gucci's, and any number of small, exclusive shops including Stuart Brent's popular bookstore. These are intermingled with I. Magnin, Bonwit Teller, Marshall Field, Lord & Taylor, and the new Neiman-Marcus in what is called Olympia Center, an office and apartment conglomeration that wraps itself behind the southeast corner of Chicago and Michigan avenues with entrances on both.

Long before you reach that intersection though, you'll easily pick out its distinctive landmark—the Water Tower—on the northwest corner, and across the street, the Water Pumping Station, home of the "Here's Chicago" multimedia promotional view of the city. Most of the area you've walked—from the Art Institute north to Chicago Avenue—was totally devastated by the fire of 1871, so any of the older buildings left in the area, other than the Water Tower and its pumping station, postdate the fire. (The fire actually started west of the Loop and swept east and north, killing 250 people and wiping out the homes of 100,000 others. One result: Chicago has long had one of the strongest building fire codes in the nation.) Today the Water Tower on the west side of Michigan houses a small air-conditioned information center where you can find out schedules and places of current happenings, from plays to festivals to concerts. There are also a visitor events line, fine arts hotline, and direct phonelines to selected restaurants.

Latecomers notwithstanding, the big event on North Michigan Avenue remains Water Tower Place, occupying the entire block bounded by Michigan, Pearson, Seneca, and Chestnut. A score of stores, eateries, and shops on the Michigan Avenue side attract literally thousands of shoppers every day—Sundays included. The complex also contains any number of offices, condominium apartments, movie theaters, and the hidden-from-view Ritz-Carlton Hotel, unique in that the hotel's main lobby is 12 floors up. When entering Water Tower Place for the first time, pass up the doors to Marshall Field or Lord & Taylor. Enter instead through the center doors on North Michigan Avenue leading to the stunning atrium lobby with its bevy of trees, a waterfall, and general feeling of solace and calm. Multilingual brochures at the information desk give the names and locations of all the stores and shops.

As you get off the second-floor escalator, you encounter an inner atrium with three glass-enclosed elevators that whisk you to the seventh floor for great views of the entire air-conditioned vertical shopping center. Watch your time: browsing here can consume a half day or more. You may want to stop on the mezzanine level at Vie de France for a croissant and cup of coffee; the light-lunch fare there is also excellent, but for heartier cuisine you may want to try the adjoining highly regarded Chestnut Street Grill.

Tea at the Ritz-Carlton is one of Chicago's genuine pleasures. Enter the hotel at ground level, immediately behind Marshall Field, and take the elevator to the 12th floor. Here you enter a two-acre fountain-centered lobby and an atrium-like greenhouse. Views to the north from the plant-bedecked greenhouse are still open enough for you to see some of Lake Michigan as you sip tea, coffee, or cocktails and munch hors d'oeuvres, usually with relaxing live piano music in the background.

Immediately north of Water Tower Place, between Chestnut and Delaware, stands towering Hancock Center, the city's third-tallest building (at one time, it held the rank of world's tallest). Some say its architecture is so-so—some even call it box-like—but the fact remains that "Big John" is tall, and the ride to the 94th-floor observation level is worth the price of admission. Or for the price of a drink you can take in cocktails on the 96th floor, or a dinner on the 95th, with unsurpassed views of the lakefront as far south as Indiana or as far north as the northernmost suburbs. The lower floors of Hancock Center are devoted to shops and offices, while the upper ones (below the observation-dining-cocktail floors) contain condominium apartments and an upper-level garage.

Directly across Michigan from Hancock Center is Fourth Presbyterian Church, home for years to some of the city's leading families (including the McCormicks). This well-endowed facility is open to visitors and worth a short stop to see the richly paneled Blair Chapel, a reincarnation of something you'd find in a classic church in England.

A contrast of sorts is presented by the building at the southeast corner of Michigan and Walton, now known as the Playboy Building but originally the Palmolive Building. It houses the editorial offices of *Playboy* magazine, now presided over mostly by Christie Hefner, daughter of founder-publisher Hugh Hefner. The beacon atop this building originally served as a navigational aid to vessels sailing on Lake Michigan, but now it's cut off from view by taller buildings in the area (including "Big John"). The Knickerbocker Hotel, across from the Drake Hotel on East Walton, has been nicely restored (it formerly was a property of Playboy Enterprises, Inc.). Its lobby provides a nice respite for late afternoon or early evening cocktails with piano music. (Due east of here, at the lakefront, are two 1920s Mies van der Rohe buildings, which are noted on Culture Bus Tours of the North Side. They are at 860–80 North Lake Shore Drive.)

The Drake, also built in the twenties, is one of Chicago's revered hotels, catering to an upscale clientele that prefers the old to the glitz of the modern. The Cape Cod Room in the Drake has a reputation for fresh seafood that predates most living Chicagoans, but if it's completely booked the hotel's other eating establishments deliver good values for the price.

A few doors east of the Drake, but with its entrance on Lake Shore Drive East, is the Mayfair Regent, one of several smaller exclusive hotels that have gained tremendously in popularity. Afternoon tea and cocktails there are recommended, as is dinner in the Ciel Blue dining room.

Among the latest in fashionable shopping and dining sites along North Michigan Avenue (at Oak) is One Magnificent Mile, a 58-story combination of shops, offices, and condominiums. Here you find a three-level designer apparel department store, Stanley Korshak (A Chicago tradition that moved a block north from older, smaller quarters), the two-story Spiaggia Restaurant featuring northern Italian cuisine, and an informal Spiaggia Cafe. There's a bread and pastries shop called Roberto Albini: Bottega del Pane and a yummy candystore, Swiss-style, called Le Chocolatier.

Oak Street, west of Michigan, continues to feature exclusive shops, boutiques, and cafes—a great area for browsing on a warm summer's day.

Rush Street Area

Rush Street intersecting Oak is synonymous with nightlife in Chicago. The street itself is less than a mile long, starting at the Chicago River just under (or behind) the Wrigley Building and stopping just north of Oak at State and Elm. From Chicago Avenue north to Elm, you'll find the glitter of discotheques and popular jazz spots: Lilly's, Billy's, Faces, and the Back Room. Singles, meanwhile, flock to Harry's Cafe, and the Division Street area just north of Elm and west of State: Yvette's, the Snuggery, Mother's, and Butch McGuire's.

If you're in the mood for less than a seven-course dinner, try the Bon Ton Café, a small, friendly, low-key storefront operation with great Hungarian entrées and an assortment of homemade mouthwatering pastries. It's on the east side of State a half-block south of Division.

To capture a sense of days gone by, continue north one block on State Street Parkway to Goethe and the twin hotels, Ambassadors East and West. Although they are owned and managed separately, the hotels attract much the same clientele; in the Ambassador East is the famous Pump Room, a place where visiting celebrities still like to dine. Just north of the Ambassador West you pass the now-empty Playboy Mansion. It was here in the heyday of his time in Chicago that publisher Hugh Hefner held court until he up and moved to the West Coast.

While you're in the area, tour Astor Street, a block east of State, to see old-style homes tucked between modern apartments. Astor is historic enough to have gained landmark status for the entire street, from North Avenue to Division. Charnley House at 1365 North Astor, a national historic landmark, dates from 1891–92; its design is attributed to Louis Sullivan and David Adler, with a touch of Frank Lloyd Wright, a protege of Sullivan, thrown in.

At the North Avenue end of Astor, occupying a block-wide lot, is the residence of the Roman Catholic Archbishop of Chicago, a huge, red-brick, multi-chimneyed structure.

Old Town

Backtrack south to Division Street again. As you move west along Division to La Salle, notice the unusual apartment building just north of Division. It's a photographer's delight, since the southerly facade is an unusual mural, and many of the windows on the building's east side are merely painted on to look like windows. At Wells and Division you encounter a Chicago tradition, the House of Glunz—the headquarters of a company that's been catering to wine lovers since the 1880s. Stop in for a taste of wine and a look at memorabilia that includes photos of the old days when this was one of meatpacker Oscar Mayer's favorite taverns.

Mayer, of course, founded the huge meat-processing plant known for the American hot dog. The original plant was located a block or so west of Wells as was Dr. Scholl's factory that produced helpful aids to aching feet. The latter, incidentally, like many former factories, is being converted to exclusive apartment units.

Walking north along Wells, you encounter any number of old stand-bys in an area that is undergoing a comeback in popularity for shopping and dining. Piper's Alley, at North and Wells, is worth a walk through as you move into to what is known as the Old Town Triangle. You will also come to the Sullivan-designed Garrick Theater, home of the always popular Second City comedy review (Mike Nichols and Elaine May are among scores of top comedy acts who got a start here). The Earl of Old Town, across Wells Street, is equally known for attracting good but relatively unknown folk music talents, many of whom find it their launching pad to notoriety—the good kind.

Northern Old Town is a good place to take a leisurely walk along the side streets west of Wells and Lincoln Avenue, where the chic and modern blends nicely with the chic and the old. Examples of architecturally worthy buildings are the Sullivan-designed town houses at 1800 Lincoln Park West that date from 1888, and many of which are beautifully restored. Other places to look for in this area of nineteenth-century nostalgia are the Crilly Court buildings at St. Paul and North Park Avenue; Concord Place; and old St. Michael's Church at Eugenie and Cleveland.

Near North

The Chicago Historical Society at North Avenue and Clark Street is one of those easily overlooked museums that is well worth a one- or two-hour visit. Over the years the Society has developed a lively center of exhibitions. Among them are a stunning array of dresses worn by Chicago's leading ladies of the late nineteenth and early twentieth centuries and a series of pioneer craft demonstrations of spinning, weaving, dyeing, quilting, and candlemaking, all by docents in authentic period costumes. The Society is best known as a center of Lincolniana, with an entire gallery devoted to a biographic diorama of the Civil War president's life, plus rare memorabilia from his Springfield, Illinois, home and his Civil War years in the White House. (Although some distance from Chicago, Lincoln-related sites in Springfield and Salem are well worth a visit.) Saturdays and Sundays are good times to visit the Historical Society because there are often films and other events of special interest. The gift shop here is quite good.

One favorite stop, north of Old Town adjoining the west side of Lincoln Park at the foot of Lincoln Avenue, is Hemingways Movable Feast, a short-order restaurant with a "mile-long" menu of king-size sandwiches. You can feast inside or on the patio, or take your meal out for a picnic in the park.

The Lincoln Park Zoo

Like Washington, D.C., Chicago still has its many free attractions that are true delights, and the Lincoln Park Zoo has to rank high on the list. Even in its moribund days, when the animals were seen in barred cages, the zoo held a fascination that drew literally thousands of visitors on a typical summer's day (the zoo is open year-round, but it's far less crowded in the fall-winter and spring). Today it is a natural-habitat-style zoo allowing the animals greater freedom and us a better look at them.

The most endearing exhibit, at the westerly entrance off Stockton Drive, is the Children's Zoo and Nursery. Although it's primarily for toddlers, you'll find that the child in you takes over, and you'll want to stop there to see the newborn of the Zoo's kaleidoscopic population. You may see tiny lion cubs frolicking in a glass-enclosed waist-high cage and tiny gorillas or chimpanzees exercising on miniature tires and other paraphernalia. There's even a petting area, where tots (young and old) reach out and touch a rabbit or a gerbil.

Nearby, seals cavort on rocks and in the water (there's an aquarium-like visitors passageway where you can see the seals swimming underwater), and in the huge lions' den, the big cats lounge in regal splendor. Most beguiling of all the mammal enclosures is the new gorilla house, where entire families of these fascinating beasts cavort on ropes and ledges to the delight of neck-stretching audiences. Polar bears also have their own swimming hole, while birds abound in the ultranatural setting of the Zoo Rookery, just off Fullerton and a block or so west of the Lake.

And there's even more. A bit south of the main entrance, off Stockton, look for the Farm-in-the-Zoo, a working farm with a fascinating array of animals indigenous to Midwestern farms: dairy cows, hogs, sheep, and horses, all working to keep the farm as in days long past. Don't expect flowing fields of grain, though; instead there's an enticing duck pond, where rental boats provide a welcome respite to all that walking you've been doing.

Just north of the zoo's western entrance you arrive at the Lincoln Park Conservatory, a Chicago landmark of sorts since the 1890s. A stunning array of live orchids greets the visitor at the entrance to the Palm House, one of four glassed buildings. Immediately beyond the orchids you'll encounter huge palm trees from India and Malaysia and a 50-foot Fiddle-leaf rubber tree from Africa. A curving walkway leads you through the Fernery and Tropical House to the Show-House, the greenhouse where major flower shows are staged, attracting thousands of Chicagoans every year. (The flower shows are usually staged over three or four weeks. They feature chrysanthemums in November, poinsettias in December, and a bewildering display of lillies at Easter. Admission, even to the major shows, is free.)

Note: If you're driving or have access to auto transportation, take the time to visit the Lincoln Park Conservatory's sister greenhouse in Garfield Park, on the West Side; it's even larger, and equally beautiful.

Lincoln Park West

Lakeview Avenue from Fullerton north to Diversey and the area of Fullerton near the Park, boast examples of old Chicago living at its finest. The streets are bordered by Lincoln Park on the east and large, high-ceilinged, tailored apartment buildings on the west, with a smattering of hotels and dining establishments in between. It's an area where nannies used to stroll babies in the park, but nowadays you're as likely to see the one-half of an up-and-coming young couple walking their Weimaraner or some other pedigree. To capture the full flavor of a bygone era, watch for the Theurer-Wrigley House at 2466 North Lakeview and Dawes House at 503 West Lincoln. Along southerly parts of Halsted near Armitage (west of where Lincoln and Armitage intersect), you'll find a grand assortment of antique shops, hardware stores, and good clothing stores as well as a large variety of bars, restaurants, and the Chicago's equivalent of New York's Off-Broadway playhouses. Nightlife in this general area is more alive with Chicagoans than tourists, but that can be a plus if you want to mingle with the locals.

Enjoy much of the same type of strolling north of Lincoln Avenue along Cleveland and Hudson Avenues (they parallel each other) all the way to Dickens, where you can turn east and head directly for the Lincoln Park Zoo. Other pleasant walking areas to tour in this mid-north area are Fullerton Avenue, from Clark to Halsted and Lincoln; the De Paul University area west of Halsted and south of Fullerton (the campus and surrounding neighborhoods have undergone extensive restoration); and Lincoln Avenue immediately north of Fullerton (look for some great bookstores as well as the restored Biograph Theater, a fine arts cinema known historically as the site where the notorious John Dillinger was gunned down by Federal agents). Lincoln Avenue, incidentally, from its beginnings just south of Lincoln Park at Clark as far north as Belmont, is dotted with antique stores, bars, and trendy dining spots. For drinks and sandwiches, try the John Barleycorn Memorial Pub at Belden and Lincoln, where recorded and live classical music is played. For an added touch, slides of works of art are projected onto screens at both ends of the bar. The Barleycorn Pub goes midly berserk every December staging Chicago's celebration of Beethoven's birthday.

The South Side (Jackson Park and Hyde Park)

If you head south on Lake Shore Drive, you'll come to Jackson Park. Chicago, a city that loves a festival, big or small, has inherited many of its cultural institutions from the World's Columbian Exposition of 1893. The Palace of Fine Arts, built in Jackson Park for the Exposition, housed the Field Columbian Museum, now the Field Museum of Natural History, from 1894 to 1920. When that museum was moved to Grant Park in 1920, the Palace of Fine Arts fell into ruin. With $1-million from philanthropist Julius Rosenwald and a $5-million bond issue to restore the exterior and reconstruct the interior, the renovation led, in 1933, to the opening of part of the Museum of Science and Industry. It is now the nation's most popular museum of its kind with an annual attendance of nearly four million—somewhat more than the population of the entire city.

Even Chicagoans who have been visiting the Museum of Science and Industry since childhood have yet to be anything but fascinated by its array of exhibits, ranging from the health sciences to physics to chemistry. One remarkable feature is the realistic indoor coal mine exhibit, where you ride an elevator down from a high point in the building to the confines of the make-believe mine. Much of the free museum reflects Midwestern business interests in agriculture (you see live chicks on display), nuclear energy (the nearby University of Chicago was the site of the first splitting of the atom), and railroading (one of the world's largest miniature railroad setups is here).

A general favorite is the annual Christmas Around the World display of evergreen trees decorated in the holiday traditions of the U.S., Korea, Japan, Germany, Denmark, and France, to name a few of the many countries represented. This highly photogenic display is staged from late November to early January. Still fascinating, too, is the permanent exhibit of the German U–505 submarine captured in 1944. Allow at least a half day for rambling among the museum's 2,000 exhibits in seventy-five different halls—it's a long walk, but an exciting one, covering some fourteen acres of floor area.

The Columbian Exposition of 1893 was also associated with the park-like Midway Plaisance of the University of Chicago, immediately west of the Museum of Science and Industry between 59th and 60th Streets. Here you enter the domain of the University of Chicago, the

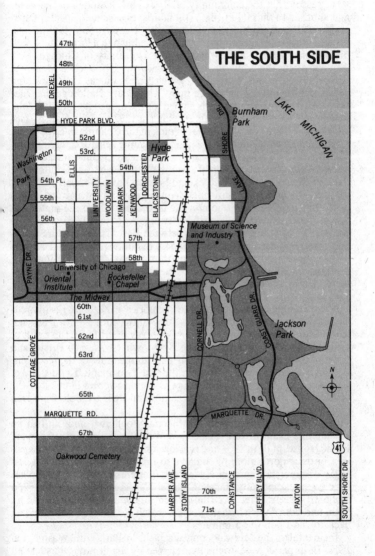

THE SOUTH SIDE

main reason that the community of Hyde Park, founded in the 1850s and annexed to the city in 1889, still flourishes as a lively locale of arts, crafts, and advanced intellectual pursuits. Novelist Saul Bellow long lived in the area, and economist Milton Friedman to a large extent built his international reputation while at the University of Chicago.

Walk along the Midway, as it's known, to Rockefeller Memorial Chapel, at 58th and Woodlawn, which stands out as the tallest and perhaps most interesting of the many University Buildings that face onto the parkway. The chapel is named for the university founder, John D. Rockefeller, who started things rolling in 1892 at Cobb Hall, at 58th and South Ellis, a year before the opening of the Columbian Exposition.

In the early '40s, some of the nation's leading scientists were assembled here on Ellis, including Enrico Fermi and Glenn T. Seaborg. It was Seaborg who led a group of scientists in the isolation of plutonium, the basic fuel of nuclear reactors, and Fermi who on December 2, 1942, directed the first successful nuclear chain reaction, which led to the development of the atom bomb. The laboratory where the plutonium was isolated is a national historic landmark: Room 405, of George Herbert Jones Laboratory on Ellis between East 57th and 58th Streets. Old Alonzo Stagg Field stadium, where the university's Big Ten football teams played, was the site of the nuclear chain reaction. The stadium is long gone; the site on Ellis between 56th and 57th Streets is marked by the Henry Moore sculpture appropriately titled *Nuclear Energy*.

More benign, certainly, are the memories evoked in the famous Oriental Institute, at 58th and Ellis, around the corner from Rockefeller Chapel. Here you'll find an amazing array of artifacts, the result of years of archaeological research in Egypt, what was once Persia, and other areas of the Middle East going back to the times of the pharaohs, Babylon, and other sites named in the Old Testament. The display of Egyptian mummies is extraordinary as are a towering likeness of the young Egyptian ruler King Tutankhamen and a winged bull (from Iraq circa 705 B.C.).

From here walk east to the corner of Woodlawn and 58th to an outstanding example of Frank Lloyd Wright's Prairie School design, Robie House, built in 1909 and now occupied by offices of the university. Continue north along Woodlawn to East 55th Street and then east to the commercial center of Hyde Park. The entire area is a great place for browsing, especially Harper Court at Harper Avenue between 52nd and 53rd Streets. There are Illinois Central commuter stations at 53d, 55th, and 59th Streets, where you can catch a train that will take you back to the Loop in 15 minutes.

Incidentally, the Midway connects Jackson Park with Washington Park. Both parks were originally designed by the firm of Olmsted and

Vaux. When Washington Park opened in 1874 it was a most fashionable place for Chicago's wealthy to roam. The 1893 Columbian Exposition brought great attention to Jackson Park, and since that time, Washington Park suffered a decline in favor. The park's main attractions are the DuSable Museum of African American History and the Lorado Taft Sculpture, *Fountain of Time*. It is used, however, on weekends by neighborhood families for ball games and barbecues.

Sheridan Road and the Northern Suburbs

From the Loop you can tour Sheridan Road, named for a Civil War general, Philip Henry Sheridan, by car or sightseeing bus. It's a drive that keeps you close to Lake Michigan and still introduces you to many outstanding neighborhoods and institutions. Sheridan Road actually begins a few blocks west of Lake Shore Drive at Diversey Boulevard, and trail-like, ambles west for a half mile or so where it right-angles into a straight north route to Devon. Reflecting the changing positions of the shoreline (Lake Michigan widens as you move north), Sheridan continues to present sharp, right-angle turns to the west and then north as you make your way into Evanston and beyond.

Your best bet is to pick up Sheridan Road at Foster Avenue, just west of Lake Shore Drive. The Saddle and Cycle, one of the city's rare surviving old-fashioned tennis clubs, is located off Foster just west of the Drive. Turning north on Sheridan, you drive past stunning high-rise apartments and what's left of the old Edgewater Beach development (for years the Edgewater Beach Hotel, now extinct, was a Chicago institution, dating from the days when the lake water literally bordered the city a short distance east of Sheridan Road, as it continues to do north of Hollywood. Most of Lincoln Park was built on landfill, which also permitted construction of northern Lake Shore Drive.

Immediately north of Hollywood, where Lake Shore Drive terminates, you will pass a score or more of high-rise apartment buildings that front on the lake. A few blocks beyond, you come to a complex that is Mundelein College and the undergraduate campus of Loyola University, the state's largest privately endowed college. (The Loyola downtown campus is in Lewis Towers, immediately west of the Chicago Water Tower.) Pull off Sheridan Road at the south entrance to the Loyola Campus and ask directions to the Madonna Strada Chapel, a little-known jewel of a church right on the lakeshore. The modern library, a few steps from the chapel, houses a small, interesting art gallery.

Continue north to the 7400 block of Sheridan, where you can spot a landmark home designed in 1915 by Frank Lloyd Wright, the Emil

Bach house. As you enter Evanston drive around Calvary Cemetery, which also fronts on the lake.

After you pass Calvary Cemetery and turn north on Sheridan once more, you'll immediately get a sense of old Chicago suburbia: large homes, large lawns, large shrubs, and frequently, large automobiles. You can turn off at practically any side street north of Main Street (which cuts into Sheridan) to view any number of extraordinary dwellings. Forest Avenue north of Main can be especially rewarding with examples of Prairie School architecture at 1000 and the old Oscar Mayer mansion at 1030. There's a Michigan Avenue in Evanston, too. It's immediately west of Sheridan Road and replete with turn-of-the-century mansions. Farther west, at 1730 Chicago Avenue, the 1865 Willard House has been restored and is open for tours. The original owner, Frances Willard, was a temperance leader, and the home now houses the national headquarters of the Women's Christian Temperance Union.

Sheridan Road actually bypasses downtown Evanston, but if you're interested in seeing a relatively thriving shopping area, turn west on Davis Street.

Not long ago, Evanston was dry as a bone—remember, it's the home of the Women's Christian Temperance Union—but now the restaurants serve beer, wine, and liquor. Being the home of Northwestern University, Evanston is something of an oversized college town. In fact the university's first president, John Evans, circa 1855, prompted the name of the town. At that time, Evans presided over ten scholars in a three-story frame structure. Today the university has two large campuses (the professional/medical one is at Chicago Avenue just west of Lake Shore Drive) with overall enrollment of some 10,000 students. The Evanston campus is primarily devoted to liberal arts and engineering, with outstanding music and drama departments. You can tour the campus on your own: pick up a self-guided pamphlet at the Norris University Center, 1999 Sheridan Road. Farther north, at 2100 Sheridan, you can visit the Shakespeare Garden, a quiet, formal garden of roses, rosemary, and other flora mentioned in the works of the Bard.

Not many remember the vice-president who served under Calvin Coolidge—in fact, many have trouble remembering Coolidge. But his vice-president, Charles Gates Dawes, lived in a turreted, 28-room chateau at 225 Greenwood Street in Evanston. The building is nicely restored and open for tours.

Just north of the Northwestern Campus, you'll spot on your right a rare Lake Michigan lighthouse, called the Grosse Point Lighthouse, which dates from 1860. The lighthouse is home to a couple who have lived there for a number of years.

Sheridan Road continues to jog to the west here, then north, as you wend your way through Evanston and into Wilmette. Wilmette is noted architecturally for the famous Baha'i House of Worship, a distinctive temple-like structure that seems to combine the dome of St. Peter's with the flying buttresses of the Cathedral of Notre Dame, but all with a definite Middle Eastern flair. This is a must stop for any photography enthusiast.

The Temple serves as the national center of the Persian-born Baha'i faith, which happened to be represented at the Columbian Exposition of 1893. Construction of the Temple began in 1903 and was completed in 1953.

Continuing north, you'll see even more opulent examples of suburban living in Kenilworth, a small, exclusive suburb tucked between Wilmette and Winnetka. Soon you arrive at a pleasant little shopping center, Plaza del Lago, with a Spanish motif. Stop for lunch or a little shopping. Burhops, one of Chicago's leading seafood vendors, has a store there, as do any number of small, classy boutiques.

The North Shore's biggest and most popular community event is the Ravinia Festival in the town of Highland Park. It plays every summer in Ravinia Park from late June through early September at a 36-acre wooded park a couple of miles west of the lake. It's a community event because countless volunteers help finance and put together the annual series of symphonic concerts, recitals, chamber music, and popular musical events from rock to country to Dixieland jazz.

Ravinia Park is to Chicago, therefore, what Tanglewood is to Boston or the Hollywood Bowl is to Los Angeles. Featured for the first eight weeks of the season is the Chicago Symphony Orchestra with its summer director, James Levine, and any number of renowned guest conductors. It's all very informal, with normally straitlaced musicians appearing tieless in short-sleeved sport shirts (white, of course).

A large percentage of the audience arrives as early as 6:00, allowing time to dine in one of two restaurants (one features buffet) or to picnic (with wine) on pleasant little tables in a delightful gazebo.

For best listening and viewing, a reserved seat in the Pavilion is definitely in order, but if you are satisfied with just hearing the music piped over loudspeakers, you can join hundreds of other concertgoers who recline on their blankets on the lawn outside the Pavilion and listen under the stars.

Commuter trains from the Chicago and North Western station at Madison and Canal provide direct service between the Loop and the Ravinia Park concerts, or you can reserve space on a chartered bus (through any major hotel).

North of Highland Park, Sheridan Road leads you past Fort Sheridan, which served as a major processing center for Army recruits during World War II. Now it's more like a country club.

Barat College on Sheridan Road, at the southern entrance to Lake Forest, is a small liberal arts college for girls operated by the Sisters of the Sacred Heart. Lake Forest itself is among Chicago's most exclusive suburbs, with tree-lined streets that are breathtaking any time of year, but especially so in October, when full fall color comes to areas along Lake Michigan.

Other places of interest nearby include the Marriott Lincolnshire Resort at Lincolnshire and Six Flags Great America at Gurnee, a few miles north and west of Lake Forest. The resort is a combination hotel/motel featuring swimming, dining areas, cocktail lounges, a well-regarded theater-in-the-round that draws professional performers, and an 18-hole golf course.

Six Flags Great America provides attractions for the entire family, from thrill rides like The Edge, a nearly vertical roller coaster, to musical shows in the Theatre Royale and the usual cast of comic characters à la Disneyland, but of a non-Disney sort: these depict Bugs Bunny and characters from the old Looney Tunes comedy movie shorts. The park is open from early May to October with a full seven-day schedule from June through early September. Admission is fairly high, so plan to arrive close to the 10:00 A.M. opening to allow time enough to enjoy all that the park offers.

Western Suburbs (Oak Park, Brookfield)

You can reach Oak Park from downtown Chicago by driving west along the Eisenhower Expressway (I-290). Oak Park is known for two major Chicago figures: Ernest Hemingway, who lived there as a youngster, and Frank Lloyd Wright, who accomplished much of his Prairie Style architecture in and near this western suburb. Vestiges of the Hemingway boyhood are hard to find, but Wright's works are easy to see. Wright and other architects of his period are well represented in Oak Park. The Hemingway birthplace, noted by a plaque, is at 339 North Oak Park Avenue, and his boyhood home is at 600 North Kenilworth.

Two of the more prominent structures on public tours of the area are the Frank Lloyd Wright Home and Studio, 951 Chicago Avenue (a National Historic Landmark built in 1889, when Wright was 22; the restored studio dates from 1898), and the Wright-designed Unity Temple (built between 1905 and 1909 at Lake and Kenilworth; it presents an interlocking complex of abstract geometric forms).

Begin your tour of the Oak Park Historic District at the Visitor Center, 150 North Forest Avenue. The center provides a slide show to introduce you to the area, an annotated walking-tour map so that you can guide yourself, a recorded tour for self-guidance, and a host of pamphlets. A guided tour that covers the temple and Wright's home and studio is offered as well. The historic district is bounded roughly by Lake, Clyde and Division Streets and Harlem Avenue.

While at the Center, also inquire about the River Forest Historic District north of Oak Park, where you can see six Wright-designed homes in one of Chicago's best-manicured suburbs. The suburb of River Forest is adjacent to Oak Park and its historic district is just a couple blocks from Oak Park's. It contains a number of houses by other architects of the Prairie School as well as some in the classical and medieval styles dating from the 1920s. Edgewood Place, just east of Auvergne, is especially rewarding.

Chicago, incidentally, is ringed by a series of massive forest preserves, and while you're in the Oak Park–River Forest area, you're close to one of the finest. Just drive west on Lake, Division, Chicago, or North Avenue to Thatcher. A Trailside Museum at 738 Thatcher, a building dating from 1874, houses a modest small-mammal zoo.

The Brookfield Zoo, 14 miles west of the Loop in suburban Brookfield (southwest of Oak Park), has been attracting animal lovers to 200 acres since 1934. It was the first zoological park in the country allowing animals to roam freely while visitors gaze at them over waist-high fences and deep protective moats. Over recent years, the zoo has added a popular dolphin show, "Seven Seas Panorama," and a delightful children's zoo. The zoo's largest addition is Tropic World, said to be the largest *indoor* exhibit of animals—mostly primates—in the world. Actually Tropic World is three "worlds" in one: Africa, Asia, and South America—each depicting the rain-forest ecology of the subcontinents.

West of Chicago

Even farther to the west, Oakbrook, one of the newest and most expensive of the Chicago suburbs, is the epitome of a planned, high-income community. The Oakbrook Shopping Center is replete with upscale shops and a major branch of Marshall Field & Co. Hotels, reflecting a trend of business to migrate closer to O'Hare Field, abound in the area. The Drake Oakbrook features a relatively low-cost weekend package that includes a welcome bottle of champagne, cocktails, dinner in the informal downstairs grill, and brunch in the elaborate dining room that overlooks a golf course and polo field.

Beyond Oakbrook, the popular Morton Arboretum, just north of the East-West Tollway at Illinois 53, is at its peak in May, when the flowers are in bloom and early October, when leaves changing turn the area into a rainbow of color. Ducks paddle in a pond near the main entrance of this 1,500-acre preserve of woody plants from around the world. The formal gardens here are especially attractive.

 SIGHTSEEING CHECKLIST. Chicago of the 1980s is undergoing a building renaissance that has lasted over 25 years. Every day, construction is underway on one new skyscraper or another as the Loop and Near North Side literally transform themselves into modern-day wonders. But there's far more to Chicago than these two areas, and so we've compiled a checklist of "must see" places not only in the city, but in outlying areas as well. You may not get to see all of them in one visit, but Chicago's the kind of place that always welcomes the visitor for a second and different look. The following are the places to plan a first- or second-time visit around, but allocate your time carefully, virtually all of them can keep you longer than you anticipate.

Sears Tower. Now the tallest building in the United States, the Sears Tower, in the Loop at Wacker Drive between Adams and Jackson, is the place to go for an overview of downtown Chicago, the city's gorgeous lakefront, and the fascinating North Side. Just picking out the tops of distinctive buildings in and around the Loop can take a half hour or more.

The Art Institute of Chicago stands out as one of the city's (and the nation's) great repositories of European paintings (especially French). It also has an outstanding oriental collection, and you can usually count on at least one temporary exhibit of national or international stature.

The Chicago Board of Trade. Now in larger quarters at the foot of La Salle Street in the heart of the Financial District, the Board of Trade is a block-size building that is great to look at from the outside and better still to browse in on any business day. Try to witness the exciting close of trading on two great trading floors around 1:00 P.M.

State Street, That Great Street. Parts of the northern section are under renewal, but the street that made Chicago famous still stands as a major attraction, especially for daytime browsing along the mall-like walkways dotted with popcorn, nut, and snack stands. Here you'll find the home base of Marshall Field & Co., Carson, Pirie, Scott & Co., the Palmer House with its great lobby, and the city's Hot Tix Booth, a bonanza for theatergoers on a budget.

The Chicago Public Library Cultural Center. Don't let the somber facade at Michigan and Randolph turn you off: walk inside to a wonderland of Tiffany glass domes, modern comfortable reading areas, and a truly delightful room in Preston Bradley Hall, third floor south.

Daley Center and the City-County Building. This complex of city and county offices plus a distinguished courthouse includes the Chicago Picasso, a lovely fountain, and a great cross section of the city. The new State of Illinois Building at the corner of Randolph and Clark is also worthwhile.

Dearborn Street in the Loop. From Madison to Jackson. Walking here is truly a great experience of seeing architecture blend the old with the new: First National Bank and its lower-level plaza; the ultramodern Xerox Building; the old Marquette Building with its colorful interior murals; and the Federal Center with the stunning sculpture *Flamingo.*

Water Tower Place and Magnificent Mile. This is a great area to begin or end a visit to Chicago. Water Tower Place is a throbbing vertical center of department stores, boutiques, restaurants, theaters, and even a world-class hotel, the Ritz-Carlton. And it's all within steps of Chicago's most distinctive landmark, the original Water Tower, which survived the great Chicago Fire of 1871. Buildings and shops along the Magnificent Mile, extending north and south of Water Tower, include the John Hancock Center, a Neiman-Marcus in Olympia Center, I. Magnin, Tiffany's, Elizabeth Arden, Saks Fifth Avenue, plus any number of art galleries, jewelry stores, etc.

The Chicago Lakefront. Seeing the city from Lake Michigan is truly a joy, and you can do so best by taking one of the boat rides from the Michigan Avenue Bridge over the Chicago River. Best time is toward the end of the day when the setting sun gives the whole city a soft, golden glow.

Lincoln Park and Lincoln Park Zoo. Animals freely roaming in large natural confines: apes and gorillas, lions and tigers, polar bears and giraffes. There's also a delightful Children's Zoo, an intriguing animal-filled Farm-in-the-Zoo, and one of the city's outstanding flora collections in the nearby Lincoln Park Conservatory. And it's all free.

Grant Park Museums. Located at Roosevelt Road and Lake Shore Drive south and east of the Loop, Field Museum of Natural History, John G. Shedd Aquarium, and Adler Planetarium always rank among the city's top attractions. The Field Museum especially is not to be missed, with its fantastically high entrance hall and labyrinth of lifelike exhibits depicting man and mammal from over the world since the beginnings of time.

Museum of Science and Industry. Located in Jackson Park on the city's South Side, this is a veritable wonderland of technology and nostalgia: exhibits touch on virtually all things scientific, mathematic, medical, and technological —from coal mining to agriculture, railroading, and nuclear energy, with a great exhibit on outer space.

OUTLYING AREAS. Baha'i House of Worship, on Sheridan Road at Linden Avenue in Wilmette. One of the area's outstanding architectural sights, a photographer's delight.

Frank Lloyd Wright Prairie School of Architecture Historic District. Dedicated to Wright and his colleagues, who literally changed the face of American homebuilding architecture early in the twentieth century. Most of it began right here in the western suburb of Oak Park in an area bounded by Harlem Avenue, Division, Clyde and Lake Streets.

Brookfield Zoo, in the suburb of Brookfield. Always well regarded, the zoo now has an added feature in its great dolphin show and Tropic World, an indoor rain-forest structure with all sorts of mammals and birds seemingly close enough to reach out and touch.

O'Hare International Airport. Just in volume of travelers and size alone, this is worth looking at, but there are other features too: an intriguing underground series of shops and restaurants, and a great cocktail lounge and dining room between two major terminals with great views of planes taking off and landing at a rate of one or more every minute.

PRACTICAL INFORMATION FOR CHICAGO

HOW TO GET THERE. By car: I–80 in the northern part of Illinois comes in from neighboring Iowa and Indiana, and I–70 in the south crosses the Mississippi River from Missouri as the 2 major east-west highways. I–90 and I–94 approach Chicago from Wisconsin to the north and I–57 slices across the state from the Kentucky border on the south.

By train: *Amtrak* serves Chicago from major cities throughout the United States and cities on the Canadian rail systems. Check for schedules and costs with your travel agent or nearest Amtrak passenger station. Call 800–USA RAIL toll free from anywhere or 558–1075 from Chicago.

By air: Chicago currently has 3 airports. O'Hare is about 18 miles west of the downtown area, accessible by I–90, 294, and Ill.–53, and has long been rated the world's busiest airport. Midway Airport is off the Stevenson Expressway (I–55) bounded by 55th and 63rd streets about 1/2 hr. from downtown. Meigs Field is at 15th St. and the lakefront, less than 15 min. from downtown. Chicago's O'Hare Airport is served by numerous major airlines, including *Delta, Eastern, Northwest Orient, United, American, Trans World, Piedmont, Ozark, Republic, Capitol, Jet America, U.S. Air, Western, Pan Am, People Express, Frontier-Horizon,* and *Continental. Mississippi Valley, Simmons,* and *Midstate Air Commuter, Air Wisconsin, Phillips, American Central, Air Midwest,* and *Britt* are other feeder airlines. There are also direct overseas flights via *Alitalia, Air France, British Airways, Lufthansa, K.L.M., Sabena, S.A.S., Icelandair, Swissair, Air Canada, Japan Airlines, Iberia, Yugoslav Airlines, El Al,* and *Mexicana. Midway Metrolink* flies into Midway Airport, which is closer to downtown Chicago than O'Hare, and private planes still use Miegs Field along the lakefront, although its future is always the subject of discussion.

By bus: *Greyhound* and *Trailways* both serve Illinois from around the country. Consult a travel agent or the carriers directly: Greyhound at 74 W. Randolph; 781–2900, covers 48 states and Canada. Trailways at 20 E. Randolph; 726–9500, also has nationwide service.

TELEPHONES. The area code for Chicago and the surrounding area is 312. You do not need to dial the area code if it is the same as the one from which you are dialing. Information (known as directory assistance) for Chicago and communities within the 312 area is 411. For numbers outside the 312 area code, dial 1 plus the area code plus 555–1212. An operator will assist you on person-to-person, credit-card, and collect calls if you first dial "0." All long-distance calls must first be prefaced by dialing 1, followed by the area code and number. Pay telephones start at 30¢.

HOTELS. Like all major cities, Chicago has had its share of glamour hotels ever since multimillionaire Potter Palmer built his grand old Palmer House. Most of the prestigious, big-name chains are here, and competition being what it is, these tend to refurbish, redecorate, and generally gussy-up their properties with some regularity. They span the super deluxe to expensive categories and feature all the high standards associated with their names.

The usual percentage of slick, ultramodern new hotels exists, catering to high-volume business and pleasure travelers. They are comfortable, full of the latest in modern conveniences, and exude a flashy veneer of sophistication.

Then there are the old grand dames, the prestige mainline names where your grandmother stayed when she came to Chicago and which feature a more formal elegance, richly paneled lobbies, acres of polished marble, genuine antiques, and service in the old manner. They offer the kind of wide aisled, grand staircase grandeur impossible to duplicate in today's world.

Over the past few years an interesting new trend has been developing toward creating small personalized English-type hotels. These tend to be very posh, low-key, and upper-class and exude the quiet rustle of old money. Their mood is understated, comparable to London's finest.

Some of the moderate finds are often so priced because of location, which may be a bit out of the center for some travelers or perfect for others. There are fashions in hotels, just like clothes. Being older, down the street, around the block, and perhaps not as "in" today simply because newer, flashier spots may have captured the limelight, some of the moderately priced hotels are excellent and have very devoted followings.

Inexpensive is a relative term. This year's inexpensive price range was probably considered deluxe not too many years ago. Those chosen here are selected from the many for specific reasons. Some are close to downtown and feature on-site parking, others cater to families interested in adequate, comfortable, and clean surroundings but who have no need of a concierge, imported bath oil, and a posh decor.

Price categories for double occupancy are as follows: *Super Deluxe* $150–$200 and up; *Deluxe* $110–$180; *Expensive* $85–$105; *Moderate* $65–$84; and *Inexpensive* $65 and under.

Interestingly, a wide spectrum of all categories offers escape weekends packages at bargain prices. So investigate before you invest. Chicago Hotel Association, 100 W. Monroe, 60603, offers a brochure outlining weekend specials.

Super Deluxe

Mayfair Regent. 181 E. Lake Shore Dr.; 787–8500. Gracious, traditional, new 220-room beauty totally refurbished. (Formerly Lake Shore Drive Hotel dating from late 1920s.) 19th-floor rooftop dining with sweeping lake view. Accent on old-world service. Arriving guests register with bilingual concierge at antique Louis XVI desk. Quiet residential Gold Coast mood close to North Michigan Ave., across from Oak St. Beach. Lobby lounge is decorated with hand-painted Chinese murals and, with its fireplace, has the living room look of a town-house mansion. 24-hour room service. Umbrella and plush robes in room. Private telephone-equipped limousines for airport transportation or local sightseeing. *Palm* restaurant. Even their garbage is refrigerated!

Park Hyatt. 800 N. Michigan Ave., on Water Tower Sq.; 280–2222. This is the former Water Tower Hyatt, and anyone who knew it then would never recognize the place. It has been turned into a remarkable Cinderella, an intimate jewel of a hotel where the arrival of each guest is treated like a special event. The doorman who welcomes you is wearing a coachman's coat and cape made of mink with black leather Gucci boots. Check-in is personalized, a concierge is there to smooth the way, and housekeepers are stationed on every floor to unpack your luggage and take care of any necessary sewing or pressing. The 255 rooms have marble-topped dressers, rosewood and Chinese lacquer pieces, designer bed linens, and hand-painted watercolors. The lobby's marble floors are covered with Oriental rugs, and Oriental art, velvet sofas, and lush palms provide a relaxing, low-key decor. The style is definitely upper echelon. This is the first of the "small wonderfuls" planned by the Hyatt chain.

Ritz Carlton Hotel. 160 E. Pearson, just off Michigan Blvd.; 266–1000. Shoppers can practically fall out of bed and into the temptations of Water Tower Place across the driveway. An unusual hotel that does not begin until the 12th floor, although there is luggage check-in at the lower level. The spectacular lobby is a marvelous place to promenade—large, splashy fountain, acres of lounge space, fountain-side dining room. The hotel offers the kind of grandeluxe service and facilities that the name implies. For the absolute ultimate in baths, the Anniversary Suite has a 5½-by-7-ft. white marble tub set on a pedestal with a chandelier overhead and silver trees etched on walls and mirrors.

Tremont. 100 E. Chestnut; 751–1900. A prestige property where there are only suites. Antique English prints and large Flemish-style vases decorate the unpretentious lobby—rather like the entrance to an English country house. Fireplaces, overstuffed chairs, everything quiet, unobtrusive, and very classy. Elizabeth Taylor likes to stay here when she's in town. Good location 1 block from Upper Michigan Ave. Its *Crickets Restaurant* is locally popular.

Whitehall. 105 E. Delaware Pl., just off Michigan Blvd.; 944–6300. Very prestigious, has the understated low-key, high-quality mood of a private upper-class London club. Everything about the place is so unique that even the dining room is private, open only to members and guests. For the ultimate, the elaborate Terrace Suite has its own formal dining room, kitchen, terrace complete with garden furniture and plants, sitting room, and bedroom. Even guests like Gregory Peck, Katherine Hepburn, Richard Burton, and Donald Sutherland have found their privacy protected here. Do not expect a lot of flash and glitter. The entrance and lobby look like a high-rent town house just off Knightsbridge. 222 rooms function with quiet efficiency, fresh Rogers and Gallet soap magically reappears in bathrooms, and the food is always good.

Deluxe

Ambassador East & West. 1300 N. State Pkwy.; 787–7200, 787–7900. These redecorated establishments remain elegant society queens among the city's hotels. Many visiting show-business celebrities stay here. No. 1 booth in the Pump

Room at Ambassador East still marks the importance of celebrities. Excellent service, beginning of quiet residential Gold Coast neighborhood.

The Barclay-Chicago. 166 E. Superior; 787–6000. Under the same management as The Knickerbocker-Chicago, it is another very special personalized hotel. Soft French Provincial decor; 75 percent of the rooms are suites. 100 suites have fully equipped kitchens and stocked liquor cabinets.

Chicago Marriott. 540 N. Michigan; 836–0100. Opened May 1978. Good location along south fringe of "Magnificent Mile" of carriage-trade shops and prestigious restaurants. Ultramodern, eclectic decor. Lots of convention business. Rooms functional but quite standard.

The Drake. 140 E. Walton Place at Michigan Ave.; 787–2200. Across the street from the Oak Street Beach. Truly deluxe suites, the kind of baronial grandeur no one can duplicate today. Some people with familiar society names maintain apartments here. Noted for variety of exceptional restaurants. Outstanding luxury in the grand manner with a sense of tradition.

Hyatt Regency. 151 E. Wacker Dr.; 565–1234. East of the Michigan Ave. Bridge. So popular it is constantly expanding, now has 2,033 rooms and large convention center. Familiar Hyatt-style waterfall lobby with tropical plants. Lots of bustle, activity, innovative entertainment, and all those "touch of Hyatt" extras. Some suites have fireplaces. Underground garage for on-site, pull-in parking.

The Knickerbocker-Chicago. 163 E. Walton; 751–8100. For a while this was the Playboy Towers. Now it has reassumed its maiden name, and the famous glass dance floor and everything else in the 265-room hotel just off Michigan Ave. has been restored. 94 of the rooms have 2 baths. You'll find Godiva chocolates on your turned-down bed and Vitabath in the tub; bathrooms are equipped with toothbrush, toothpaste, and dental floss. The blond oak-paneled walls of the *Prince of Wales Room* are a mellow background for the harp music played at dinner.

The Lenox House. 616 N. Rush St.; 337–1000. (Formerly the Croydon). Mostly suites, kitchens in all units. Completely refurbished.

Palmer House. State and Monroe; 726–7500. Millionaire founder Potter Palmer would be happy to check in here any time. One of the truly grand old hotels. Now a Hilton property. Built in an elaborate gilt-edge style no longer possible to duplicate, the Empire Room is one of the most beautiful dining rooms in the city. Second-floor lobby that leads to it is also worth a visit. Fine restaurants, lounges, excellent downtown location only steps away from all major State St. department stores. New luxury section in the Tower.

Raphael. 201 E. Delaware; 943–5000 or 800–327–9157. An elegant find with European atmosphere. 172 guest rooms on the Gold Coast one block east of Michigan quality far surpasses its prices: such touches as a box of chocolates on arrival and Perrier water in your room refrigerator.

Westin Hotel. 909 N. Michigan; 943–7200. Formerly the Continental Plaza. Settle down into spacious quarters with period furniture and remote control TV. Newest "in" spot for the new generation Hollywood set. Another excellent location for shoppers along the avenue.

Expensive

Americana-Congress. 520 S. Michigan Ave.; 800–228–3278 in Illinois, 800–223–2672 outside the state. (Formerly Pick-Congress.) Another of those sturdy structures built to last. Modernized, face-lifted, and facing toward the Art Institute. 5 restaurants.

Chicago Hilton and Towers. 720 S. Michigan Ave.; 922–4400. Its 1620 rooms make it one of the world's largest hotels, almost a self-contained city in itself. Big and busy. South of downtown with beautiful views overlooking Grant Park and the lakeshore. Ideal location for museum-goers. Art Institute, Goodman Theatre, Field Museum, Shedd Aquarium, and Adler Planetarium all close by. Big face-lifting and refurbishing completed in 1985 cost over $150 million.

Hotel Continental (formerly the Radisson). 505 N. Michigan; 944–4100. At one time the building housed a private athletic club, and the pool resembles a Roman bath, truly Olympic in size. *Kon Tiki Ports* is a popular restaurant. Next door to *Chicago Tribune.*

McCormick Center Hotel. 23rd St. and S. Lake Shore Dr.; 791–1900. A convention hotel-motel with 650 rooms. Always operating at full steam as conventioneers rush in and out for nearby McCormick Place. Fine for its purpose, but nonconventioneering families would find it noisy and fast paced. There is a health club with sauna, steam bath, and whirlpool.

Midland. 172 W. Adams; 332–1200. A recently refurbished hotel that has turned into a real European-style beauty while still preserving its rich architectural integrity. One of the new celebrities on the local hotel scene. In the heart of the financial district. Good food, definitely a rising star. 100 guest rooms have personal computers (Dialcom) with access to electronic mail as well as stock market, sports, airline, and entertainment information.

Ramada Executive House. 71 E. Wacker Dr.; 346–7100. Overlooks Chicago R. just ½ block off Michigan Ave. Located just north of the Loop. Caters to expense account travelers, very modern mood. Rooftop restaurant.

Richmont. 162 E. Ontario; 787–3580. (Formerly the Eastgate.) Another of the intimate-sized new finds located among the boutiques, galleries, and restaurants of North Michigan Ave. Rates include Continental breakfast. Completely renovated and decorated with European flavor.

Sheraton-Plaza. 160 E. Huron; 787–2900. A special bonus here is a rooftop pool offering a dramatic view of the city. Concierge.

Moderate

Allerton. 701 N. Michigan; 440–1500 or 800–621–8311. Recently renovated. 350 rooms at about the lowest rates to be found in the pricey North Michigan Ave. area. Older, but clean and a real bargain for budget travelers.

Ascot Motel. 1100 S. Michigan; 922–2900 or 800–621–4196. Large motel south of shopping and business district but close to McCormick Place and South Side attractions. Outdoor heated pool, 14 cabana rooms. Free parking. 200 rooms.

Avenue Motel. 1154 S. Michigan; 427–8200 or 800–621–4196. 80 rooms south of the city. Room service, waffle shop, cocktail lounge, and free parking. Decor is Far Eastern.

Bismarck. 171 W. Randolph; 236–0123. Well-known older hotel with loyal following. Located across from County Building-City Hall. *Chalet* restaurant is noted for Swiss-German specialties, and the hotel has something of a Germanic flavor. Good dollar value. Some recent remodeling in bedrooms. Garage facilities.

Blackstone Hotel. 636 S. Michigan; 427–4300. Has been around a long time and still going strong. Became known as a favorite with visiting Presidents a long time ago, but it has been a long time since one stayed there. Across from Grant Park and the Art Institute, close to the Auditorium Theater and Roosevelt College.

Essex Inn. 800 S. Michigan; 939–2800 or 800–621–6909. Recently redecorated and well located for those headed for McCormick Place Convention Center and south-of-the-city attractions. Free bus to the Loop makes getting around easy. Outdoor heated pool, some cabana rooms. Free parking.

Holiday Inn. This chain maintains 3 quite sophisticated hotels near the downtown area: **Number one** is at 644 N. Lake Shore Dr.; 943–9200. A 33-story motor hotel with revolving rooftop restaurant and entertainment. Close to Navy Pier and convenient to downtown, with nice location near lake. The **Mart Plaza** sits high atop the chic new Apparel Center at 350 N. Orleans St. across from the Merchandise Mart; 836–5000; and **Chicago City Centre** is on Ohio just off Michigan; 787–6100. All are high rise and offer in total over 2,000 rooms.

Hyde Park Hilton. 4900 S. Lake Shore Dr.; 288–5800. Only 5 min. to the Museum of Science and Industry and McCormick Place. Also a neighbor to the University of Chicago and the treasures of the Oriental Institute. 330 newly appointed rooms and suites, a lake-view restaurant, lounge, and large outdoor swimming pool and sun deck. Lots of free parking. Hourly free shuttle service to North Michigan Ave.

Many other chain motels have what they consider showcase properties here. **Rodeway Inn,** 506 W. Harrison St.; 427–6969; with 154 rooms, is considered a convenient location. So is the 150-room **TraveLodge** at La Salle and Ohio Sts.; 467–0800; with its year-round rooftop swimming pool and free parking. Near the Merchandise Mart. **Quality Inn** is at 1 S. Halsted St. and Madison St., just off Kennedy Expressway (I–94); 829–5000.

Inexpensive

Lake Shore Hotel. 600 N. Lake Shore Drive; 787–4700. A good address close by Northwestern University's Downtown Campus and the furniture Mart. Just across from lakefront Olive Park.

Comfort Inn of Chicago. 601 W. Diversey; 348–2810. 100 completely remodeled and modernized rooms with complimentary breakfast and hotel service. Close to Lincoln Park, beach, and about 10 min. from downtown. Coffee shop, cocktail lounge.

La Salle Motor Lodge. 720 N. La Salle; 664–8100. Called "the affordable motor hotel in downtown Chicago." Location is an important factor here. Just

7 blocks north of city center, within walking distance of Merchandise Mart and Apparel Center. You can park next to your room. 70 rooms, restaurant. No meeting facilities available.

Ohio House. At La Salle and Ohio, near the Merchandise Mart; 943–6000. This is a surprising find—a 2-story, 50-room motel complete with coffee shop and at-door self-parking and near the heart of the city. There is a free courtesy car to the Loop and major attractions. Easy access to expressways.

O'HARE AIRPORT AREA

Deluxe

Hyatt Regency O'Hare. 9300 W. Bryn Mawr Ave.; 696–1234. Striking copper mirrorlike exterior makes this a landmark. 1,100 rooms overlook 12-story atrium lobby in dramatic Hyatt tradition. All those "touch of Hyatt" extras. Close to O'Hare, but also only 20 min. from the Loop. Health club for stress-bound travelers, 4 restaurants and 2 lounges.

Marriott-O'Hare Motor Hotel. 8535 W. Higgins Rd. at Cumberland interchange on Kennedy Expressway; 693–4444. Business executives tend to gather here for fly-in corporate meetings. Families often come along to enjoy its 2 pools, ice skating, health club, and tennis.

The Westin Hotel, O'Hare. 6100 River Rd., Rosemont; 698–6000. Opened January 1984. Its 535 rooms are 4 min. from O'Hare. Facilities include year-round swimming pool, health club, and 2 racquetball courts. There are 2 restaurants and a sleek lobby lounge in the Westin tradition, plus an entertainment lounge.

Expensive

O'Hare Hilton. Directly across from main terminals in the world's busiest airport; 686–8000. All 886 rooms are soundproofed. Usual Hilton standards, lots of conference space and 7 restaurants to accommodate guests. Underground moving sidewalks offer direct access to airport terminals.

Sheraton O'Hare North. 6810 N. Mannheim, Rosemont; 297–1234. This 500-room facility is 3 miles north of the airport. Features indoor and outdoor pools, sauna, and recreation facilities. Recently renovated.

Moderate

The Hamilton Stouffer Hotel. 400 Park Blvd.; west of airport, near Itasca; 773–4000. Eye-opening, 12-story atrium lobby; 370 luxurious rooms; complete health facilities.

Holiday Inn. Two additional locations near airport: Touhy Ave. and Mannheim Rd., Des Plaines; 296–8866. 1000 Busse Hwy., Elk Grove Village; 437–6010.

Ramada Hotel O'Hare. 6600 N. Mannheim Rd.; 2 miles north; 827–5131. Hotel and motor inn with indoor and outdoor pools, health club; 727 rooms; home of well-known *Henrici's Restaurant.*

Rodeway Inn. 3801 Mannheim Rd., Schiller Park; 678–0670.

Inexpensive

Quality Inn. 3939 N. Mannheim, Schiller Park; 678–4800. $5 million spent to completely refurbish Manny Skar's onetime headliner.

TraveLodge. 3003 Mannheim Rd. at Higgins Rd. 1 mi. north of airport; 296–5541. This smaller, 2-story facility has 95 rooms and offers family rates as well as a free airport shuttle bus.

For rock bottom economy, there is **Royal 6,** 6450 Touhy Ave., I–94 (Niles); 647–7700; and **Regal 8 Inn,** 2448 N. Mannheim (Franklin Park); 455–6500.

 BED AND BREAKFAST. Bed & Breakfast, Chicago. P.O. Box 14088 Chicago, 60614. (312) 951–0085. $35–$120 double with breakfast. Some hosts multilingual. Contact for information on 90 different locations in homes, high rises in Evanston, Chicago, and North Side.

 HOW TO GET AROUND. By bus: Chicago has an extensive bus system that will take you long distances for 90¢. For 10¢ extra you can get a transfer that allows you to spend an hour shopping or sightseeing before you ride back. Only change may be used—no dollar bills. If you need information on public transportation, call RTA 24-hour information at 836–7000. Tell them where you are, and where you want to go, and they will tell you how to get there. *CTA Culture Bus* operates every Sunday and holidays from the Art Institute, mid-April through September, on 3 routes that serve over 30 museums and cultural attractions. These operate between 11:00 A.M. and 5:15 P.M., allowing passengers to get off at a particular destination, then later reboard another bus. Fare is $2.00 adults, 70¢ children.

By subway: Subway maps are available from *Chicago Tourism Bureau* and the same fare structure applies.

From the airports: O'Hare Airport, at Mannheim and Kennedy Expressway, is by far the most frequently used. Many hotels have their own airport shuttle service. For $6.00, *Continental Air Transport* will take you to downtown Chicago. The stops for the limousine are listed by hotels, so just get out at the hotel nearest your destination. A rapid-transit train offers direct service to Chicago in about 34 min. Free courtesy buses are provided by about 30 O'Hare area hotels. (See *O'Hare Airport Area* hotel listings.) Midway Airport, only 11 mi. from downtown, is connected to Chicago by Continental Air Transport at $5.00 per person.

By taxi: Taxis currently charge $1.00 base fare and 90¢ for each additional mile. There is a 50¢ charge for each additional rider. **Note:** Fares are constantly being changed. There is a shared system from O'Hare and Midway airports via taxis identified by orange "Shared Ride" pennants. Minimum load is 2, maximum 3.

By car: Get a good road map and be wary of parking regulations; they are strictly enforced. Beware of parking in a posted area or you may fall victim to one of the infamous local towing companies and their extortionlike rates. Downtown State St. is now a pedestrian mall closed to cars, and there are many one-way streets complicating matters. The Roosevelt S curve just south of Grand Ave. and over the Chicago River is closed for a several year straightening project. U-turns are not permitted at intersections in Chicago, but are allowed in middle of block, unless prohibited by signs. In most suburbs, the opposite is true. Right turns are permitted on red lights after stopping if there is no oncoming traffic and signs do not say otherwise. Garages are increasingly expensive, with city-owned lots offering lower, but not cheap, rates.

By limousine: For those who want to arrive in style, there are a number of limousine services advertised in the Yellow Pages. *Carey Limousine Service* (tel. 663–1220 or 800–336–4646), *Chicago Limousine Service* (726–1035 or 800–621–7307), and *Metropolitan Limousine* (751–1111 or 800–368–5623), are a few of them. *E & M Enterprises* offers Rolls Royce rental (769–4054).

By rental car: *Avis, Budget, Dollar, Hertz, National, Rent A Wreck, Thrifty, Ajax, Econo-Car, Airways,* and *Sears* are among car rental agencies.

By boat: The summer shuttle service from the boat dock below Michigan Ave. Bridge to Northwestern Station is a popular ride. Commuters use it regularly, but visitors also enjoy it. Runs April through September, takes 10 min., and transports passengers along the Chicago R. in comfort for 65¢ each way (tel. 337–1446). 7:45–8:45 A.M. from station, 4:45–5:15 P.M. from bridge.

On foot: Several areas are ideal for walking. Michigan Avenue's Magnificent Mile, the Downtown Loop, Old Town, and Near North neighborhoods are examples. In all cases, no matter what conditions may appear to be, make local inquiries as to the safest way to go. As in all cities, there are certain trouble spots, and the world being what it is, it does not pay to take chances.

By horse-drawn carriage: *Chicago Carriage Company* has a stand at Pearson St. and Michigan Blvd. just south of Water Tower Place and offers carriage rides daily from 9:30 A.M. to 3:30 P.M. and again from 7 P.M. to 3 A.M. (tel. 280–8535) *Coach Horse Livery* is located 1 block west of Michigan Blvd. between Chicago Ave. and Pearson St. with rides available Monday – Friday from 10 A.M. to 3:30 P.M. and 7 P.M. to 2 A.M. and Saturday and Sunday from 10 P.M.–2 A.M. (tel. 842–8500). Rates vary but average $20 for one-half hour for 1–4 people.

Getting out to the suburbs: A number of major expressways, some paralleled for part of their route by elevated trains, make access to suburban areas easy. Dan Ryan (I–90 and I–94) goes south, Stevenson (I–55) southwest, Eisenhower (I–290) west, Kennedy (I–90) north-northwest, and Edens (I–94) north. Tri-State Tollway (I–294) skirts the metropolitan area on the south and west. For the most spectacular drive, follow the Outer Drive both north and south along the lake. The North-West Tollway feeds into Chicago from Beloit, Madison, and Janesville, Wisconsin, and the East-West Tollway (Ill. 5) comes in from Iowa.

Northwestern Railroad leaves Northwestern Station at Canal and Madison and heads north to Evanston, Wilmette, Kenilworth, Winnetka, Glencoe, Highland Park, Highwood, and Lake Forest, carrying executive commuters to their lakeshore suburbs. The railroad also has a northwest run to Des Plaines, Arlington Hts., Mt. Prospect, Palatine, Fox River Grove, Cary, and Crystal Lake. The *Milwaukee Road* angles slightly northwest en route to Glenview, Northbrook, and Deerfield. The *Illinois Central-Gulf* extends south to Park Forest. *Burlington Northern* goes west, and *South Shore* south.

City Streets

Travel around Chicago is made easy by a simple grid pattern. It all begins at the intersection of State and Madison in the heart of downtown, which is the zero-zero point. From this center the numbers go up in all directions covering about 100 numbers to a block. If you are looking for an address at 2000 North State, expect to find it 20 blocks north of that corner. One at 400 E. Madison would be 4 blocks east and very close to the lake. The suburbs are another story, although many of the old traditional ones follow a similiar simple system. New subdivisions are more apt to be meandering with a penchant for cutesy-poo names. If all else fails, a call to a local police department will bring helpful directions.

 TOURIST INFORMATION SERVICES. Contact the *Chicago Convention and Tourism Bureau,* McCormick Place on the lake, Chicago 60616 (tel. 312–225–5000). Their *Visitor Eventline* (225–2323) gives information on special events, theater, entertainment, and sports 24 hours daily. The new *Chicago Visitor Information Center* is in the historic Water Tower, open 7 days a week; multilingual. The state maintains a walk-in information center at 310 South Michigan Ave. (tel. 793–2094), and the *Conservation Department* is at 100 W. Randolph St. (tel. 793–2070). *International Visitors Center* is at 520 N. Michigan Ave. (tel. 645–1836). In a language emergency call 332–1460. *Travelers Aid* has facilities at the Greyhound Bus Station (tel. 435–4537); Union Train Station (tel. 435–4543); and O'Hare International Airport (tel. 686–7562). There are nearly 50 foreign consulates in the city, ranging from Argentina to Yugoslavia, who can help native residents with problems.

For information on facilities for the handicapped call 744–4016.

Both newspapers, the *Chicago Tribune* and *Sun Times,* are good sources of information, listing current attractions, entertainment, and special events. The *Tribune* has a Friday section, titled "Weekend," full of suggestions and ideas for local and out-of-town visitors.

Chicago magazine, published monthly and available on newsstands, covers restaurants, shopping, and entertainment in depth. *North Shore Magazine* does the same for the suburbs stretching north along the lake. A variety of local newspapers geared to what's going on downtown on the restaurant and entertainment scene are available free at hotels and parking garages. *State of Illinois Office of Tourism* publishes *Illinois,* covering 82 pages of statewide attractions, including Chicago. Their twice-yearly calendar of events is also helpful. Write 310 S. Michigan, Chicago 60601. Businessmen can keep up with what's happening by reading *Crain's Chicago Business.* O'Hare International Airport has a multilingual service at 686–2304.

For weather forecasts dial 976–1212, time 976–1616. For Police, Fire, or Ambulance dial either 911 or 0. Medical Referral Service is 670–2550; Dental emergency 726–4076.

CBS has an all news station (80 on radio dials) that has frequent updates of local expressway traffic conditions.

 SEASONAL EVENTS. January and February bring a flurry of boat, travel and outdoor shows. With them comes the latest in everything from rowboats to ocean-worthy yachts. North country fishing-camp owners are on hand to fascinate anglers with tales of their wilderness adventures. Assorted attractions from artificial trout streams to casting contests attract visitors.

Meanwhile out in Chinatown, a dragon leads the way as a gala parade and celebration welcome the *Chinese New Year.*

February means flowers as the azalea and camelia flower shows bloom at Lincoln and Garfield Park conservatories. Celebrity sports figures appear at the *Chicago Sport Show,* which tends to change locations some winters. Stars of the *Ice Capades* make it all look so easy at the Chicago Stadium. The late February–early **March** auto show features everybody's dream buggy.

They put dye in the Chicago River to turn it green for *St. Patrick's Day* in March, and an always grand and glorious parade follows the green line painted down State St. come rain or shine.

Old Town Art Fair brings out artists and admirers in **June.** From June through September the *Ravinia Festival* takes place in Ravinia Park, Highland Park. This annual event is a series of symphonic concerts, recitals, chamber music, and popular music events that include rock, jazz, country, and you name it.

The **July** 4 holiday attracts food samplers with dozens of big-name restaurants dishing up *A Taste of Chicago* and serving their most popular specialties in Grant Park. Massive crowds, long lines, and some rowdyism and reports of underage drinking have been reported. A pickpocket's haven. Attendance last July 3rd was three-quarters of a million, creating a traffic jam of mammoth proportion.

Big names in golf make sports headlines at July's *Western Open Golf Tournament* held at the Butler National course in suburban Oak Brook. Lake Michigan's version of the Tall Ships depart for the challenging Chicago to Mackinac race the third weekend in July. Free Wednesday, Friday, and Saturday evening concerts begin in Grant Park in the Petrillo Music Shell at the northeast corner of Jackson Blvd. and Columbus. Phone 294–2420 since hours may vary.

A series of weekend neighborhood ethnic festivals was formerly climaxed by *Chicago Fest,* a 12-day musical extravaganza in July or August, featuring music from rock to jazz, and blues to country. A couple years ago it was one of the city's headline events attracting huge crowds to Navy Pier. More recently there have been boycotts of performances. It did not do well in a new location at

Soldier Field in 1983 and was cancelled in 1984. Still, many are struggling to keep the idea alive and the very popular event may resurface in the future.

The *Gold Coast Art Fair,* usually in **August,** on Rush St. and Wabash, attracts the arts and crafts crowd. *Venetian Night* later in the month inspires colorful animated floats and brilliantly illuminated yachts, turning Monroe St. into a sort of St. Tropez for a night.

A special Olympics for the handicapped is held in Grant Park during late summer. Giants of jazz show up for another free, city-sponsored event, the 7-day *Chicago Jazz Festival* around Labor Day (first Monday in **September**). Its continuance in 1986, however, is dependent on the same factors influencing Chicagofest.

International Folk Festival is next, a **November** salute to the ethnic heritages of Chicagoans, focusing on their foods, traditional costumes, and music.

In **December,** Santa Claus arrives for the *State Street Parade* and the Museum of Science and Industry opens it month-long exhibit *Christmas around the World,* displaying Christmas trees from most major countries, along with their traditional foods.

Chicago is a parade town and any occasion calling for a celebration gets a much-applauded march downtown. Make local inquiries; if it's not Columbus Day, Veterans Day, the Shriners, American Legion, or whatever, it is just as liable to be a welcome home to astronauts.

TOURS. By land: Chicago and nearby areas of interest are covered in tours offered by *Gray Line of Chicago,* 33 E. Monroe (tel. 346–9506), *American Sightseeing Tours,* 530 S. Michigan Ave. (tel. 427–3100). Everything from Chinatown and some surprising city sites to plush suburbs and after-dark destinations. They have such a variety of half-day and full-day tours that there is something to fit most tastes. These operate year-round.

On The Scene Tours, 505 N. Wells (tel. 661–1440), covers just about any aspect of the city one can imagine. They offer special Amtrak all-inclusive packages into Chicago and are noted for guided tours of the massive, otherwise off-limits Merchandise Mart. There are "Hot Tix" discounted theater tours, leisurely excursions along the North Shore to the Baha'i Temple, or "Go Go Chicago" for a basic overview of the city's high points. Their guides also conduct specialized Art Institute tours. "Offbeat Chicago" visits the very different Graceland Cemetery, with its grandiose Victorian monuments and tours the University of Chicago and the antiquities of its Oriental Institute. There are History and Landmarks tours, adventures to Six Flag's Great America, lunch in the architectural splendor of 35-room Glessner House—you name it, they will arrange it. Anything from Abraham Lincoln's carriage to a multimedia recreation of the Chicago fire. These range from a couple hours to all day, and this very creative organization is constantly coming up with new tour ideas.

Amtrak has an ever-changing collection of all-inclusive package tours into the city, as do various airlines and bus companies. Chicagoland hotels offer special packages throughout the year with budget-priced fringe benefits. *Chicago*

Convention and Tourism Bureau can tell you about them; so can your travel agent.

For something really different, consider the *Chicago Supernatural Tour,* "America's only coach bus guided tour to haunted and legendary places." These are held Saturday and Sunday afternoons at 1:00 P.M. and last 5 hrs. The $18.50 fee includes snacks. Departure is from De Paul University, Lincoln Park campus. Call 735–2530 for reservations. Tour usually includes what guides label "psychic hot spots, some interesting burial grounds, and a search for Resurrection Mary, Chicago's most famous ghost." Also some evening trips.

By water: There are boating tours on Lake Michigan by the *Mercury Scenicruiser* (tel. 332–1353) and *Wendella Streamliner* (tel. 337–1446). Both offer views of the photogenic shoreline and skyline and leave from below the Michigan Ave. Bridge, passing through locks at the mouth of the Chicago R. into the lake. A dazzling, eye-opening view, even for residents. *Wendella* operates from mid-April to mid-September, weather permitting and offers 1, 1½, and 2 hr. trips at 10:00 A.M., 11:30 A.M., 1:15 P.M., 3:15 P.M., and 7:30 P.M. Prices are $4.50, $6, and $7.50, children under 12 half price. *Mercury* has 1½ and 2 hr. trips variously scheduled at 10:00 A.M., 11:30 P.M., 1:15 P.M., and 3:15 P.M., for $6 adults, $3 under 12. Their 2-hr. 7:30 P.M. cruise costs $7.50 adults, $3.75 children. They also have a program of 1-hr. lake rides. These are not operated on a fixed schedule, but generally leave at 10:20 A.M., 2:30, 5:00, 8:45 P.M. and also at 6:00, 10:00 P.M., and 11:00 P.M. weekends. It is wise to check both lines, since schedules change.

Shoreline Marine Sightseeing (tel. 427–2900) offers numerous 1-hour lake cruises from 3 locations: Shedd Aquarium, the Planetarium dock and evenings from Buckingham Fountain. These operate from Memorial Day to Labor Day, plus off-season weekends weather permitting. Fare is $3.50 adults, $1.50 children under 10. S.S. *Clipper,* now docked at Navy Pier, was built in 1905 and once cruised the Great Lakes. Last major renovation was in 1940, so it is wonderfully Art Deco. It has now been restored and is open for 1-hr. tours, which roam from the steam engine to the captain's bridge and staterooms. Open roughly from Memorial Day to Labor Day. We strongly suggest that you call ahead as 1986 hours were not firm at press time. Guided tour $4.00, children $2.00 (tel. 329–1800).

Star of Chicago, P.O. Box 39, Oakbrook Terrace, 1–800–782–7827. On the pricey side. $21 luncheon cruise, $39.50 buffet dinner cruise, moonlight cruises, Sunday brunch, TGIF Friday afternoon cruises. New in 1983 and sails from Navy Pier.

 SPECIAL INTEREST SIGHTSEEING. For an overview, start at the country's tallest building, 110-story *Sears Tower,* at Wacker, Adams, Jackson, and Franklin streets (tel. 875–9696). 2 nonstop elevators rush up to the skydeck 103 floors above the city, open daily 9:00 A.M. to midnight. Same hours apply to the only slightly shorter John Hancock Center Observatory, 875

N. Michigan (tel. 751–3681). On a clear day Michigan, Indiana, Wisconsin, and the Illinois prairie are visible, with superb shoreline views along Lake Michigan.

Chicago is a thriving financial center and institutions connected with its prosperity provide fascinating tours. The *Board of Trade,* housed in an imposing Art Deco structure with *Ceres,* the gilded Goddess of Grain, on the roof, is the largest commodities futures market in the country. Hostesses conduct continuous 15-min. tours 9:30 A.M.–1:15 P.M., Monday–Friday and help unravel the mysteries to budding brokers (tel. 435–3617).

International Monetary Market and *Chicago Merchantile Exchange,* 30 S. Wacker Dr., are the places to learn all about trading in gold, silver, and hogs. Hours and phone numbers are the same for both: 930–8200, Monday–Friday, 7:30 A.M.–3:15 P.M. Closed holidays. Noon tour.

The *Federal Reserve Bank,* 230 S. La Salle (tel. 322–5322) is certain to send visitors away with a better understanding of our monetary system, and so are the *1st National Bank of Chicago,* Dearborn and Madison streets—the world's tallest (tel. 732–6037)—and *American National Bank & Trust Co.,* La Salle and Washington (tel. 661–5897), which also offer tours.

To see what helps make this "the city that works," here are a few behind-the-scenes tours. You've been hearing about Chicago politics for years, why not tour *City Hall* at 121 N. La Salle St., complete with a visit to the Mayor's Office (tel. 744–3370).

Some of Chicago's "finest" will guide visitors through the *Chicago Police Department,* 1121 S. State at 10:30 A.M. and 1:30 P.M. One weeks notice required, children under 12 not admitted. (tel. 744–5571). Tour includes a look at the crime lab and some background on the city's livelier past.

Ever since Mrs. O'Leary's cow kicked over the lantern that legend insists started the Chicago fire, fire protection has been Chicago's prime concern. Here at 558 W. DeKoven St., where the fire supposedly started, the *Robert Quinn Fire Academy* trains future firefighters. To join an illuminating tour, call 744–4728. These are offered Monday through Friday at 11:00 A.M. and 1:00 P.M. by appointment only.

It seems appropriate that some of the country's best-tasting water comes from the world's largest water filtration plant. 50-min. tours at *James Jardine Water Purification Plant* at Navy Pier cover the entire purification process (tel. 744–3692). Advance notice required.

O'Hare International Airport, the world's busiest, also offers behind the scenes tours, Mannheim Rd. and Kennedy Expressway (tel. 686–2200).

If you're beginning to think Chicago specializes in the biggest, largest, tallest, etc., there is some truth in that. Even the post office is the largest postal building in the world (perhaps offering that many more nooks and crannies in which the mail can get "delayed"?). 2-hour tours daily except December (tel. 886–3360).

If "all the news that's fit to print" is your interest, both the *Tribune,* 435 N. Michigan (tel. 222–3993) and *Sun Times,* 401 N. Wabash (tel. 321–2032) offer tours—80-min. tours at the *Tribune* and 45-min. tours at the *Sun Times.* The Tribune Building, once labeled "exuberant Gothic Revival," is architecturally interesting and contains bits and pieces of such buildings as Westminster Abbey, the Arch of Triumph, and the Taj Mahal, near the entrance.

Here comes another "world's largest," this time the gigantic Kennedy family-owned *Merchandise Mart* at the Chicago R. and Wells St. This giant showcase of wholesale furniture, clothes, and gifts and furnishings measures displays by the mile and is usually closed to the public, but tours can be arranged when trade shows are not being held. Call 661–1440.

What is a submarine doing in Lake Michigan? It's the U.S.S. *Silversides,* a survivor of World War II lovingly restored and at the lakefront's Navy Pier. It is open daily noon–6:00 P.M., May–October, but weekends only November–April. Tour takes 30 min. Since this is a volunteer effort, of dedicated submarine enthusiasts, call 884–6312 to check times.

Rockefeller Memorial Chapel on University of Chicago campus is a vaulted Gothic wonder noted for its 72-bell carillon. Tours after Sunday services, 5850 S. Woodlawn.

GANGSTER TOUR

"Scarface" Al Capone, "Machine Gun" Jack McGurn, "Baby Face" Nelson, Dutch Schultz, Bugs Moran, Paul "The Waiter" Ricca, Tony "Big Tuna" Accardo, Jake "The Barber" Factor, John Dillinger: not exactly a list of Chicago's Who's Who. But their names, for better or worse, became so indelibly associated with the city that nothing can ever erase them.

Certain city officials breathe a sigh of relief every time an old gangland monument like the infamous St. Valentine's Day massacre garage is torn down. But no one can ever forget that seven Bugs Moran henchmen were gunned down by other mobsters wearing policemen's uniforms at what used to be 2122 North Clark St. (The wall the seven were lined up against is now part of a restaurant in Vancouver, BC.) When asked who shot him, dying Frank Gusenberg said, "Nobody shot me."

Big Jim Colosimos Café (now an empty lot beside Lions Barb-B-Q at 2126 South Wabash) is where it all started. His own bodyguard reputedly arranged the underworld leader's "demise" in 1920, then assumed his empire. Honorary pallbearers included three judges, two congressmen, an assistant states attorney, assorted aldermen, and a future federal judge.

Dion O'Bannion, like Capone a graduate of the newspaper circulation wars, was shot down in his flower shop at 738 North State Street across from Holy Name Cathedral, and 26 flower cars followed his $10,000 casket to the cemetery. When Michael Merlo, head of Unione Siciliane, died, friends ordered a $25,000 floral tribute, including a wax effigy of him for the funeral cortege. Ironically, O'Bannion had been working on Merlo's funeral flowers when he was shot. The flower shop is gone, but the cathedral, which was riddled with 38 machine gun bullets two years later when O'Bannion's lieutenant Hymie Weiss and chauffeur were murdered, is still there.

By the time Capone assumed power, the Better Government Association wired the U.S. Senate, "Chicago politicians are in league with gangsters and the city is overrun with a combination of lawless politics and protected vice."

Then the massacre really began. In the first four months of 1926, there were 29 gang murders in Chicago, and at the end of four years over 200—with no convictions. Capone's income in 1927 was estimated at $105 million, and it was income tax evasion that ultimately sent him to prison. Today, he lies in an inconspicuous grave in Mt. Carmel cemetery in Hillside. The headstone was stolen in 1972.

Estimates put the number of assassinations on the corner of Oak and North Cleveland, in the heart of what was once the bootleg brewery district, at anywhere from 15 to over 40. And there was no safety in numbers for Antonio Lombardo, head of Unione Siciliane, gunned down near State and Madison, the world's busiest intersection, walking with two bodyguards.

Capone headquartered at the Metropole Hotel, 2300 South Michigan, where he occupied 50 rooms on two floors. He also had offices in another hotel connected to it by tunnel. His other known residences included 2222 South Wabash (the Four Deuces Brothel), 7244 South Prairie, and a summer home in Mercer, Wisconsin, where his brother Ralph died several years ago.

When Al went to the theater, he rode in a seven-ton bulletproof car with combination locks so no one could open it and plant a bomb inside. Eighteen bodyguards in tuxedos went with him. Today's visitor might feel more comfortable in the same kind of car when seeking out those South Michigan and South Wabash neighborhoods. (They're about three blocks west of McCormick Center Hotel and two or three blocks north off the expressway.) Neighborhood character changes within blocks in Chicago.

Jake Lingle, *Chicago Tribune* reporter who was also on Capone's payroll, was gunned down in the lower-level concourse of the Illinois Central Station, Randolph and Michigan, in 1930.

One by one these landmarks are disappearing—some making room for other construction, others through mysterious fires, to become vacant lots. But the alley just south of the still active Biograph Theatre, 2433 North Lincoln, where bank robber John Dillinger was shot, is still there. He had been hiding out in a flat behind the theater at 2420 North Halsted. The theater's Art Deco theme has been preserved, and it is still very much as it was the night Dillinger and "the lady in red" saw Dillinger's last film there.

The bullet-riddled car of "Baby Face" Nelson was found abandoned on the Winnetka Avenue bridge over the North Branch of the Chicago River in Northfield. His body was found dumped in a Skokie cemetery.

Grudges last a long time here. It was seven years and one day after the St. Valentine's Day massacre that 38-year-old "Machine Gun" Jack McGurn got his, gangland style, at what was then a bowling alley at 805 Milwaukee Avenue. He was always suspected as Capone's hit man for the St. Valentine's Day headliner, and he was indicted, but the case never came to trial. Yes, he really did carry his machine gun in a violin case.

Roger "The Terrible" Touhy had been convicted on what he considered a "trumped up charge" involving kidnapping Jake "The Barber" Factor during Prohibition, and he spent more than 25 years in prison. There were always those who said he knew too much to survive. Twenty-three days after his release from Statesville Penitentiary in 1959 he was shotgunned down on the steps of his sister's house at 125 North Lotus.

Some local Chicago publications actually print the addresses and connections of surviving notorious residents, identifying them as "suspected gunman in the St. Valentine's Day massacre," "generally considered Capone's triggerman," and people ride around peering at them as though on some Hollywood movie star house tour.

In those early days, gangsters were an interesting ethnic mix; Sicilian, Irish, Jewish, Polish, etc. Things have changed. But they are a lot quieter now and Thompson .45-caliber machine guns are very passé. When reputed mob boss Sam "Momo" Giancanna was shot in his basement in suburban Oak Park a few years ago, his assassin used a .22-caliber revolver with a silencer, and his houseman very mysteriously disappeared.

The Chicago Crime Commission releases lists of syndicate-controlled businesses—these are regularly published in the paper, everybody knows about them, talks about them, and continues to patronize them. Chicago has always had a unique attitude about such things, a "live-and-let-live" philosophy, which also applies to business.

Yet any talk or questions about this colorful past that so intrigues visitors is enough to cause cardiac arrest in some city employees, who would rather bury it all forever and pretend it never happened and in some cases is still happening.

Tourists, incidentally, need not worry. These fellows are only interested in killing each other off and go about it very professionally.

ARCHITECTURAL SITES

This is where the skyscraper originated and names like Louis Sullivan, Burnham and Root, Mies van der Rohe, and Frank Lloyd Wright emerged as strong influences. So much has happened here architecturally that professionals refer to all the innovations as "the Chicago School" and a number of associations offer tours of major landmarks.

Chicago Architecture Foundation. Maintains the Archi-Center, 330 S. Dearborn, 60604 (tel. 782–1776), sponsoring a full schedule of walking tours, bus tours, and even bicycle expeditions to districts of architectural interest. They maintain 2 of Chicago's very historic houses. One is Glessner House, 1800 S. Prairie, near McCormick Place. Renovated 35-room Romanesque mansion designed by H.H. Richardson, in the historic district known as Millionaire's Row, which is now undergoing restoration. (tel. 326–1393). The other is the Widow Clark House, also located in the Prairie Avenue Historic District (tel. 326–1393).

Sears Tower. 233 S. Wacker Dr. The tallest building in the world, 110 stories and 1454 ft. high. Observation platform.

The Rookery Building. 209 S. La Salle. Vintage 1886, is one of the remaining early skyscrapers. Frank Lloyd Wright designed the lobby in 1905.

Monadnock Building. A few blocks away at 53 W. Jackson. Designed by Burnham and Root. Its 16 stories were completed in 1891. It is the tallest building with load-bearing walls in the world.

Robie House. 5757 S. Woodlawn (tel. 962–8370). This house, forerunner of the modern "prairie house," is one of the most important buildings of our century. Offers tours Monday–Saturday at noon and at 1 P.M. summer Saturdays.

Oak Park. There are 16 Frank Lloyd Wright buildings in Chicago, but suburban Oak Park, 25 min. from downtown, boasts 30, including the home and studio where he lived and worked for more than 20 years. The home is open to the public, guided tours. Call *Oak Park Visitors Center* (848–1978). The Center at Forest and Lake avenues is open daily 10:00 A.M.–5:00 P.M. and provides maps, guidebooks and an audio-visual program, "Lightning on the Prairie." There are guided tours as well as tape-recorded walking tours in English, German, or Japanese. Guided tours of both Wright's home and the Unity Temple he designed are $3.00 each, $1.50 children and seniors. A $5.00 discount coupon includes the tour and the tape-recorded walking tour. Schedule is complicated so calling first is advisable. Annual house walk, covering a number of Wright-designed homes, is held 3rd Saturday in May and is a popular sellout. A property of the National Trust for Historic Preservation.

Pullman Community. 104th St. to 115th St. at Calumet Expressway. The first company town in America. Founded in 1880 by George Pullman, inventor of the Pullman sleeping car, it is an outdoor museum of architecture, city planning, and labor history. Victorian Hotel Florence serves lunch Sunday through Friday. Guided walking tours 1st Sunday of month, May–October. Open-house tours annually, 2nd weekend in October. Tours start at the Historic Pullman Center, 614 E. 113th St. at 12:30 P.M. and 1:30 P.M. Adults $3.50, students $2.00 (tel. 785–8181). A national historic landmark.

Auditorium Theater. 70 E. Congress. Designed by Louis Sullivan and beautifully restored. *Carson, Pirie, Scott & Company.* 1 S. State St. The cast iron in the store entrance, known as the rotunda, is often referred to as "iron lace." Also designed by Louis Sullivan. Both the exterior and vestibule interior were restored to their original style in 1979 to celebrate the company's 125-year anniversary, and the result is definitely a "designer original."

Marquette Building. 140 S. Dearborn. A 16-story steel-framed beauty finished in 1894. The life of Jesuit missionary Jacques Marquette, who wintered in Chicago in 1674–75, is shown on bronze reliefs above the main entrance. Inside, impressive mosaics trace Chicago history.

Illinois Institute of Technology. 10 W. 33rd St. Campus architecture designed by Ludwig Mies van der Rohe is the subject of a 1-hr. tour. Reservations (tel. 567–3025).

State of Illinois Building, covering square block bounded by Randolph, Lake, Clark, and La Salle streets. Completed in 1985, this steel and glass conversation stopper continues to generate controversy.

University of Illinois, Circle Campus. 750 S. Halsted. Tours (tel. 996–8686).
University of Chicago. 122 E. 59th St. Special tours. Buildings designed by Eero Saarinen, Edward Durrell Stone, Mies van der Rohe, and Frank Lloyd Wright's Robie House (tel: 962–8374).

Baha'i Temple. Sheridan Rd. at Linden Ave., Wilmette. Looks like a modern Persian version of the Taj Mahal along the lakeshore. National Center for the Persian-born Bahai faith, it took 50 yrs. to build and is unique in this hemisphere. Construction started on the white-faced ornamented dome in 1903 and by 1953 the lacy-looking marvel was finished. It is on the National Register of Historic Places. The faith came to the U.S. during the Columbian Exposition held in Chicago in 1893 and a site near the city was selected for the first Baha'i temple in the Western world. Open daily May 15–October 14, 10:00 A.M.–10:00 P.M. and October 15–May 14, 10:00 A.M.–5:00 P.M.

Chicago's Famous Buildings: A Photographic Guide, Third Edition, edited by Ira J. Bach; *A Guide to Chicago's Public Sculpture* by Ira J. Bach and Mary Lackritz Gray; *A Guide to Frank Lloyd Wright and Prairie School Architecture in Oak Park* by Paul Sprague; and *A Walk Through Graceland Cemetery* by Barbara Lanctot are sources for further information. These publications are generally available in the 2 shops of the Chicago Architecture Foundation.

Landmarks Preservation Council of Illinois, 407 S. Dearborn St. (tel. 922–1742), sometimes offers tours of Illinois historic architectural sites, both in the city and elsewhere in the state. Their members are active in working for historic preservation. *National Trust for Historic Preservation,* 407 South Dearborn St., (tel. 353–3419) is also becoming increasingly involved in local preservation.

PLAZA ART

It seems appropriate that the city that made such a name for itself architecturally should have equally unique art work decorating its buildings. There is practically a competition in which plazas try to outdo one another. In summer, office workers picnic, sunbathe, and in the case of Daley Center and First National Bank, enjoy free concerts in these plazas.

Bertoia Sculpture. Standard Oil Plaza, 200 E. Randolph. Truly unique "sound sculpture" in a reflecting pool. Meant to be heard as well as seen; natural wind currents determine the sound.

Calder. Federal Center Plaza at Adams and Dearborn. His 53-foot-high, 50-ton red stabile, entitled *Flamingo,* is here, while his mobile *Universe* decorates the lobby of Sears Tower.

Chagall Mosaic. First National Plaza, Monroe and Dearborn. Colorful 70-foot-long mural utilizes marble, stone, glass, and granite.

Henry Moore's Nuclear Energy. Recalls the historic spot on the University of Chicago campus where the first atom was split.

Miro's Mystery. Brunswick Plaza, 69 W. Washington. A 1981 addition, still the subject of much speculation.

Claes Oldenburg's Batcolumn. Social Security Administration Plaza, 600 W. Madison. Stands 100 ft. high with 1,608 pieces of welded steel.

Picasso Mystery Sculpture. Daley Plaza, Dearborn and Washington. Remains a 50-foot-tall object of considerable attention. It was a gift from that famed artist to the city. It has been variously described as a woman, a dog . . . or a vulture prepared to prey on the taxpayer. See what you think.

PARKS. Chicago had the good sense to do something few other cities considered—use its lakefront as a beautifully manicured frontyard rather than a series of docks and warehouses. Seemingly endless miles of parks stretch along the lake like jewels, interspersed with yacht harbors, a city golf course, some surprising statues, a conservatory, and grand views of the shore. *Lincoln Park.* Along the lake between North Ave. and Hollywood Ave. It houses the renowned Lincoln Park Zoo, Farm-in-the-Zoo, conservatory, outdoor gardens, lagoon, athletic fields, tennis courts, golf course, jogging paths, shooting range, and more. *Jackson Park.* 56th St., 67th St., Stony Island Ave., and the lake are its boundaries. This was site of the Columbian Exposition of 1893 and includes the exceptional Museum of Science and Industry. *Grant Park.* East of Michigan Ave. between Randolph St. on the north and Roosevelt Rd. on the south. 300 acres of attractively landscaped parkland adjacent to the Loop. The Field Museum, Adler Planetarium, Shedd Aquarium, and Art Institute are here (see *Museum* listing). Also noteworthy:

Buckingham Fountain, presented to Grant Park in 1927 by Miss Kate Sturges Buckingham in memory of her brother. A much larger version of one she admired at Versailles, it operates daily, Memorial Day to Labor Day, from 11:30 A.M. to 10 P.M., ending with a rainbow of color nightly. It is a dramatic spectacle, with waters rising 135 ft. above the marble base.

Petrillo Music Shell, also in Grant Park, is the setting of free concerts from popular music to classics during summer (tel. 294–2420).

ZOOS. *Lincoln Park Zoo* covers 35 acres just north near the lake and is especially noted for its gorillas. The Great Ape House has everything from chimpanzees to orangutans amusing viewers in their own private rain forest. The 550-lb. Bushman, most famous of them all, is now stuffed and in the Field Museum. Youngsters (and adults) who have never visited a farm are fascinated with the Farm-in-the-Zoo. Free. Contains about 2,500 mammals, birds, and reptiles. Its Rookery walkways wind past waterfalls, ponds, and bird sanctuaries. A world apart, yet minutes from downtown at 2200 N. Cannon Dr. in Lincoln Park. Open daily 9 A.M. to 5 P.M. (tel. 294–4660). Free.

Brookfield Zoo in suburban Brookfield, 11 mi. west, was the first zoo in the country to develop a moat system with completely natural outdoor landscaping, which makes it look like the animal is not caged. Monkey island can keep anyone amused for hours. A tropical African rain forest populated with gorillas, birds, monkeys, reptiles, and a pygmy hippo is one of its newest attractions. It was built complete with waterfalls and scheduled thunderstorms. Several dolphin shows are presented daily in the Seven Seas Panorama, and steam trains and motor safari trains make the zoos 200 acres easier to visit. Open daily from Memorial Day to Labor Day, 8:30 A.M. to 6:00 P.M., other seasons to 5:00 P.M. Adults $2.25, seniors and children 75¢ (tel. 242–2630). Free Tuesdays. Parking $2.00. Both zoos have children's petting zoos, which are well maintained and tremendously popular.

 GARDENS. Partly because of the unique way Chicago's lakefront has been developed, the city seems to have a long, continuous garden strip for a frontyard. Within that strip, or often adjoining it, are several exceptional gardens, although some of the major botanical finds are a drive away.

Garfield Park Conservatory. 300 N. Central Park Blvd. Considered the largest in the world under one roof and covers 5.5 very exceptional acres. Special shows are seasonally scheduled, but the regular displays are always worth a trip. There is also a 175,000-sq.-ft. formal garden on the grounds and a Garden for the Blind. Open daily 9:00 A.M. to 5:00 P.M., 10 A.M.–6 P.M. during shows. Free (tel. 533–1281).

Grant Park Rose Garden near Buckingham Fountain. Over three dozen carefully manicured rose beds with 8,000 bushes.

Lincoln Park. Really a three-in-one delight. Grandmother's Garden, between Stockton and Lincoln Park West, dates back to 1893 and specializes in gorgeous old-fashioned flowers. 40,000 plants brighten this 130,000-sq.-ft. slice of tranquillity. The 3-acre Conservatory is the year-round pièce de résistance, with seasonal shows and rooms devoted to some of the most spectacular palms in captivity. Part of the Conservatory dates from 1891 and the great Victorian fondness for potted palms is part of its inheritance. There are also tropical plants and ferns in prime condition at all times. The flower garden to the south has over 25,000 plants surrounding Bates Fountain. The conservatory is open daily 9:00 A.M. to 5:00 P.M., 10 A.M.–6 P.M. during shows. Free (tel. 294–4770).

Marquette Park Rose Garden. 3540 W. 71st St. Features 4,000 of those beauties, plus a pool with live swans. Like parks in so many places in the world, these are all best enjoyed in the daylight. It is not wise to wander around in them after dark.

Chicago Botanic Garden. Lake-Cook Road just east of Edens Expressway in suburban Glencoe. 300 acres of gardens still undergoing development. Owned by Forest Preserve District of Cook County and managed by the Chicago Horticultural Society. Building open 9:00 A.M. to 6:00 P.M., park open 8:30 A.M. to sunset. Admission free, but $1.00 parking and tram ride $1.50 adults, 75¢ children and seniors. (tel. 835–5440).

Shakespeare Gardens on Northwestern University's nearby Evanston campus is planted with flowers Shakespeare wrote about in his plays.

BEACHES. Chicago has miles of beautiful sand beaches fully staffed with lifeguards in season. Open mid–June, closed Labor Day. Hours 9:00 A.M. to 9:30 P.M. Admission free. *Oak Street Beach,* which stretches along the Gold Coast, attracts a younger, avant garde city-dweller type, while *North Avenue Beach* attracts a mixed group. These 2 beaches are also most favored by vacationers. Up-to-the-minute information on all beaches is available by calling the Park District's Beach Information number, 294–2333. Swimming from rocks along Lake Michigan or in unpatrolled area is foolhardy and dangerous. Many suburban beaches along the North Shore accept paying guests and are frequented by affluent residents of those high income bracket communities. Heed red warning flags, which indicate undertow or other conditions that make swimming hazardous. Do not expect tropical temperatures—water in the 60s is normal; 72° here is considered absolutely spa-like!

PARTICIPANT SPORTS. Bicycling: Getting more popular every year. These several standout trails. *Chicago Lakefront Path* covers 20 mi., utilizing the city's lakefront parks, harbors, beaches, and ever changing skyline to great advantage. Park hours are 6:00 A.M. to 11:00 P.M., but for safety sake, it is wise to confine your cycling to daylight hours. *Illinois Prairie Path* extends 40 mi. into the western suburbs. A growing number of communities are utilizing abandoned railroad beds and parks to develop routes. *Schwinn Bicycle Co.* (tel. 292–2900), 1856 N. Kostner, Chicago 60639, is good source of information. *Spokes for Folks* rents bikes (and roller skates) daily during summer at Lincoln Park at Fullerton Parkway, and Cannon Drive. Open daily 10:00 A.M.–7:00 P.M., May 1–Labor Day and weekends in April, September, and October, depending on weather. $4.00 first hours, $3.00 each additional hour, for bikes or skates. Also at North and Clark Streets. (tel. 389–3967).

Boating: Big, broad, and deep, Lake Michigan is at the city's front door. Mooring slips are taken long in advance, but there are *launching ramps* at Diversey Harbor, Burnham Harbor, Calumet Park, Rainbow Beach, Wilson Avenue, and Jackson Park. There are 2 free launching ramps on Des Plaines and Calumet rivers. *Chicagoland Canoe Base,* 4019 N. Narragansett (tel. 777–1489), offers wide variety of canoe rentals, and many charter boats are available for fisherman attracted by Lake Michigan's coho runs. Hours, sunup to sundown. Summer Paddleboat rentals in Lincoln Park Lagoon; $4.00 for ½ hr., $7.00 per hour. $5 deposit.

A word of warning. Lake Michigan often displays the temperament of the inland sea it is. Never venture out in a boat before checking weather predictions. Sudden squalls are not uncommon. Call 298–1413 for extended forecast, including Lake Michigan wave and weather conditions. Also be wary of overloading small boats and heading too far out in small craft.

Golf: Chicago Park District has 6 public courses and provides free winter golf school. *Waveland,* 3800 N. Lake Shore Dr. along the lake; *Columbus* at 5800 W. Jackson; *Marquette Park,* 67th St. and Kedzie; *South Shore Park,* 71st St.

and South Shore; *Robert A. Black,* 2045 W. Pratt (the old Edgewater course) and *Jackson Park,* 1 block east of 63rd and Stony Island. All are 9 holes except 18-hole Jackson Park. Open daily dawn to dusk, April–September. Weekends and holidays $4.00, weekdays $3.50 for the 9-hole courses, and $5.50 weekends, $5.00 weekdays for the 18-hole course. Driving range is at *Lake Shore Drive and Diversey* along with a miniature-golf course, and another driving range in Jackson Park, open 8:00 A.M.–10:45 P.M. daily. Large bucket of balls costs $2.50. Park District phone is 294–2274. Many other fine courses are available for a greens fee in Chicago and suburbs. *Butler National* in Oak Brook is site of the Western Open.

Racquetball: *Pottawattomie Park,* 7340 N. Rogers. Call 743–4313 for information and reservations.

Tennis: Park District has over 650 free tennis courts. Add to this the hundreds of courts in the suburbs and at the resort hotels. There are 2 major tennis facilities in the downtown district. Both are open daily April–October. *Daley Bicentennial Plaza,* Randolph and Lake Shore Dr. (tel. 294–4792), $5.00 per hour, 12 lighted courts, reservations required, and *Grant Park Tennis Courts,* 9th and Columbus Dr. (tel. 294–2307), $2.00 per day or $20 annual permit. 12 lighted courts, no reservations needed.

 SPECTATOR SPORTS. Baseball: Baseball's National League *Chicago Cubs* play at Wrigley Field on the North Side. Season: April–October (tel. 281–5050). Daytime games only. The American League *Chicago White Sox,* at White Sox Park on the South Side, play ball April–October (tel. 924–1000). This is definitely a big baseball city, often with more news emphasis on major league scores than national events.

Basketball: *Chicago Bulls* play at Chicago Stadium, October–April (tel. 346–1122), which is also host to many college games and tournaments. Loyola, Northwestern, and DePaul usually field strong and exciting teams. The latter's *Blue Demons* have been in the headlines ever since they stepped into the limelight a few years ago as the nation's Number 1 team.

Football: *Chicago Bears* now play at Soldier Field, September–December (tel. 663–5408). *Northwestern* plays Big Ten and other teams at Dyche Stadium in Evanston.

Hockey: *Chicago Black Hawks* play at Chicago Stadium, making headlines October–April (tel. 733–5300). Newest team on the scene is the *Chicago Sting* soccer team, which plays at Soldier Field, outdoors May–September and at the Chicago Stadium indoors November–April (tel. 558–5425).

Horse Racing: Flat racing at *Arlington Park,* May–September (tel. 775–7800), and *Hawthorne,* September–December (tel. 652–9400). Harness racing, mostly nights, at *Sportsmans Park,* February–October (tel. 242–1121), and *Maywood Park,* February–May and October–December (tel. 626–4816).

Tournaments: *Western Open Golf Tournament* is held in early summer at Oak Brook's Butler National. Sailors hope for a breeze the 3rd weekend in July for *Chicago to Mackinac boat race. Norge Ski Jump* at Fox River Grove has slide tournament in January. *Polo* matches at the Chicago Armory and at Oak Brook, May–October (tel. 654–3060), where some spectators cultivate such a way-out look that they compete with the ponies for attention.

For latest results on major sports nationwide, call *Sportsphone* 976–1313.

 CHILDREN'S ACTIVITIES. Both *Lincoln Park* and *Brookfield Zoo* have exceptional children's petting zoos, (see *Zoos* section in this chapter for details), and the *Lambs Farm* near Libertyville also has a children's farmyard, pet shop, and special programs ranging from pumpkin parties to hayrides and pony rides. The Sunday buffet breakfast, 11:00 A.M.–3:00 P.M. is popular with families (tel. 362–4636). Farmyard hours are 9:00 A.M. to 5:00 P.M. daily except holidays.

All the major museums offer very worthwhile programs for youngsters. The *Art Institute* has a Junior Museum, with unusual changing exhibits and attention-holding events. *Field Museums's* trained volunteers guide children on carefully planned tours. At the *Museum of Science and Industry,* the thousands of gadgets, Colleen Moore's dollhouse, a newborn chick display, World War II submarine, and the working coal mine win youngster applause. *Adler Planetarium* has special Saturday morning Sky Shows for children. The kids would also enjoy seeing *Ripley's Believe It Or Not Museum* at 1500 N. Wells. See *Museums* section in this chapter for further details on hours and telephone numbers.

Six Flags Great America. North of the city off Rte. 94 at Gurnee. Theme park covers 200 acres, with roller coaster rides, cartoon characters, fantasy worlds, and enough general whoop-de-do to keep the whole family entertained. A 7-story-high movie screen almost puts viewer in the picture. New American Eagle roller coaster attracts the adventurous on a spine-chilling 66-mile-an-hour ride labeled the world's highest, longest, and possibly scariest. Open daily summer; weekends only in spring and fall (tel. 249–1776). Hours vary. Admission $13.95 plus tax, under 3 free and over 55 $8.95 plus tax. Parking $3.00.

Ebenezer Floppenslopper's Wonderful Water Slide. Rte. 83 at Roosevelt Rd. in Oak Brook. Brings squeals of excitement from those who like to slide and splash on a warm summer day (tel. 832–4386). Open 10:30 A.M.–11:30 P.M. weather permitting.

McFetridge Sports Center. 3845 California Ave. Operated by the Chicago Park District and features ice skating and a hockey rink. Figure skating and hockey lessons. Rental skates available (tel. 478–0210).

Goodman Theatre. 200 S. Columbus Dr. (tel. 443–3800). Has a special children's theater.

Second City. 1616 N. Wells St. (tel. 787–8220). Youngsters are encouraged to participate at children's theater. This well-known talent center has been the launching pad for many big name stars.

The *Chicago Public Library Cultural Center.* 78 E. Washington. Features storytelling hours, puppet programs, films, and youth-oriented lectures. Call for recorded schedule. (tel. 346–3278)

The *Chicago Architecture Foundation.* Has special tours for youngsters to help them learn about buildings and what makes them special. Reservations necessary (tel. 326–1393 and 922–3432).

Hundreds of dolls make their home in an 1883 mansion at suburban Naperville's 11-acre *Naper complex,* 201 W. Porter Rd., (tel. 420–6010). Open May through October on Saturday, Sunday and Wednesday from 1:30 P.M. to 4:30 P.M. There is also a firehouse and old-time fort. Aurora has the *Blackberry Historical Farm and Village,* with a replica steam train ride to an 1840s farm, complete with a carriage museum housing 40 vintage buggies of all shapes and descriptions. Craftsmen demonstrate their skills in the village's 11 stores. Open May–Sept. 10:00 A.M.–4:30 P.M. (tel. 892–1550).

For those who like to plan ahead, there is the *Bozo Show.* There's a LONG waiting list to watch the clown with orange hair. To get your name on that list, write WGN TV, 2501 W. Bradley Pl. 60618.

HISTORIC SITES. The picturesque *Water Tower* at Michigan and Chicago avenues is one of the most famous survivors of the disastrous Chicago fire, which swept across the city in 1871 and left much of it in ashes, including the central business district.

Just across the street, *Here's Chicago* is a new attraction utilizing the historic Water Tower Pumping Station at Michigan Ave. and the Water Tower. Also a survivor of the Chicago Fire, its museum section emphasizes that disaster. A tour of the Pumping Station is followed by multimedia shows in 2 different theaters. Some critics feel the presentations do not do justice to Chicago's attractions. It's more of a people show than a place show. Open daily 10:00 A.M. –8 P.M., Friday and Saturday to 10 P.M. Adults $3.75, children and seniors $2.00. Cheerie O'Leary's is their on-site gift emporium emphasizing Chicago collectibles (tel. 467–7114).

Fort Dearborn. Just south of the Michigan Ave. Bridge. The site of Chicago's first settlement. The city's early history is depicted on bronze tablets on the bridge.

Old Town. Running from 1200 to 1700 north on Wells St. Includes some of Chicago's finest restored Victorian residences. It is a cosmopolitan area populated with distinctive shops, restaurants, and pubs. The entrance to 19th-century Pipers Alley at 1608 is marked by a large Tiffany lamp.

Hull House, 800 S. Halsted. Part of the famed social settlement established in 1889 by Jane Addams. Two buildings have been restored and are National Historic Landmarks. Open 10:00 A.M.–4:00 P.M., Monday–Friday, also summer Sundays from noon to 5 P.M. (tel. 996–2793). Located on University of Illinois Chicago Circle campus. Ramp for handicapped.

Chicago Historical Society. In Lincoln Park at Clark St. and North Ave. Has everything to acquaint you with Chicago's history. Particular emphasis is placed on the state's popular native son, Abraham Lincoln, and the Civil War. There are exceptional exhibits pertaining to Illinois pioneer life and the Chicago Fire, plus an impressive costumes display. Pioneer craft demonstrations recall the frontier way of doing things. Hours are 9:30 A.M.–4:30 P.M., Monday–Saturday, and noon–5:00 P.M., Sunday. Adults $1.50, children and seniors 50¢. Admission free Monday (tel. 642–4600).

Chicago Public Library Cultural Center. 78 E. Washington St. and Michigan. The land was once part of old Fort Dearborn military reservation. When the city library outgrew this post-Chicago Fire landmark, it was preserved, with the soft-spoken help of Mayor Daley's wife, for its exquisite Tiffany glass domes, mosaics, grand staircases, and general architectural beauty. Built in 1897 in the style of an opulent Italian Renaissance palazzo. Noted for its changing exhibits and G.A.R. collection. Many cultural programs and exhibits are regularly cosponsored by the *Chicago Council on Fine Arts* and the *Public Library.* To find out what's on schedule call (tel. 346–3278). Open Monday–Thursday, 9:00 A.M.–7:00 P.M., Friday to 6:00 P.M. and Saturday to 5:00 P.M. To arrange for special guided tours call 269–2922. Admission is free.

Evanston just to the north has 3 sites worth a detour. *Grosse Point Lighthouse* off Sheridan Road dating from the 1860s, has a Maritime Museum and Nature Center dedicated to native wildlife. Lighthouse tours are available Saturday and Sunday afternoons during May–October (tel. 864–5181). The mansion-museum of former Vice-President *Charles Dawes* at 225 Greenwood St., a block from Lake Michigan, is now home of the Evanston Historical Society. Its 28 rooms are full of antique furniture, artifacts, and historical displays. Open 1:00 P.M.–5:00 P.M. Monday, Tuesday, Thursday, Friday, and Saturday. Adults $1.00, children 50¢. Friday is free (tel. 475–3410). The museum-home of *Frances Willard,* Women's Christian Temperance Union founder, is the 3rd site (tel. 864–1397).

MUSEUMS AND GALLERIES. Chicagoans tend to be modest when it comes to boasting about their cultural riches. But the treasures in their museums and art galleries are right up there in the big league with the best of them.

Adler Planetarium. 1300 S. Lake Shore Dr. A great observatory on the lakefront. Probably the best view of the city is across the water from this promontory (tel. 322–0300). Its exhibits range across history from man's earliest navigating techniques using antique instruments to the most modern astronomical developments—everything from navigating a historic sailing schooner to a space vehicle. Open daily 9:30 A.M.–9:00 P.M. from mid-June through August. Other times Monday through Thursday to 4:30 P.M.; Friday to 9:00 P.M.; Saturday, Sunday, and holidays to 5:00 P.M. Exhibits free. Elaborate Sky Show presented in Sky and Universe Theaters focuses on nearby planets, galaxies, and distant stars. Sky Show costs $2.50 adults, $1.50 kids. Children under 6 are not admitted to Sky Show, but there is a special children's Sky Show on Saturday mornings. Senior citizens free.

Art Institute. Michigan at Adams St. Truly one of the world's great art museums. Noted for its Impressionist collection, Renaissance oils, Thorne miniature rooms, garden restaurant, and children's museum (tel. 443–3500).

There are works by El Greco, Monet, Renoir, Rembrandt, Cézanne, Degas, and Picasso. Grant Wood's *American Gothic* is a popular favorite. More current additions are the reconstructed old Stock Exchange trading room, the Rubloff paperweight collection, and stained glass windows by Marc Chagall. Open daily, Monday, Wednesday, Thursday, and Friday, 10:30 A.M. to 4:30 P.M.; Tuesday to 8:00 P.M.; Saturday, 10:00 A.M. to 5:00 P.M.; Sunday and holidays, noon to 5:00 P.M. Free on Tuesday. Suggested contribution: $4.50 adults, $2.25 seniors and children. Several very special exhibitions are planned for 1986. From January into April, "Lazlo Moholy—The Evolution of a Photographer's Vision." June through August, "In the American West: Photographs by Richard Avedon."

Bradford Museum of Plates. 9333 N. Milwaukee Ave., Niles, across from Golf Mill Shopping Center. A permanent newly enlarged exhibit of the most actively traded collector's plates. Open Monday through Friday, 9:00 A.M. to 4:00 P.M.; Saturday and Sunday 10:00 A.M. to 5:00 P.M. (tel. 966–2770). Visitors can also watch the current price quotes as these actively traded plates fluctuate on the exchange. $2 adults, $1 seniors; free Saturdays.

Cantigny. 115 Winfield Rd., Wheaton. The generation who grew up listening to Saturday night operettas on WGN in the 30s and 40s will remember Colonel Robert McCormick's endless intermission speeches, usually covering some event during the American Revolution. His fascination with war is reflected on his estate, where the late publisher of the *Chicago Tribune* filled part of the 500 acres with tanks, field artillery, and memories of war. The home is also open to tours. Daily in summer, noon to 5:00 P.M.; other times, Wednesday through Sunday to 4:00 P.M.; closed January in the mansion. The war museum is open daily 10:00 A.M. to 5:00 P.M. in summer; 10:00 A.M. to 4:00 P.M. the rest of the year; and closed Mondays and January (tel. 668–5161). Free.

Chicago Academy of Sciences. 2001 N. Clark. Oldest science museum in the Midwest features exhibits depicting natural history of the area, including a coal forest and swamp. Emphasis is on the Chicago region. Open daily 10:00 A.M.–5:00 P.M. $1.00 adults, 50¢ children and seniors. Phone 549–0606 for information on special exhibits. The South Gallery will feature changing exhibits. There is a winter lecture series each Tuesday and field trips to places like the Indiana Dunes and Starved Rock State Park.

Du Sable Museum of African American History. 740 E. 56 Pl. Emphasis is on black history and African art. Many documents pertaining to the history of black Americans, fine African masks, varied sculpture, paintings, a photography collection, and library on the history of midwestern blacks (tel. 947–0600).

Field Museum of Natural History. In Grant Park at 12th St. World's largest museum of natural history exhibits. It has a dazzling collection of precious and semiprecious stones. Trace the history of man through lifelike exhibits. Superb exhibits on American Indian culture, China, and Tibet.

New permanent exhibit on plants of the world is considered largest of its kind, with plant models representing 60 yrs. of work. A Pawnee Earth Lodge is an unusual permanent exhibit where visitors sit on buffalo robes in a reconstructed 38-ft. Pawnee lodge and view and handle Pawnee treasures. Maritime Peoples, a newsmaking exhibit in 1983, is now permanent and highlights the

Arctic and Northwest Coast. Open daily 9:00 A.M.–5:00 P.M. Admission free Thursdays, other times $2.00 adults, students $1.00, seniors 50¢ and families $4.00. There are facilities for the handicapped (tel. 922–9410). Dazzling new Gem Hall opened as a permanent exhibit in November 1985, with a special Adornment Hall showing how jewelry and adornments have been used in different parts of the world. Display includes the Chalmers Topaz. A special Maori exhibit is planned for March 1986.

International Museum of Surgical Sciences. 1524 N. Lake Shore Dr. Traces medicine from prehistoric times to the present. Everything from medicine men's dolls to an old apothecary shop and the history of healing herbs. Located in 2 impressive old mansions, headquarters for the International College of Surgeons. Open 10:00 A.M.–4:00 P.M., Tuesday–Saturday; 11:00 A.M.–5:00 P.M., Sunday. No children under 11 admitted (tel. 642–3555). Free.

Museum of Contemporary Art. 237 E. Ontario St. Offers changing exhibitions of one-man, group shows, historical shows. Exceptional museum store and The Site Restaurant featuring Charles Simonds wall-long work, "The Dwelling." Free gallery talks Tuesday at noon, Saturday 1 and 3 P.M.; Sunday 2 P.M. No reservations required. Call 280–2660 for details. Hours are 10:00 A.M.–5:00 P.M., Tuesday–Saturday, and Sunday noon–5:00 P.M. Admission adults $3.00, seniors and children $2.00. Tuesday is free. Completely wheelchair accessible.

Museum of Science and Industry. In Jackson Park. A 5-star magnet that attracts kids and senior citizens alike with its 14 acres of exhibits in engineering, industrial, and medical progress. Tour a simulated operating coal mine or a captured Nazi submarine. There is an antique car display, Main Street of Yesterday; a must for all ages. You could spend days here. Lots of push-button displays. Building was erected as Palace of Fine Arts for 1893 Columbian Exposition. Open daily 9:30 A.M.–5:30 P.M. in summer. Winter 9:30 A.M.–4:00 P.M., Monday–Friday; Saturday, Sunday, and holidays to 5:30 P.M. Admission and parking free (tel. 684–1414). Some special shows scheduled for this year include "A Bauhaus Exhibit" June 12–September 1, and a lively display on "Robots" June 15–July 30. A permanent architecture exhibit was slated to open this spring. Big head-liner will be the $12 million new Crown Space Center which opens July 1 in a special new addition. It will have an Omni Max theater which promises to be a real eye-opener. The season's grand finale is "Christmas Around the World" which begins the Saturday before Thanksgiving and features elaborate Christmas trees, along with the customs and traditions of many nations.

Oriental Institute. University of Chicago. Has exhibits dating back to 5000 B.C. Scholarly archaeologists from here have been involved in major digs around the world. Artifacts from Egypt, Persia, Anatolia, Syria, Palestine, and Mesopotamia. Call 962–9507 for further information about their special exhibit, which will run through 1986. "The Quest for Prehistory: The Oriental Institute and the Origins of Civilization in the Near East" will focus on their work at prehistoric sites in Iran, Iraq, and Turkey. The central exhibit will be a full-scale reproduction of a 9,000-year-old prehistoric house excavated at Jarmo, Iraq. Admission is free and tours are at 10:00 A.M., 11:30 A.M., 1:00 P.M., and 2:30 P.M.,

Tuesday–Saturday. Sunday hours are noon to 4:00 P.M., and free films are offered as well as tours.

Peace Museum, 364 W. Erie St. Tel.: 440–1860. Explores the issues of war and peace by means of visual and performing arts. Open Tuesday, Wednesday, Friday and Sunday from 12 A.M.–5 P.M., Thursday 12 A.M.–8 P.M. Admission $1.50, 50¢ for seniors and children.

Polish Museum of America. 984 N. Milwaukee. Has notable stained glass, Polish and American art, sculptures, Paderewski and Kosciuszko rooms. Source of great pride to the city's Polish population, 2nd only in size to that of Warsaw. Open 12:00 P.M.–5:00 P.M. daily (tel. 384–3352). Free. No children under 12.

Ripley's Believe It Or Not Museum. 1500 N. Wells. Shows fabulous exhibits of often bizarre oddities collected by Robert L. Ripley during his foreign travels. Daily. Summer hours noon–10:00 P.M. daily, Friday and Saturday to midnight. Call 337–6077 for winter hours. $4.50 adults, $2.50 children.

John Shedd Aquarium. Across Lake Shore Dr. from Field Museum. So many species on display here that you will be an ancient mariner before you are able to remember them all. Plans for special exhibits were not yet formulated at press time, but 5,000 fish of over 560 species are highlighted by a 90,000-gallon Coral Reef where divers hand-feed fish daily at 11:00 A.M. and 2:00 P.M. Summer hours 9:00 A.M.–5:00 P.M., vary other months. 939–2438. Adults $2.00, children $1.00, seniors 50¢. Thursday free.

Spertus Museum of Judaica. 618 S. Michigan. One of the world's largest private collections of Jewish artifacts, manuscripts, and ceremonial objects. Fridays are free. "History of Zionism", a photo essay from Israel, will be exhibited March 2–June 22. "Mouton Rothschild: Paintings for the Labels" is a unique show on loan from London's Victoria & Albert Museum April 27–August 17, featuring all the Rothschild labels by top artists of the world—from Miro and Picasso to Dali, Warhol, and Chagall. Admission $1.00 for seniors and students, $2.00 adults. Monday–Thursday, 10:00 A.M.–5:00 P.M.; Friday to 3:00 P.M.; and Sunday to 4:00 P.M. (tel. 922–9012).

Telephony Museum. 225 W. Randolph. Traces the history of the telephone from Alexander Graham Bell's time to the present. A phone used by him in 1892 is here. Open 8:30 A.M.–4:00 P.M. weekdays. Admission free (tel. 727–2994).

Morton B. Weiss Museum of Judaica. 1100 E. Hyde Park Blvd. (Isaiah Israel Congregation). Collection of unusually illuminated marriage contracts and rare manuscripts in Judeo-Kurdish and Judeo-Persian. Open after worship services and by appointment (tel. 924–1234). Free

Terra Museum of American Art. 2600 Central Park, Evanston. Showcases the private art collection of a North Shore industrialist's 19th- and 20th-century treasures. Emphasis is on 200 yrs. of American painting. Tuesday–Saturday, 11:00 A.M.–5:00 P.M., Sunday, 1:00 P.M.–5:00 P.M. $3.00 (tel. 328–3400).

Fox River Trolley Museum. On Rte. 31 in South Elgin. Has electric street-cars on display and operating. Offers 30-min. ride along the Fox R. via early 1900s trolley cars, along with displays of such vintage vehicles as the oldest interurban rail car in America. Open from 11:00 A.M. to 6:00 P.M. the 3rd Sunday

The Art Institute of Chicago

Lower Floor

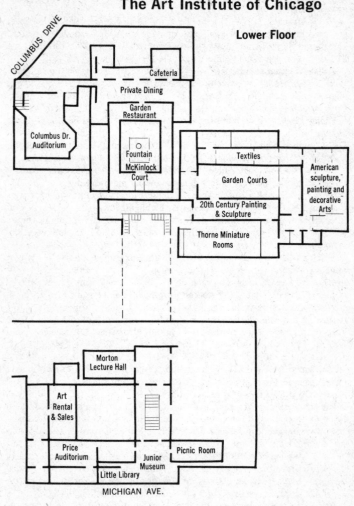

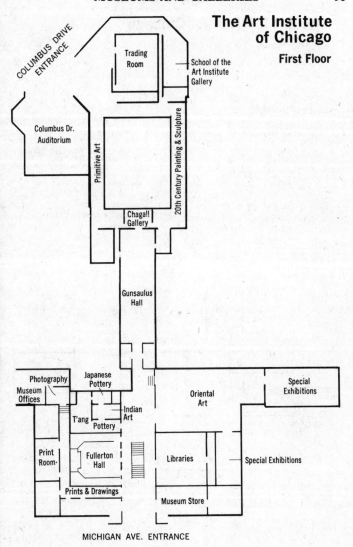

The Art Institute of Chicago

First Floor

COLUMBUS DRIVE ENTRANCE

Trading Room

School of the Art Institute Gallery

Columbus Dr. Auditorium

Primitive Art

20th Century Painting & Sculpture

Chagall Gallery

Gunsaulus Hall

Photography

Museum Offices

Japanese Pottery

Indian Art

T'ang Pottery

Print Room

Fullerton Hall

Prints & Drawings

Oriental Art

Special Exhibitions

Libraries

Special Exhibitions

Museum Store

MICHIGAN AVE. ENTRANCE

The Art Institute of Chicago

Second Floor

Points of Interest

1) Earlier Painting and Sculpture
2) 13th, 14th, 15th century Italian
3) 15th century Flemish
4) 15th, 16th century German
5) 16th, 17th century Italian
6) 17th century Spanish and Italian
7) 17th century Dutch (*Rembrandt*)
8) 17th, 18th century Italian (Baroque)
9) 18th century English Period Rooms
10) 18th century Italian (Neoclassic))
11) Burnham Library of Architecture Gallery
12) Late 18th century British Portraits
13) 19th century English and French (Romantic)
14) Impressionist
15) Late 19th century French
16) Late 19th century Painting and Sculpture
17) 20th century Painting and Sculpture
18) Special Exhibitions

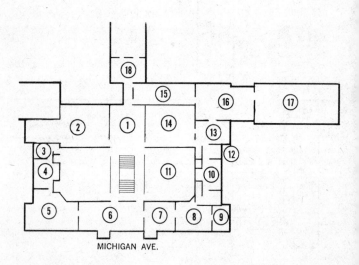

MICHIGAN AVE.

of the month, May–October. Also Saturdays, 1:00 P.M.–5:00 P.M. in July and August. $1.50 adults, 75¢ children (tel. 697–4676).

Illinois Railway Museum. At Union. Features electric railway equipment, locomotives, tours, and a special railroad library. Open daily during summer, 10:00 A.M.–5:00 P.M. During May and September on Saturday and Sunday, 11:00 A.M.–5:00 P.M., and Sunday only in March, April, October, and November. Closed December–February. Adults $3.50, children $2.00 (tel. 923–2488). Also at Union is **Seven Acres Antique Village and Museum,** a pseudo-western town jammed with antiques and a noteworthy phonograph collection. One of the country's largest antique phonograph auctions is held there in June. Youngsters enjoy the daily gunfights and often insist on staying for several. Weekend antique sales and auctions. Open daily 9:00 A.M.–6:00 P.M. April–October; and 10:00 A.M.–5:00 P.M., Saturdays and Sundays, November, February, and March. Closed December and January. Adults $3.50, seniors $2.50, children 6–12 $2.00, under 6 free (tel. 923–2214).

Lizzardo Museum of Lapidary Art. 220 Cottage Hill Ave., in Wilder Park, Elmhurst (tel. 833–1616). This private collection has everything from fossils and petrified wood to exotic carvings on onyx, jade, and agate, plus educational programs and films. Open all year Tuesday–Friday and Sunday, 1:00 P.M.–5:00 P.M.; Saturday from 10:00 A.M. Friday free. $1.00 adults, 50¢ from 13–18, and seniors.

MOVIES AND MOVIE PALACES. In the gilt-edged 1920s, spurred on by the popularity of those newfangled movies, imaginative architects returned from Europe with elaborate ideas for creating standout theaters. The *Chicago Theatre,* 175 N. State Street St., ranked among the nation's most impressive and it still does—a bedazzling, wonderfully baroque, ballroom-like collection of pillars, posts, and statuary, it is part Versailles, with a touch of Roman bath and Greek temple added for good measure. No matter what's playing, it's worth attending a movie here to observe the opulent atmosphere. Inquire locally about occasional concerts on the theater's superb organ. Real estate developers would like to tear it down and replace it with some multistory marvel—the battle lines are drawn between preservationists and developers, a battle too often won in Chicago by people with a high-rise mentality. It looks like the preservationists are winning, but it has been an uphill battle.

Chicago is a strange city when it comes to films. An award winner may have left outer-Saskatoon long before it ever arrives here, and many classic art films that achieve success elsewhere never come to town. The *Carnegie,* Rush at Oak (tel. 944–2966), *Fine Arts,* 418 S. Michigan (tel. 939–3700), along with the well-maintained Art Deco *Biograph,* where John Dillinger attended his last film, before he was ambushed in the alley (tel. 348–4123), tend to feature the unusual in films. *Facets Multimedia* concentrates on the foreign, arty, and offbeat. It has 2 locations: 1517 W. Fullerton (tel. 281–9075), in the kind of neighborhood where one likes to park directly in front of the theater, and north at the Community Center in suburban Glencoe (tel. 281–4114). *Chicago Library* in one of the city's architecturally prized settings, 78 E. Washington St. (tel. 744–6630), regularly revives old favorites.

To find out what's playing where, check the entertainment sections of the local newspapers for daily schedules.

 MUSIC. From classical to new wave, there's a home in Chicago for every musical taste. Devotees of classical music flock to *Orchestra Hall* at 220 S. Michigan (box office phone is 435–8111), to hear the *Chicago Symphony Orchestra,* acclaimed as one of the world's finest, under the direction of Sir Georg Solti. Chicago's *Civic Opera House,* Madison St. and Wacker Dr., is the home of the *Lyric Opera Company,* which frequently hosts guests performances by opera notables such as Pavarotti (tel. 346–0270). The impressive structure was built by then multimillionaire Samuel Insull. Once Thomas Edison's confidential secretary, Insull rose to power and prestige as president of Chicago Edison Company. At his peak he sat on the board of directors of 85 companies, chairing 65 of them. His overextended empire crashed during the Depression, and when he died in a Paris subway in 1938, he had 85¢ in his pocket.

The fortresslike appearance of the *Auditorium Theater,* 70 E. Congress, gives little indication of the beauty to be found inside. The theater, with its ornately decorated walls and ceilings, has been declared an architectural landmark, but its real beauty (for music lovers, at least) lies in its acoustics, which are said to be almost perfect. It seats close to 4,000, mostly for classical or "conservative" concerts, but occasionally you'll find a pop or rock act scheduled here. The building was designed by Dankmar Adler and Louis Sullivan in 1889, but declined when millionaire Samuel Insull built the Civic Opera House. After years of neglect, millions were spent to restore its gilded beauty—a rare success story in Chicago, where historic buildings are frequently demolished despite protests of preservationists (tel. 922–2110).

For more contemporary musical tastes, indoor concert facilities include *Park West,* 322 West Armitage, on the city's near north side. Since liquor is served, you must be 21 or over. If you meet the age requirement, you'll have a choice of rock, R&B, jazz, soul, new wave, and even folk and country/western acts—and from time to time, you can see big-name acts that don't usually appear in this type of intimate night-club style setting (500-person capacity on the main floor, 250 in the balcony) (tel. 929–5959).

Although the *Chicago Stadium,* 1800 W. Madison, hosts large concerts less frequently than in the past, it sometimes offers concerts by rock, soul, and country/western acts, squeezed in between rodeos, hockey games, and ice shows. The *Arie Crown Theater* in McCormick Place, 23rd St. and the lake, has put a lot of money into improving its acoustics, but it still is used primarily for the road companies of Broadway shows rather than for concerts (tel. 791–6000).

Topline rock, country/western, and contemporary performers appear at *Rosemont Horizon* near O'Hare Airport, Mannheim Rd. and Lunt Ave. (tel. 635–9800), a huge stadium that seats close to 20,000. It's also used for rodeos, circuses, family-style reviews, and home games of DePaul University's basketball team.

Jazz came to Chicago in the early 1920s and went on to become a national preoccupation. After a decline, jazz is staging a great comeback. *Andy's,* 11 E. Hubbard (tel. 642–6805); *Backroom,* 1007 N. Rush St. (tel. 751–2433); *Joe Segal's Jazz Showcase* at the Blackstone, 636 S. Michigan (tel. 427–4300); *Rick's Cafe Americain,* Holiday Inn Lakeshore (tel. 943–9200); *Manhattan,* 1045 Rush St. (tel. 751–2001), are among headliners. Jazz Institute Hotline is 666–1881.

Summertime is really the best time for Chicago (and out-of-town) music lovers, with an abundance of outdoor concert facilities and plenty of free concerts in parks and downtown plazas. On almost any summer business day (most frequently during the noon hours), you're likely to hear a free outdoor concert at the *First National Bank Plaza* on Monroe between Clark and Dearborn, where you can enjoy the Chagall mosaic while you listen to the concert; the *Daley Center Plaza,* home of the Picasso sculpture; or at the *Chicago Tribune's Pioneer Court,* 435 N. Michigan. The Park District offers 70 concerts at 49 park sites throughout the city. For schedule call 294–2320.

Classical music lovers who enjoy the outdoors are treated in the summer months to outdoor concerts by the *Chicago Chamber Orchestra,* the *Chicago Chamber Brass,* and other small classical groups, mostly at outdoor plazas, as well as at the *Art Institute's* beautiful outdoor garden at Michigan and Adams; the *Museum of Science and Industry,* 57th Street and the lake; and *St. James Cathedral,* Michigan Ave. and Chestnut. Carillon recitals are held at Rockefeller Memorial Chapel, 5850 S. Woodlawn on the University of Chicago campus (tel. 962–6002). The entertainment sections of both major newspapers give complete listings. During colder weather, small-scale classical concerts are also abundant, particularly at the *Cultural Center,* Michigan and Randolph (tel. 744–6630), and at the downtown colleges. Again, check newspaper listings.

Poplar Creek Music Theater in suburban Hoffman Estates, highways 59 and 72 at Northwest Tollway (tel. 599–1212), an hour's drive from downtown, is a beautiful outdoor concert facility that offers terrific acoustics and great sight lines for those seated either in the pavilion or on the less-expensive lawn seats farther from the stage. You can bring a picnic dinner to enjoy before the concert at Poplar Creek, or at Highland Park's *Ravinia Music Festival Theater.* Ravinia is an established outdoor concert facility that offers summer concerts by the *Chicago Symphony Orchestra,* dance troupes, and contemporary performers. If you choose a lawn seat at Ravinia, you can hear, but not see, the performers. Ravinia is at the south end of town at Lake Cook and Green Bay roads. For information on the season, which runs from late June through mid-September, call 728–4642. Northwestern University has summer band concerts on their Evanston Campus. For dates and times of these popular events call 491–5441.

ChicagoFest, the city's summer festival, has become embroiled in politics, boycotts, and other problems, and was not scheduled for two years, but there is some hope it will be back on a future calendar. A new program of 1-day *Neighborhood Festivals* was introduced in 1981. They are held during June and

July and feature ethnic entertainment and food in the city's Jewish, black, Polish, and Mexican neighborhoods. Again, check local papers for schedules.

For discount ticket information, see Note at end of *Theater* section in this chapter.

 DANCE. Although Chicago is home to several excellent dance companies, few of them have their own theaters. Maria Tallchief's *Chicago City Ballet* (tel. 943–1315), the *Gus Giordano Dance Company* (tel. 866–9442), and the *Hubbard Street Dance Theater,* 218 S. Wabash, 3rd Floor (tel. 663–0853), perform throughout the city at various locations, as do the many ethnic dance troupes, so it's best to check newspaper listings for times and places. For the most part, the high-powered dance attractions in Chicago are still the touring companies of domestic and foreign dance troupes, and their appearances are generally well advertised. *Mo Ming Dance and Arts Center,* 1034 W. Barry Ave. (tel. 472–9894), hosts dance and musical performances of both local and out-of-town artists and also provides space for art exhibits. Their summer series "Dance for a Dollar Ninety-Eight" showcases talents of local dancers and choreographers and really costs only $1.98.

For discount ticket information, see Note at end of *Theater* section in this chapter.

 THEATER. Chicagoans choose from Broadway plays and musicals, revivals, original works by established playwrights and newly emerging local talent, avant-garde offerings, and lighthearted revues.

The *Goodman Theatre,* part of the Art Institute cultural complex at 200 S. Columbus Dr., is the home of the city's oldest locally produced theater, and one of the best-known regional theaters in the country. Plays first presented at the Goodman have gone on to Broadway, the Kennedy Center in Washington, D.C., and the National Theatre in England. The Goodman's *Studio Theater* is a very intimate space, seating about 100 and specializing in experimental productions and cabaret. For convenient preshow dining, the theater houses *Ingrid's,* Wednesday–Saturday, open at 6:00 P.M. You pay a set price, then enjoy the freshly prepared gourmet buffet. Reservations advised. Call Goodman Theatre box office (443–3800).

"Off-Loop" Theaters. In recent years, Chicago's off-Loop theaters have consistently provided professional legitimate theater offerings at a lower cost and in a more intimate atmosphere than the city's larger facilities. Several plays and musicals that had their beginnings in Chicago, eventually became top Broadway shows, notably *Grease, Mornings at Seven,* and Lily Tomlin's *Appearing Nitely.* If you take advantage of the off-Loop offerings, you may be able to boast one day that you enjoyed a play or musical long before it came to Broadway.

Off-Loop theaters located in the city and accessible by public transportation or cab are the *Wisdom Bridge Theater,* 1559 W. Howard St. (tel. 743–6442); *Victory Gardens Theater* and *The Body Politic Theater,* both at 2261 N. Lincoln (tel. 871–3000); the *Organic Theater,* 3319 N. Clark (tel. 327–5588); the *Apollo Theater,* 2540 N. Lincoln (tel. 935–6100); the *Court Theater* of the University of Chicago, 5706 S. University (tel. 753–4472); the *Theater Building,* 1225 W. Belmont (tel. 327–5252); *Practical Theatre,* 703 Howard St. (tel. 328–4151); and *Steppenwolf Theatre,* 2851 N. Halsted St. (tel. 472–4141).

Downtown Theaters. Chicago companies of Broadway shows most often settle in at the city's downtown theaters, conveniently located in the heart of Chicago's business district. They are a pleasant walk from downtown hotels and only a short cab or bus ride from popular near North Side hotels.

The Shubert Theater, 22 W. Monroe (tel. 977–1700), specializes in Broadway musicals; *The Blackstone Theater,* 60 E. Balbo (tel. 977–1700), is most often used for Broadway dramas and comedies. The renovated *Auditorium Theater,* 70 E. Congress Parkway (tel. 922–2110), boasts what many consider to be the city's finest acoustical system, but it is used more frequently for concerts than for theatrical productions.

Although some Broadway offerings remain at the downtown theaters for as long as 2 years, traveling companies of other shows often choose McCormick Place's *Arie Crown Theater,* Lake Shore Dr. and 23rd St. (tel. 791–6000), because of its size. Since it seats 4,300 people, shows are made available to a larger number of people in a shorter period of time—an important consideration when a road company is scheduled for a short run. The *Playhouse* at McCormick Place (tel. 791–6000) generally offers smaller-scale musicals and comedies in a less-spacious theater. Because McCormick Place is the city's primary convention center, it is accessible by public transportation and, of course, by taxi.

No mention of Chicago theater would be complete without highlighting *Second City* at 1616 N. Wells. The theater's hilarious, frequently outrageous, comedy revues have been the training ground for dozens of nationally known personalities, including Mike Nichols and Elaine May, Alan Arkin, and John Belushi (tel. 337–3992).

Note: The *Hot Tix Booth,* on the west side of State St. between Madison and Monroe, offers half-price, day-of-performance tickets to most of the city's theater, music, and dance offerings. A limited number of tickets are available beginning at 11:00 A.M., and many people are pleasantly surprised to find that seats are occasionally the best in the house. Call to find out what's going on that day (977–1755).

 SHOPPING. Whether you're looking for a budget bargain or for a designer original, Chicago will come as a very pleasant shopping surprise. As the transportation crossroads of America, merchandise flows in from all directions. Its inland port status and overseas service via nearly a dozen foreign airlines also makes it an unexpected center for imports.

Some of America's most famed merchandising names also got their start in Chicago, sending what became known as their "dream book" catalogs to the most isolated corners of the country. Sears Roebuck, Montgomery Ward, and Alden's are still headquartered here.

Where to begin? Why State Street, that Great Street, of course. Each of the giant department stores that line this shopper's heaven contains floor after floor of everything imaginable. Let's start with 130-year-old *Marshall Field & Company*, a prestige store synonymous with shopping in Chicago. This is such a marvel that the visitor will be tempted to follow the example of locals and spend the whole day there. From its Tiffany-domed ceiling of Favrile iridescent glass to its superb Victorian Antique Jewelery Department, the store is as much a sightseeing attraction as a great emporium.

Field himself set the tone with his motto "Give the lady what she wants." And with 73 acres of floor space, the store has just about everything anybody ever wanted, always displayed in a very special way, whether it's a Russian lynx coat, a find from the bargain basement, or one of the treasures from the famed Antique Furniture Department. Field's makes its own flavorful Frango mints and bakes taste-tempting homemade pastries, and the store restaurants are justifiably popular, fashion shows and all. Right on the premises, the store's fine craftsmen will fix your great grandfather's watch, restring your pearls, reweave your antique tapestry, and restore an ancestral portrait. Everything, whether it be a modest purchase or a designer original from the *28 Shop*, goes out in boxes Chicagoans have labeled "Marshall Field Green." It is still considered fashionable to meet under the massive Field's clock that hangs at State and Washington, where it has been since 1907, replacing an even earlier one. Today, there are 18 stores in the Chicago division, but the State Street Store is the granddaddy of them all. There are guided tours of the store and a staff of interpreters speak over 3 dozen languages. Onetime employee Gordon Selfridge was so impressed he went to London to build one like it. It can be summed up in one sentence: Field's is definitely finer. There is quality here in all price ranges. The bargain basement is actually a store within a store. 111 N. State St. (tel. 781–1000). Open 9:45 A.M.–5:45 P.M., Monday–Saturday and Monday and Thursday evenings to 7:00 P.M. Accept American Express, Master Card, Visa.

Give a Chicagoan a present in a *Peacock* box and it speaks volumes. This is *the* prestige shop for jewelery. The reputation dates back to 1837, when Elijah Peacock opened a small shop making watches and ships' chronometers. Today, the shop at State and Monroe is ultra genteel, with bronze peacock doors opening onto a green marble interior with crystal chandeliers as sparkling as the diamonds they illuminate. The store is also noted for fine English bone china, silver, leather goods, crystal, and other quality gifts. There are now branch shops at Old Orchard, Oak Brook, and other shopping centers. 101 S. State St. (tel. 630–5701). Hours at the State St. store are 10:00 A.M.–5:30 P.M., Monday–Friday and 10:00 A.M.–5:00 P.M. Saturday. Accept American Express, Master Card, Visa.

Carson, Pirie, Scott & Company has come a long way since manager Mac-Leish stood on State St. during the Chicago Fire shouting, "50 silver dollars for every wagonload of merchandise you save out of this building." Passing teamsters rescued about 40 percent of the merchandise before the store burned. The company managed to survive. By 1909, the store moved into an elaborate new Louis Sullivan-designed building so famous today that visitors rate it as a sightseeing attraction. Although the company operates over 2 dozen retail stores, this Chicago landmark is still the flagship store. Interpreters can answer questions in nearly 2 dozen languages, and there is a quality selection of fashionable clothes, accessories, and furnishings. Their 7th floor *Kitchentech* is a special housewares attraction, a fully equipped demonstration kitchen featuring cooking classes, famous chef appearances, and product demonstrations Monday through Friday. There are 7 different dining areas. *Carson's Eighth-floor Grill* is especially popular for its buffet table. 1 S. State St. (tel. 744–2000). Open at 11:30 A.M., Monday–Saturday, until 3:00 P.M. Accept Master Card and Visa.

Nine blocks of State Street from Wacker Drive to Congress is now a landscaped mall closed to regular traffic, and shoppers seem to enjoy the more leisurely mood. Shops of all kinds extend down both sides, ranging from *Charles Stevens*, 25 N. State St. (tel. 630–1500), with a fine reputation for women's clothing, to *Broadstreets*, 123 S. State St. (tel. 726–8902), noted for traditional men's clothes and furnishings and leisure sportswear. Tall women head for *Tall Girls Shop*, 17 N. State (tel. 782-9867) and *Tall Togs*, 105 S. Wabash (tel. 782-2915) where there's a good selection of styles. The fuller-figured shopper does well at *Lane Bryant* on the next block at 9 N. Wabash Ave. (tel. 621–8700), which specializes in larger sizes, half-sizes, and overweight juniors. *Pendleton Woolen Mills* has a shop full of jackets, shirts, robes, blankets, and everything woolen in the Palmer House Arcade, just off State St.—beautiful fabrics in hard-to-resist plaids, 17 E. Monroe St. (tel. 372–1699).

Henry C. Lyttons, 235 S. State (tel. 922–3500), is top drawer for men and women. Another big State St. department store is *Wieboldt's*, 1 N. State (tel. 782-1500).

Sears Roebuck, Montgomery Ward, and *Goldblatts* have closed their State St. department stores, and at press time there is talk of establishing a permanent home for the Chicago Library in the Goldblatt building.

THE MAGNIFICENT MILE

Head 2 blocks over to Michigan and start north, and the mood definitely changes. Anyone with stamina and sales resistance can spend a glorious morning or afternoon window-shopping his or her way along what is known locally as "The Magnificent Mile." Block after block of ultra-posh shops lining Michigan Ave. are frequented by the city's moneyed class. These range from classic French silk scarfs and purses at *Hermes*, 875 N. Michigan (tel. 787–8175), to status-symbol Italian loafers and luggage at *Gucci*, at 713 (tel. 664–5504). *Lord & Taylor* (tel. 787–7400) and *Marshall Field* (tel. 781–1234) share the limelight at Water Tower Place, 835 N. Michigan Ave., which has over 100 imaginative boutiques all under one roof. For those who can't resist taking home a Chicago-oriented souvenir, *Accent Chicago* (944–1354) there is an unusual specialty shop where all gifts have unique city-oriented themes. Even if you aren't interested in shopping, Water Tower Place is so dramatic and interesting that it deserves a visit.

Next door at John Hancock Center's street level, *Bonwit Teller* (tel. 751–1800) offers chic fashion with a special flair. There's more high style at *Saks Fifth Avenue,* 669 Michigan (tel. 944–6500); *I. Magnin,* 830 (tel. 751–0500); *Stanley Korshak,* 940 (tel. 280–0520), all of which cater to the carriage trade. You can buy a conversation-stopping French original or an Americanized adaptation at any of them. *Brittany Ltd.,* at 642 (tel. 642–8560), pleases the classic, tweedy set, while *Courreges,* 835 (tel. 337–0606), is always avant-garde. *Laura Ashley,* 835 (tel. 951–8004), emphasizes classic tradition.

The list is long and very glamorous. For a real "Maine Chance" kind of day or half day, *Elizabeth Arden,* at 717 Michigan (tel. 266–5750), offers the whole treatment, pampering customers with facials and the luxury of spa treatments. The store is also noted for its lingerie. *Neiman Marcus* (tel. 642–5900) has opened its largest store outside Texas at the corner of Michigan Ave. and Superior St., occupying 4 floors of the 63-story retail-commercial-residential Olympia center complex. The very luxe store carries everything from designer apparel to prestige furs. Its epicure food complex is one of the most extensive in the Neiman Marcus chain, and there will also be a Petrossian shop, featuring caviar, smoked salmon, trout, and sturgeon. *Ilona of Hungary,* 45 East Oak (tel. 337–7161), also stands ready to glamorize visitors for a special occasion, as does *Marilyn Miglin Model Makeup,* 112 East Oak (tel. 943–1120). *Georgette Klinger* has a salon in Water Tower Place, 835 N. Michigan (tel. 787–4300), where your travel-tired face can get a facial and mask.

Spaulding & Company, 959 N. Michigan (tel. 337–4800), has been selling jewels in the city since 1854. *Tiffany & Company,* 715 (tel. 944–7500), is a more recent addition.

Jackie Renwick, 19 S. LaSalle (tel. 236–4353), and 65 E. Oak, (tel. 266–8269), focuses on clothes for the business woman. If the need arises to come up with a fancy costume, *Broadway Costumes* at 932 W. Washington Blvd. can send you off as a queen, a clown, or anything in between (tel. 829–6400).

We're assuming no one is going to sip champagne from your slipper, as visitors once did at Chicago's famous-infamous Everleigh Club—but labels from these shops are definitely fashionable enough, with prices to match. *Joyce Selby Shoes,* 845 N. Michigan (tel. 664–8281), and 112 N. State (tel. 236–0592), *Charles Jourdan Boutique,* Water Tower Place, 835 N. Michigan (tel. 280–8133), and *Naturalizer* at 636 (tel. 337–2255), as well as Water Tower Place (tel. 266–7315). For hard-to-fit sizes, *Nierman's Tall Girl Shoes,* 17 N. State, carries sizes 5 to 14 from quad A to double E (tel. 346–9797). So does *Hy Miller* Shoes, 125 N. Dearborn (tel. 236–3534). *Chandler's* at 27 N. State (tel. 263–8157) and 650 N. Michigan (tel. 944–9375), and *Bakers,* 133 S. State, carry modestly priced copies of the latest shoe fashions. Incidentally, *Woolworth's,* 18 N. State (tel. 236–9265), has fast repair service in the basement if your favorite walking shoes collapse. *Hanig's Shoes,* 660 N. Michigan (tel. 642–5330), and 1 S. LaSalle (tel. 263–1365), can fit men from sizes 6 - 15 and AAA to EEE.

Almost as many of these specialty shops cater to men and women and there are all kinds of prestige names—*Capper and Capper,* 1 N. Wabash (tel. 236–3800), and *Brooks Brothers,* 74 E. Madison (tel. 263–0100), are only a few.

Jaeger International, 835 N. Michigan (tel. 642–6665), is typical of many quality establishments that feature both men's and women's things. *M. Hyman and Son* has several stores, all specializing in clothes for unusual sizes. One is at 835 N. Michigan (tel. 266–0060). *Eddie Bauer,* 123 N. Wabash (tel. 263–6005), is an expert at outfitting outdoorsmen, and century-old *Hart, Shaffner, Marx* has a wide selection of quality things sold at *Capper & Capper, Baskins* and *Charles Stevens. Morris,* 4200 S. Halsted (tel. 927–3887), is the place where stockmen bought their Stetsons in the city's stockyard days. The store is noted for western boots, including Tony Lama, Justin, and Lucchese. *Bally Shoe Salon,* 919 N. Michigan Ave., (tel. 787–8110), is noted for its Bally of Switzerland products, including belts, attaché cases, and carry-all bags. *Marks, Ltd.,* 2756 N. Racine Ave. (tel. 883–4477), caters to men under 5'8" in sizes 34–50. Even ties are custom-made for shorter men.

Things have been changing on the shopping scene so fast in the past few years that it is impossible to include all the shops worth a detour. Real estate developers work so fast in Chicago that a building can be torn down and another one on its site by the time a book goes to press. And the turnover percentage in prime locations like Water Tower Place is high enough that it always pays to call before making a special trip to a particular shop. 3 new prestige addresses were recently built along Michigan Ave.—One North Michigan, Olympia, and One Magnificient Mile. Ralph Lauren and Stanley Korshak have shops at the Magnificient Mile location.

People in the know seem sure a Bloomingdale's is also about to appear on the Magnificient Mile. *Beagle & Company* is also there (tel. 337–8002), with a large collection of Snoopy and Peanuts treasures for fans of all ages.

More and more European branch shops have also opened, like *Liberty of London,* 845 N. Michigan (Water Tower) (tel. 280–1134). And of course, for those who like the classic look, *Burberrys* brings their traditional English weatherwear to 633 N. Michigan Ave. (tel 787–2500).

Those who arrive in a winter snow may have a special interest in heading for *Rosenthal Furs,* 940 N. Michigan Ave. (tel 943–1365), and *Evans Furriers,* 36 S. State St. (tel. 855–2000).

Caravans Awry, 318 W. Grand at Franklin (tel. 644–5395), has been making news in the budget-priced rug world. *Douglas Kenyon, Inc.,* 1357 N. Wells St. (tel. 642–5300) features art of John James Audubon.

LOOKING FOR BARGAINS

Because it has always been America's center for mail-order catalog sales, Chicago has some exceptional bargains at special surplus stores operated by those companies. These feature overstocked merchandise, discontinued items, returns, sometimes scratched, dented, or whatever. *Sears Catalog Supplies* at 5555 S. Archer (tel. 284–3200), offers varies merchandise at 20–80 percent savings.

These warehouse type, no-frill stores in the pipe-rack display tradition usually spell big savings for the shopper, but they're often well-kept secrets, since retail shops normally are not overjoyed by the competition. *Clothing Clearance Center,* 1006 S. Michigan (tel. 663–4170), offers men's designer suits at substantial savings. *Chicago Shoe Outlet,* 3167 N. Lincoln Ave. (tel. 348–0555), has men's shoes at a discount. *Gingiss Formal Wear Warehouse,* 555 W. 14 Place (tel. 829–1188), sells new, used, close-out, and irregular formal clothes at savings of 40 percent and more. *Handmoor,* 300 N. Michigan Ave. (tel. 726–5600), is known for good-quality clothes at good prices, normally 20 percent off, with frequent sales. *Cut Rate Toys,* 2424 W. Devon Ave. (tel. 743–3822), has walls lined with toys and stuffed cardboard boxes marked 3 for $1.00.

Frye Factory Outlet has a no-frills store at 2727 N. Mannheim, Franklin Park (tel. 451–0024). Frye products sold at a discount there are boots, shoes, bags, and briefcases with minor factory defects. *Lands End Outlet* has 2 places on N. Elston, 2317 and 2241 (tel. 384–4170 and 276–2232). Overstocked merchandise, factory seconds, and discontinued items are sold at 10–60 percent off. For the ultimate experience, consider Maxwell Street, the old pushcart market where many immigrant merchants got their start. *Coats, Coats, Coats, Willow & Phingston,* Glenview (tel. 291–0333), features top name designer fashions at 30–50 percent off.

For the ultimate experience, consider Maxwell Street, the old pushcart market where many immigrant merchants got their start. The buyer can still expect high pressure and lots of bargaining.

SPECIAL INTEREST SHOPPING

Book lovers seek out *Abraham Lincoln Bookshop,* 18 E. Chestnut (tel. 944–3085), where Lincoln-expert Ralph Newman has an overwhelming collection of Lincolniana and Civil War history. *Kroch's and Brentano's,* 29 S. Wabash (tel. 332–7500), is one of the giants, a massive operation with 16 branch stores; *B. Dalton* and *Waldenbook's* each has several bookstores scattered across the city and suburbs. For the rare and unusual, collectors will be interested in *Hamill and Barker,* 400 N. Michigan (tel. 644–5933), with first editions and early English classics, and *Kenneth Nebenzahl,* 333 N. Michigan (tel. 641–2711), where the emphasis is on early American works, plus rare prints and maps.

Local museums like the *Art Institute* and *Field Museum* have interesting gift shops that carry colorful prints, books, and items relating to the treasures on display.

If cooking is your thing, *Crate and Barrel* with 7 locations has everything imaginable in the way of gifts. The food section at *Marshall Field* (tel. 781–3668) has an excellent gourmet shop.

People drive from miles around to browse through *Hubert Hoffmann & Sons Florist,* Ridge (Gross Point) Road at Isabella on the Evanston-Wilmette border across from Lovelace Park. Acclaimed by local food editors for the year-round selection of over 50 different herbs (including specimen-sized bay laurel trees, rosemary bushes, lavender, thyme, and old-fashioned scented geraniums), this large garden center and florist dates from 1908 and specializes in the unusual (tel. AL 1–3300). Closed mid-July to November.

For antiques, there's *Donrose Galleries,* 751 N. Wells (tel. 337–4052), crammed with French, English, and continental wonders of all sizes and descriptions. And *Sothebys* now has an office at 840 N. Michigan (tel. 280–0185). But for the ultimate discovery, read the want ads and locate a genuine house sale, either in the city or on the North Shore, where a lifetime collection of basement-to-attic treasures is often sold at estate sales. So many people turn up looking for bonanzas at these things that numbers are distributed on a first-come basis—but even so, some estates yield rare finds.

TEATIME. Several of Chicago's most posh hotels have a very definite upper-class, understated English mood— the kind of places where one hears the rustle of quiet old money in low key but elegant surroundings. In many of these places, tea carts, laden with rich, tempting pastries, bite-size sandwiches, and the sort of taste temptations more often encountered in Britain, roll out at 3:00. Relaxing music usually drifts across the lobby while these hotels pour:

The Drake, 140 E. Walton Place at Michigan Ave.; 787–2200. Eight different varieties of teas served in the Palm Court from 3–5:30 P.M. $8 fee includes hot scones with clotted cream and jam, currant buns, assorted finger sandwiches and a selection from the pastry cart. Harpist and pianist alternate, providing the mood music. **Mayfair Regent,** 181 E. Lake Shore Drive; 787–8500. Served in Lobby Lounge decorated with hand-painted Chinese murals from 3–5:30 P.M. $9 complete or selections may be made à la carte. 18 varieties of tea available. Violin, piano or harp music is always played, adding to the atmosphere. **Park Hyatt Hotel,** Water Tower Square, 800 N. Michigan Ave.; 280–2222. Served in the Park Hyatt Salon from 2:30–5 P.M. 6 different teas offered. Cost is $2 for tea only, or $9.50 for tea including sandwiches and pastries. Live piano music except Monday. **Ritz Carlton Hotel,** 160 E. Pearson at Water Tower Place,; 266–1000. Served in the Greenhouse. 15 teas featured daily from 3–5 P.M. Service includes a selection of finger sandwiches, scones and miniature pastry. Monday–Friday. **Whitehall Hotel,** 105 E. Delaware,; 280–3097. Everything here is usually done with a special flair. Tea is served in the lobby bar from 2:15–4:15 P.M.

DINING OUT. Ever since its days of brawling adolescence, Chicago has been identified as "strictly a meat and potatoes town." However, residents who do even a modicum of dining out these days are well aware that this characterization has long since become obsolete. For the rest of the world, though, the image dies hard.

Excellent meat, with or without potatoes, will doubtless continue to be a prime factor in the repertoire of the city's restaurants. The significant point is that it is no longer the only feature of dining out in Chicago worth noting. A diner who fancies continental cuisine, Mexican-style trout prepared with cucumbers and cilantro, or tandoori murg from India currently can indulge his dining whims almost as easily as can one who wants a 2-in. porterhouse with a baked potato and sour cream on the side.

In recent years Chicagoans have shown a greatly increased interest in fine food of all kinds. This may be due to the influence of the diverse ethnic groups that have been drawn to the city or the great popularity of international travel, which has exposed Chicagoans to the delights of fine food from Paris to Tokyo and points in between.

To cater to the public's expanding tastes, more and more restaurateurs have sought out chefs with backgrounds in the classic European schools of cuisine or in various ethnic styles of cookery.

The result is a lively and infinitely varied reservoir of restaurants. Some statistically minded observer employed by the city's Convention and Tourism Bureau calculated that Chicago's eating establishments are so numerous that a person could dine out in the city every day of his or her life without duplicating a single restaurant. Such an itinerant diner would, of course, encounter some exceptionally bad food along the way. But he would also be served many meals that range from satisfactory to memorable.

As an aid to finding meals in this last category we offer a carefully selected list of recommended establishments. The price categories we use are approximate; figure for an average 3-course meal (appetizer, main course with vegetable, dessert) at a given establishment, per person. This does not include wine or drinks, taxes, or gratuities. For outstanding service you may wish to tip 20 percent, with another percent for an especially helpful maître d'.

Super Deluxe restaurants will cost $45 and up. **Deluxe** establishments will generally fit into the $40 range. **Expensive** dinners will usually cost about $30. **Moderate** meals should run about $20. A tab at an **Inexpensive** restaurant will cost an average of $15.

Today, credit cards, "plastic money," are a very acceptable commodity. Most—although not all—restaurants accept credit cards. These are indicated by the following abbreviations, which appear at the end of each listing; AE - American Express; MC - MasterCard; CB - Carte Blanche; V - Visa; DC - Diners Club.

AMERICAN-INTERNATIONAL

Deluxe

Arnie's. 1030 N. State St.; 266–4800. The striking Art Nouveau décor can't help but impress with its abundance of stained glass, campy graphics, undulating mirrors, and rococo statuary. All this plus a glass-walled atrium chock full of greenery. There's a wine bar, and dancing to the Myles Green trio. Specials include pasta primavera, capellini with bay scallops in a pesto sauce, roast duckling, and broiled swordfish. Appetizer choices range from escargots baked in pastry to fried brie with tomato sauce. A good place for a fun evening. AE, CB, DC, MC, V.

The Bakery. 2218 N. Lincoln Ave.; 472–6942. The restaurant is as distinctive as its chef-owner Louis Szathmary, who has gained fame as a cookbook author, newspaper columnist, radio commentator, and culinary consultant, as well as a restaurateur. A bright and lively atmosphere pervades, providing a fine setting for unpretentious furnishings, snowy white linens, and a tuxedo-clad serving crew. There's no printed menu. Instead, your waiter or waitress describes the 8 to 10 entrées available each evening as part of a 5-course dinner that includes a duo of superb patés, stockpot soups, and selections from a dessert cart. Entrées usually include Chef Louis' justifiably famous beef Wellington, duck with cherry sauce, and roast pork loin stuffed with Hungarian sausage. AE, CB, DC, MC, V.

Cricket's. 100 E. Chestnut; 280-2100. A collection of business-corporation artifacts decorates the walls and hangs overhead in this bright, carefree spot that very successfully achieves a chic, clubby ambience reminiscent of New York's "21" Club. The kitchen is first class, the Continental menu innovative and extensive (18 appetizer selections, for example). A good way to start your meal is with crême Senegalaise, a chilled, velvety smooth chicken soup with just the perfect hint of curry seasoning. Top entrées include venison, quail, veal sweatbreads, and fettuccine with prosciutto and shrimp. Brunch Saturday and Sunday. AE, CB, DC, MC, V.

Eugene's. 1255 N. State Parkway; 944-1445. Right across the street from the Ambassador Hotels, Gene Sage, one of Chicago's best-known restaurateurs, opened a spot he modestly dubbed Eugene's. It's fun and kitschy. For example: desserts range from chocolate mousse to a frozen Milky War bar. An extensive menu done with Damon Runyonesque prose offers some 2 dozen entrées, including Soft Sell Sollie's shrimp de Johnge and Irish Hymie's double rib lamb chops. Décor is an eclectic, hodge-podge. Serves late. AE, CB, DC, MC, V.

J.W.'s. Chicago Marriott Hotel, 540 N. Michigan Ave.; 836-0363. Top hotels throughout the world frequently house one special dining facility designed to cater to the comforts and palates of really knowledgeable diners. The Chicago Marriott is no exception. Done with dark stained-wood paneling, plush carpets, and subdued lighting, the room is reminiscent of a fine private gentleman's club. There's a definite French accent to the menu, but outstanding dishes really represent a variety of culinary heritages. For openers try a nicely seasoned lobster bisque, followed by veal medallions with wild mushroom sauce. Finish with a flambé dessert. AE, CB, DC, MC, V.

The Ninety-Fifth. John Hancock Center, 875 N. Michigan Ave.; 787-9596. It's a lofty view from the 95th floor of "Big John," but the cuisine also rises to commendable heights. Although à la carte prices also tend to be on the lofty side, a *prix fixe* dinner that includes appetizer, sorbet, salad, fish and meat courses, dessert and coffee, provides excellent value in luxury dining. Conch fritters, paté of hare en croute, and quennelle of sole are recommended appetizers, while good entrée choices are tournedos Rossini, stuffed pork loin with fig sauce, and various lobster specialties. The wine list has more than 300 entries, and the cocktail lounge, one floor up on the 96th, offers a spectacular view of the city and Lake Michigan. AE, CB, DC, MC, V.

The Pump Room. 1301 N. State Parkway; 266-0360. A far cry now from the operation that used to be a favored gathering spot for film folk stopping off in Chicago to change trains on journeys east or west. The Pump Room has shifted to a more contemporary approach. Décor is now far less pretentious, with clean lines and a feeling of spaciousness. Culinary offerings have been pared to a shorter listing, but the choices are imaginative and palate-pleasing, with nice extra touches. There is a varied and reasonably priced menu and an extensive dessert selection designed to placate even the most insatiable "sweet tooth." Lavish complimentary buffet during the cocktail hour. AE, CB, DC, MC, V.

Tango. 3172 N. Sheridan Rd.; 935–0350. Off the lobby of the Belmont Hotel, this chic "in" spot is attractively done with unusual and interesting art, plus an assortment of greenery, all showcased against rather austere basic décor. The kitchen staff is particularly adept with seafood, which is often prepared in traditional French style or grilled over mesquite coals. Most days, several fish specials are offered. They're described in fine fashion by the serving crew who perform consistently at a high-professional level. Meat dishes are also superior, along with soups, which come by the crock, vegetables such as battered eggplant fingers and fried potato skins, onion bread, and calorically sinful desserts. Serves late. AE, MC, V.

Zaven's. 260 E. Chestnut St.; 787–8260. The menu reads like a chef's tour around the world, with dishes that owe their culinary heritages to France, Italy, Spain, Russia, England, Austria, and India, plus those drawing on the Armenian background of host/owner Zaven Kodjayan. A charming, intimate setting successfully blends sophistication with a feeling of relaxed casualness. Service is warm and hospitable. Particular attention is paid to selection, presentation, and pouring of wines. Hors d'oeuvres are particularly noteworthy, as is the fine salad that is included with each main course. AE, CB, DC, MC, V.

Expensive

Di Leo's. 5700 N. Central Ave.; 774–6900. A large, elaborately furnished restaurant, Di Leo's always seems to be filled with customers. They're lured back time and time again by the attractive décor, the warmth of the staff, and the praiseworthy Continental and American specialties. In addition to a series of dining rooms on the main floor, the restaurant has first-rate banquet facilities. Many of the dishes have an Italian accent, but other styles of cookery are well represented. Steaks and lobster tail are also popular choices. AE, CB, DC, MC, V.

Empire Room, Palmer House, 17 E. Monroe; 726–7500. Probably the single most dramatic room in all Chicago, it looks like a gilded transplant from a European palace. Lunch only, also Sunday jazz brunch 11 A.M.–2 P.M. includes eggs Benedict and champagne. AE, CB, DC, MC, V.

Hillary's. Water Tower Place, 845 N. Michigan Ave.; 280–2710. There's lots of brass, glass, and greenery at this chic watering hole and eatery. If you like your hamburgers in a sophisticated setting, try the half-pounder here. It comes plain or juicy or flavored with minced vegetables. Quiches are popular, and the salads are well made. If you're hungry (or want to share), try the huge fried-onion loaf as an appetizer. Nachos also are good starters. Rounding out the menu are steak and seafood selections and rich cheesecake for dessert. AE, DC, MC, V.

Manhattan Tavern & Grill. 1045 N. Rush St.; 751–2001. This sleek Art Deco emporium, reminiscent of a 1930s nightclub, has live entertainment and a glittery bar that attracts the stylish Rush St. bar-hopping crowd. It also is a surprisingly good spot to eat, with a small but thoughtful menu. Included are prime, dry-aged steaks; tender calves liver, thinly sliced and sautéed with onions, green peppers, and lemon; and Long Island duckling with either an orange or cherry sauce. Poached salmon comes with a mustard caper sauce and red snapper is unusually and piquantly flavored with ginger. You may wish to split a pasta dish on the side or share an appetizer platter of hot shellfish. Chocolate mousse cake is a recommended dessert. AE, CB, DC, MC, V.

Raphael Dining Room. 201 E. Delaware Pl.; 943–5000. This cozy dining room in one of the many small, charming hotels in Chicago's prestigious Gold Coast area offers American/Continental cuisine in an intimate, European-like atmosphere. Appetizers, for example, range from all-American steamed clams in a bucket to country paté and escargot served Andalusian style. Entrées include rack of lamb, Boston baked scrod, medallions of beef in a burgundy tarragon sauce, garlicky scallops Marseilles, and Kansas City sirloin steak. The house salad combines romaine and spinach leaves with mushroom slices, water chestnuts, cherry tomatos, and garbanzo beans. AE, CB, DC, MC, V.

Don Roth's River Plaza. 405 N. Wabash Ave.; 527–3100. Nestled alongside the Chicago R. between the Wrigley and Sun-Times buildings, this attractive, bi-level restaurant is a popular after-work meeting spot. There's a small outdoor café, and complimentary build-your-own tacos during cocktail hour. Appetizers include nachos and baked brie, while entrées encompass crisp, meaty ribs, steaks, and broiled fresh swordfish, salmon or grouper. An excellent accompaniment is cream spinach, a Don Roth specialty. Formal dining room upstairs. AE, CB, DC, MC, V.

Wrigley Building Restaurant. 410 N. Michigan Ave.; 944–7600. Although it is now dwarfed by taller neighbors, the wedding-cake Wrigley Building is still one of the outstanding landmarks of the city's skyline. This twin-tower edifice houses a restaurant whose fare seems to be unfailingly pleasing to a legion of regulars who somehow just never seem to go anywhere else for lunch. There are so many of them the general air is almost that of a club. The varied menu includes steaks, whitefish, chops, special salads, and unusual appetizers and desserts. Steak tartare, with raw egg and anchovies, is a long-time menu favorite. If you sample one of the martinis, you'll know why the bar always does a stampede business. Dinners, too. AE, CB, DC, MC, V.

Moderate

The Berghoff. 17 W. Adams; 427–3170. This Chicago institution tends to defy classification. Certainly, it is German, with excellent roulade of beef, Wiener schnitzel and kassler rippchen. But you'll also find such selections as mahi mahi, grilled or broiled fresh swordfish steak, Boston scrod, and broiled tournedos au poivre. Appetizers, too, are an international melange with bluepoint oysters, cherrystone clams, escargot, and Bismarck herring. The dessert menu is largely Teutonic with strudel, tortes, and Black Forest cake. Draft beers are custom-brewed for Berghoff's. This 2-level, spacious old dining establishment has oak paneling and bustling, black-attired waiters. No cards.

The Cheese Cellar. 1204 N. State St.; 266–8181. The name says it all! The atmosphere is that of an attractive European wine cellar. Cheeses are the star item on the menu. Appetizers include baked brie and a version of traditional Swiss raclette—a sizzling hot cheese-and-potato platter. If you're a dyed-in-the-wool cheese lover, you'll probably want to opt for the cheese board. You make your selections from 16 cheeses and 4 different types of sausage—lots of fun, here, reacquainting your palate with old favorites and experimenting with untried cheeses. Various fondues also are available on a menu that is rounded out with some sandwich selections and "Look of Lean" low-calories meals. If becoming or staying svelte doesn't concern you, try chocolate fondue for dessert. AE, CB, DC, MC, V.

Chicago Claim Company. 2314 N. Clark St.; 871–1770. With bricks and barn sidings, an old rooming house has been happily transformed into a comfortable and handsome setting. Juicy, charbroiled hamburgers, made with top-quality meat, are the attraction here. Try the "Motherlode," a huge hamburger with any of 4 cheeses and other accessories, or the steak sandwich with tomato, bacon, cheese, and onion. A fresh salad bar has a choice of 10 toppings and 5 dressings. Serves late. Brunch Saturday. AE, MC, V.

City Tavern. 33 W. Monroe St.; 280–2740. In the heart of the Loop financial district, this restaurant gets crowded during lunch but gives you plenty of elbow room during dinner. The menu is eclectic, ranging from sandwiches with absurd names to nicely grilled seafood, as well as omelettes and steaks. Brook trout and scallops are regularly featured, and daily specials include such items as broiled salmon, pork chops, lamb chops, and a pasta dish. A good appetizer—but probably big enough for 3 or 4 persons—is a loaf of deep-fried onions. This is a handsome dining room, with rich woodwork, attractive lighting, and greenery. AE, MC, V.

D.B. Kaplan's. 845 N. Michigan Ave.; 280–2700. Essentially a deli, but what a deli. Thoroughly delightful, semisophisticated atmosphere on the 7th level of the Water Tower Place shopping complex. A 3-ft.-long menu offers hundreds of items and provides great reading with its collection of outrageous puns. Single item sandwiches are available, but the larger ones are more intriguing. Also omelettes, soups, knishes and other side dishes, fish platters, and desserts. Naughty double-entendre ice cream and drink menus; friendly, outgoing waitresses. For at-home entertaining, special party sandwiches up to 6 ft. long are available. Serves late. No cards.

Geja's. 340 W. Armitage St.; 281–9101. More than 100 different wines and nearly 3 dozen varieties of cheese. That's only the beginning here. There's also an outdoor café with umbrellaed tables and chairs, very reminiscent of a Paris bistro; inside, romantic booths, classical music, and guitarists. Portions of cheese are served with French bread and pumpernickel. If you want more substantial fare, there are fondues—cheese, chicken, beef, seafood, chocolate—and other tasty treats. For a finale, try one of the hot coffee and liqueur combinations topped with whipped cream. Serves late. AE, CB, DC, MC, V.

Hamburger Hamlet. 44 E. Walton Pl.; 649–6600. As the name implies, you find hamburgers here—giant, juicy things seasoned to perfection and served with a choice of toppings. But that's only the starting point in this extraordinarily handsome dining emporium. Patrons sit on various levels in a variety of nooks and crannies surrounded by dark wood walls, expanses of mirrors, and antique lighting fixtures—all done with the best of taste. An efficient staff provides imaginative salads, fish and beef dishes, hearty homemade soups (the chili is excellent!), and marvelous desserts. AE, MC, V.

My Place For? 7545 N. Clark St.; 262–5767. Reds dominate the color scheme, accented by wood-paneled walls, and the menu, featuring good, fresh fish, offered by Dennis, Steve and John Dorizas, is reasonably priced. Red snapper prepared Grecian style and broiled, whole sea bass are stars of the menu, along with roast duck, a seafood platter, and shrimp de Jonghe. Fresh Lake Superior whitefish also deserves high billing, as do the barbecued ribs and fried chicken. Beef eaters have a choice of several steaks or shish kebab. Complimentary taramosalata (creamy fish-roe spread) with crusty bread. Serves late. AE, CB, DC, MC, V.

Printer's Row. 440 S. Dearborn; 461–0780. Imaginative use of an old printer's building dating to 1897 provides an unusual setting. Where else could you discover duck ravioli with blue cheese, escalloped minestrone and ragout of venison shank. AE, MC, V.

R.J. Grunts. 2056 Lincoln Park W.; 929–5363. Humorous graphics and copy make the menu here a delight to read, and set the stage for fun, casual dining. Among the wide range of offerings, burgers, sandwiches (particularly the roast beef), nachos, and soups are good choices. Plus there's an imaginative, all-you-can-eat salad bar. Portions are immense, and prices moderate; service friendly and efficient. First-rate desserts include a fine cheesecake and unusual ice cream concoctions. Serves late. Brunch Sunday. AE, MC, V. In Glenview: 1615 N. Milwaukee Ave.; 635–7707.

Sessions Pullman Club. 605 E. 111th St.; 785–7578. One of Pullman's famous mansions has emerged as a pleasant place to dine while touring that community's many historic sites. Menu at the entrance changes seasonally, but fresh fish, veal, steak, and lamb chops are available year round. AE, CB, DC, MC, V.

Inexpensive

Corona Café. 501 N. Rush St.; 527–5456. Long a favorite of Chicago's fourth estate, this is the place where reporters, photographers, and printers gather. They're joined by numbers of advertising men, artists, and other folk who are looking for good food at reasonable prices. The Moroni brothers offer their guests a blend of diversified American fare, plus a variety of Northern Italian specialties. AE, CB, DC, MC, V.

Santa Fe Cafe. 800 N. Dearborn Parkway; 944–5722. One of the most recent regional food trends to reach Chicago is the smoky cookery of the Southwest. This corner, fast-food restaurant is an example of the genre at its best and cheapest. Slabs of tangy, barbecued ribs may be savored sitting down, at stand-up tables, or from carryout containers. Other smoked selections, available in sandwiches, include pork loin, brisket, ham and turkey breast. Grilled chicken is crispy outside, moist inside. Side orders of smoky beans and slaw accompany barbecued orders. A meaty chili is satisfyingly hot and spicy. Décor includes bare brick and stucco walls, posters, hanging plants, and massive steer horns. No cards.

GAME

Expensive

Café Bohemia. 138 S. Clinton St.; 782–1826. Virtually a landmark on the near west side, Café Bohemia dispenses authentic cuisine of the land its name honors. However, it's the multitude of wild game on the menu that has made the restaurant famous. Dishes prepared from pheasant, quail, and duck seem almost prosaic when compared with entrées using venison, moose, buffalo, and bear. Serves late. AE, CB, DC, MC, V.

SEAFOOD

Deluxe

Cape Cod Room. 140 E. Walton St.; 787–2200. If it swims, crawls, or slithers in ocean, lake, river, stream, or brook, you're sure to find it at this premier seafood restaurant in the Drake Hotel. There are more than a dozen preparations of lobster alone. Fresh clams and oysters are shucked to order. Soft-shelled crabs are cooked to perfection; the famous Bookbinder red snapper soup is superb. Décor is nautical and the staff both knowledgeable and attentive. AE, CB, DC, MC, V.

Nick's Fish Market. First National Bank, 1 First National Plaza; 621–0200. The finest seafood available flown in fresh from seemingly everywhere is the big drawing card at Nick's here in Chicago, in Beverly Hills, or at Waikiki. These restaurants have attracted a sophisticated clientele who don't mind paying a lot for excellently prepared sea delicacies from far and local waters. You'll find abalone and whole baby salmon on the menu, as well as Hawaiian mahi mahi and opakapaka. Serves late. AE, CB, DC, MC, V.

Shucker's. 150 E. Ontario St.; 266–6057. Named for the folk who shuck (open) fresh oysters and clams for a living, this restaurant properly puts the emphasis on fresh fin and shellfish preparations. Housed in a former private club, the operation serves guests either on a lower bar/lounge level or in a balcony area. Shucker's New England clam chowder has won critical acclaim as one of the best in the city and, accompanied by a hot loaf of bread and a well-made spinach salad, makes a nice light lunch. AE, CB, DC, MC, V.

Expensive

Chestnut Street Grill. Water Tower Place, 845 N. Michigan Ave.; 280–2720. Fish cooked over an open grill is a rare treat and it's done to perfection over Mexican mesquite coals at this charming restaurant. Décor features turn-of-the-century-style architecture and an open display kitchen where you can watch fish being grilled. Swordfish and sea bass are perennially popular choices, as is fried calamari with tartar sauce as an appetizer. Other grilled selections include brook trout, seafood brochette, lemon sole, lobster tail, prawns, salmon, and scallops.

Pork chops and sirloin occasionally share the charcoal with the seafood. Sourdough bread accompanies entrees. On the lighter side are a seafood quiche, seafood omelette, and shrimp and crabmeat salad. Cappuccino ice cream is a delicious dessert. AE, CB, DC, MC, V.

La Ciboulette. 1260 N. Dearborn St.; 944–2506. Excellent food served in relaxing surroundings. A menu with imagination combines fine seafood with nouvelle cuisine. Grilled salmon is a special favorite, so are scallops. For dessert, try the apple tart ladled with caramel sauce. Seafood soups are among favorites here. AE, CB, MC, V.

Ireland's. 500 N. La Salle St.; 337–2020. Seafood reigns supreme here at what the owners claim is Chicago's oldest fish house. Patrons dine in relaxed surroundings catered to by a youngish, friendly service crew. Seafood selections range from clam chowder to full clambakes. Extensive fin fish choices include grouper, trout, whitefish, and red snapper. Shellfish preparations utilizing shrimp, crab, clams, and oysters are even more extensive. There's a 40-item salad bar and a raw bar that offers 2-for-1 oysters, clams, and shrimp during the cocktail hour. Serves late. AE, CB, DC, MC, V.

Nantucket Cove. 1000 N. Lake Shore Dr.; 943–1600. New England clambake dinners are featured here in a fishing village atmosphere. Included are clams, shrimp in the shell, a yam, corn on the cob, and a whole lobster, all steamed together in a large casserole. Trout wrapped in vine leaves is another specialty. Menu includes fresh fish, king crab legs, scallops, shrimp, and Long Island oysters. The décor is guaranteed to give any transplanted Yankee a twinge of nostalgia for the stern and rockbound coast. AE, MC, V.

The Waterfront. 1015 N. Rush St.; 943–7494. In a nautical setting of weathered wood, ropes, and nets, the restaurant serves up a variety of fin and shellfish fare. Sole en sacque—filet of sole with thinly sliced ham, tiny shrimp, mushrooms, and olives in sherry sauce, baked in paper—and prawns in a wine-garlic butter sauce served in their shells in the cooking pan with mushrooms, are two of the interesting choices. Cioppino, a spicy, tomato fish stew, is a house specialty. Serves late. Brunch on Sunday. AE, MC, V.

Moderate

Charley's Crab. 1160 N. Dearborn; 337–6617. Part of a national restaurant chain, Charley's has a surprisingly extensive menu of seafood selections. Cold starters range from raw-bar items to smoked salmon, sushi, and gazpacho. Hot appetizers include mussels, steamed clams, eggplant crepe stuffed with 3 cheeses, and sherry-buttered bay scallops. Ambitious specialties include paella and bouillabaisse. The menu also offers several pasta choices, including shrimp and artichoke linguine. AE, CB, MC, V.

Grover's Oyster Bar. 2256 W. Irving Park Rd.; 588–4662. A casual, informal place for relaxed dining. The restaurant's motto, "Soon to be famous . . . since 1973," sets the upbeat, fun-oriented mood. And don't let the location throw you off. Although West Irving Park is far from the poshest section of town, and Grover's facade is far from imposing, the interior is warm and inviting. Actually the name is somewhat of a misnomer. Oysters are always readily available, but the offerings from the kitchen encompass a much wider range of palate-pleasing specialties, including gumbo and chowder. Desserts include cheesecake, sundaes and an assortment of pies. AE, DC, MC, V.

STEAKS AND BEEF

Deluxe

Gene & Georgetti's. 500 N. Franklin; 527–3718. Beef's the thing to order here, although pasta offerings are also commendable. The steaks are among the best to be found anywhere, and come in huge portions that often overlap the edges of the generous-sized platters on which they are served. A house salad and crispy cottage fries accompany all entrées. Side orders of pasta are also available. Friendly relaxed service by old-time waiters sporting long white aprons. Unpretentious, yet somehow sophisticated, ambience. A popular, crowded bar at which you're liable to spot more than one well-known personality. No reservations, but the bar wait can be fun, and you will be well rewarded by the food. AE, CB, DC.

Morton's. 1050 N. State St.; 266–4820. This basement restaurant in Newberry Plaza deals superbly with those bottom-line favorites of American taste: steak and lobster. The open grill is central to the wood-and-stucco décor. Make your selections from a cart presented by your waiter: 24-oz. T-bones, double-cut prime rib with the bone in, sirloin, 3-lb. lobsters, and cheese-breaded veal chops. Everything comes with a 1-lb. baked potato or perfect, golden hash browns. There's not much to the rest of the menu: salad, fresh asparagus with hollandaise sauce, good oysters on the half shell. There are dessert soufflés. Order one when you sit down, and it will emerge at just the right time, high and golden crowned. Serves late. AE, CB, DC, MC, V.

The Palm. 181 E. Lake Shore; 944–0135. Located off the lobby of the Mayfair Regent Hotel, this steak house is a branch of a duo of successful New York restaurants. There's sawdust on the floor, old-fashioned fans whirling beneath the tin ceiling, and cartoons depicting famous patrons. The restaurant specializes in two entrees—steak and Maine lobster—and renders them both extremely well. The steaks are thick and juicy—top quality for top dollar; lobsters are exceedingly tender and large enough to split with a steak order. Tomato and onion slices make a simple, compatible appetizer. If you've room for dessert, the New York-style cheesecake is worthwhile. AE, DC, DC, MC, V.

That Steak Joynt. 1610 N. Wells St.; 943–5091. The former home of Pipers Bakery has been artfully transformed into an elegant setting that's reminiscent of a Victorian Valentine's Day card. A collection of antiques, quality oil paintings, and Tiffany lamps is set off against plush red velvet. In the food department, as the name implies, steak is king. Here varying cuts and sizes are offered in your choice of 4 different preparations: char-broiled, sautéed, studded with garlic, or with fresh peppercorns. The menu also offers excellent barbecued ribs and fresh fish. There is an extensive wine bar and a popular piano bar. AE, CB, DC, M, V.

Expensive

Eli's the Place for Steak. 215 E. Chicago Ave.; 642–1393. Table for table, this restaurant nestled in the Carriage House provides some of the best celebrity watching in town. It's a favorite of show business, sports, and political names, as well as hosts of other folk. The menu concentrates on superb beef, along with a limited number of poultry and seafood dishes and the best beef liver in town. Eli's also has become equally well known for its scrumptious cheesecake, varieties of which include chocolate chip, cinnamon raisin, blueberry, and strawberry. AE, CB, DC.

Lawry's Prime Rib. 100 E. Ontario St.; 787–5000. As its name implies, this is a specialty restaurant—housed in an elegant old mansion—and it delivers its raison d'etre very well indeed. Prime rib is tender, juicy, and sliced to the desired degree of thickness and doneness from a slab rolled to your table on a silver cart. Accompaniments are traditional, puffy-light Yorkshire pudding, plus baked potato skins, and a vegetable. Simple, but delicious. Luncheon offers a more varied menu, including salads and fish-of-the-day. Serves late. AE, CB, DC, MC, V.

Miller's on Kinzie. 33 W. Kinzie St.; 644–7470. Victorian décor provides a perfect backdrop for enjoying fine beef, chops, and other fare. Although the restaurant is primarily a steak house with excellent prime meat in an assortment of cuts, the kitchen crew also does a commendable job with seafood. If you're a steak lover, be sure to try the 16-oz. T-bone. Barbecued ribs are also first-rate, with either a tangy tomato-based sauce or a sweet honey one. A salad bar offers fresh greens, condiments, vegetables, and dressings, plus chopped liver, marinated herring, and garbanzo beans. AE, CB, DC, MC, V.

CUISINE BY NATIONALITY

ASIAN

Moderate

Seoul House. 5346 N. Clark St.; 728–6756. An interesting assortment of authentic Korean dishes is available at this storefront restaurant. All are cooked to order, and come with rice and kim chee, fiery-hot pickled vegetables that are almost a staple of Korean meals. Be sure to try fried mahndoo, which is somewhat like a won ton, with a seasoned filling of ground beef, bean sprouts, onion, cabbage, and green onions. Many dishes are spicy-hot. Among the milder selections are shrimp tempura and chap chae (beef with vegetables and noodles). Serves late, MC, V.

Thai Room. 4022 N. Western Ave.; 539–6150. Your taste buds will run the gamut at this Thai restaurant. Curried dishes, for example, are hot enough to start a fire in your throat, while salads featuring chicken or squid or beef are decidedly peppery. Shrimp-and-lemon-grass soup is a good starter, as are the ubiquitous egg rolls. Try barbecued sausage or one of the fried-noodle dishes, served with shrimp or pork. The menu offers almost 50 choices from soup through dessert. CB, DC, MC, V.

BRITISH

Moderate

Altantic Fish & Chip Restaurant. 7115 W. Grand; 622–3259. A no-nonsense place with the area's largest selection of English, Welsh, Irish, and Scottish foods and potables (many of draught). Roast beef with Yorkshire pudding, meat-and-potato pie, Cornish meat and onion pasties, black pudding, mixed grill with lamp chop, pork sausage and thick Irish bacon, soda bread, and other simple, good dishes in a family-run establishment. Rousing entertainment on weekends. Darts in an English-style pub. Buffet Sundays. MC, V.

CHINESE

Deluxe

The Abacus. 2619 N. Clark St.; 477–5251. Chinese cuisine at its gourmet best, with dishes from 4 of the country's most popular regional styles of cookery: Mandarin on the north, Cantonese on the south, Shanghai on the east, and Szechuan and Hunan on the west. Imaginative preparations make use of subtle seasonings to produce palate-pleasing delights. In addition to upwards of 100 tempting menu items, there are specialty dinners—including Peking duck—for a minimum of 4 persons. AE, CB, DC, MC, V.

Expensive

Chiam. 2323 S. Wentworth Ave.; 225–6336. 50-some meat, poultry, and seafood courses, not counting more than a dozen different chow meins, chop sueys, and egg foo yung variations. As if that weren't enough, the management goes on record as being prepared to produce any other Chinese or American dish. One of the better known of the Chinatown restaurants, Chiam features family-style dinners that are suitable for groups of from 2 to 8. The food is American-Cantonese in style. Try the diced lobster prepared with mushrooms, snow peapods, bok choy, bamboo shoots, water chestnuts, and crushed almonds. AE, CB, DC, MC, V.

Chinese Tea House. 6248 W. North Ave.; 237–3073. Mandarin dishes are the feature: hot-and-sour soup, chicken with peanuts and Szechuan pepper, thousand-year eggs, moo-shu pork, the classic Peking duck, crispy duck, smoked duck (they smoke it themselves), and Hung-shao duck. (All duck dishes should be ordered a day or two in advance.) The adventurous way to dine here is to call a few days ahead of time and let the chef choose your dishes. It's most fun if you go in a party of 6 to 8. A newly acquired liquor license means you can order your favorite cocktail. MC, V.

House of Hunan. 535 N. Michigan Ave.; 329–9494. An impressive range of Mandarin dishes, including several not usually found at other local restaurants, indicates the creativity of the establishment's chefs. Knowledgeable gourmets have high praise for such entrées as beef with tender sliced scallops in hot sauce, Szechuan noodles in spicy vegetable-shrimp sauce, and chicken stir-fried with bamboo shoots and garlic sauce. It's fun to come with a group and share. AE, CB, DC, MC, V.

Inexpensive

Cantonese Chef. 2342 S. Wentworth Ave.; 225–3232. In the heart of Chicago's Chinatown, this restaurant is done in attractive modern style with pleasant Oriental touches. It's a perfect place to stop for a meal before or after browsing through the many interesting shops in the area. The menu offers all the usual Cantonese favorites, with interesting preparations of beef, pork, chicken, duck, and seafood. Unusual dishes are also available. Try going with a group so you can share many different selections. AE, CB, DC, MC, V.

Lee's Canton Café. 2302 S. Wentworth Ave.; 225–4838. Some of the best food in Chinatown is to be found in this lunchroom modern setting. You'll do well enough stepping in off the street and ordering at random. The ideal approach is to have a knowledge of Chinese cookery or a Chinese friend to guide you in selecting some of the more unusual dishes. AE, CB, DC, MC, V.

EASTERN EUROPEAN

Expensive

Miomir's Serbian Club. 2255 W. Lawrence Ave.; 784–2111. Attractive decor, recreating European street scenes, is a perfect setting for superb food. Start your meal with corba (traditional Serbian soup with beef and vegetables) or with 2 tasty and unusual spreads—kajmak (fermented milk) and ajvar (grilled eggplant, sweet green peppers, and celery in olive oil). Then proceed to other Serbian specialties—all delicously seasoned. Try, perhaps, chicken cooked in wine sauce or skewered pork tenderloin. There's an extensive selection of wines to go with your food. Entertainment and dancing on weekends with Gypsy fiddlers, Cossack dancers, and assorted singers and vocalists. MC, V.

Sayat Nova. 157 E. Ohio St.; 644–9159. Named for a 17th-century Armenian troubadour-balladeer, the restaurant serves Middle-Eastern food in a striking setting. Their menu is small but liberally sprinkled with fine versions of grape leaves stuffed with meat, rice, and spices; shish kebab; lamb broiled with green peppers; and homemade yogurt. Appetizers include bulgar salad and stuffed eggplant. Finish with baklava and Armenian coffee. Serves late. MC, V.

Moderate

Hungarian Restaurant. 5062 N. Lincoln; 334–4850. Authentic Hungarian cookery is found in this neighborhood restaurant, a friendly and unpretentious place. The 33-item menu offers chicken paprikash, beef goulash, stuffed cabbage, and debreceni paros (sausage), as well as szekely goulash, a glorious combination of cabbage and meat that have been simmered together. Delicately seasoned hunter's stew is superb and hearty enough for big appetites. A combination plate offers smaller portions of about half the entrées. Hungarian wines and liquors add further appeal. Strolling Gypsy violinists on weekends. No cards.

FRENCH

Super Deluxe

Ciel Bleu. 181 E. Lake Shore Dr.; 951–2864. This showcase restaurant on the 19th floor of the Mayfair Regent Hotel offers a stunning view of Lake Michigan. As you sit and watch the billowing sails by day or shimmering lights at night, you'll bask in elegant surroundings and enjoy cosseted service by white-gloved waiters and a watchful maitre d'. As an appetizer, try snails and mushrooms in a puff-pastry shell or duck terrine with oranges. Not-to-be-missed entrées are bay scallops with raisins and red-wine butter sauce, served with wild rice, and sweetbreads with morel mushrooms marinated in port wine. There is a fine version of vichyssoise and an admirable creamy tomato soup. The dessert cart is laden with sinfully rich temptations. AE, DC, MC, V.

Le Perroquet. 70 E. Walton; 944–7990. A tiny private elevator takes you to the 3rd floor, where you alight in a spacious, cheerful, and elegantly appointed dining room. The walls are adorned with Persian and Turkish rugs and vivid foliage murals by Chicago artist Meg Abbot. The tables lining the room are decorated with fresh flowers in lovely, delicate vases. Mussels are a great beginning to a nouvelle cuisine dining experience that is excellent throughout. Ris de veau à l'orange, pigeon en cocotte paysanne, and truite soufflé Veronique are just a few of the superb entrées. But save room and a few superlatives for the pastries and soufflés. AE, CB, DC.

Deluxe

La Fontaine. 2442 N. Clark St.; 525–1800. Classic French cuisine is served here in an elegantly remodeled town house. The owner-partners serve as chef and maître d', so there's great personal interest and attention to detail. The serving staff, clad in tuxedos, follows suit. Menu offerings include nearly a dozen-and-a-half regular entrées, plus daily specials, a host of appetizers, and 4 or more soups. Veal Normande done with a Calvados-spiked cream sauce is outstanding. Also worthy of top ratings are sautéed sweetbreads with truffled goose-liver sauce and paupiette of salmon with crabmeat stuffing. Even if you visit the restaurant in warm weather, be sure to try the delicious split pea soup. Serves late. AE, CB, DC, MC, V.

Le Francais. 269 South Milwaukee Ave., Wheeling; 541–7470. Days and weeks after dining at Le Francais, you will be saying that Jean Banchet prepares and serves the best food on this planet! You may have to wait weeks, or months, for a reservation, but a visit should take priority on any discriminating diner's calendar. The cottage in Wheeling is of modest architecture; the kitchen is larger than the dining room, but guests are not crowded. the ambience is genial and comfortable, but not ostentatious—the whole show is the food. Desserts are visible at the entrance, the menu is shown in a presentation of dishes on silver platters, glistening with chaud-froid aspic, decorated, some carved, some cooked, all appetizing and enlightening. Banchet, a perfectionist, tastes every dish that leaves his kitchen. He works 12 to 14 hrs. a day, 6 days a week. This is serious dining on culinary creations that you are unlikely to find anywhere else—from delightful seafood mousses, through roast veal loin wrapped in pastry, to elegant dessert-cart selections. AE, CB, DC, MC, V.

Jovan. 1660 N. LaSalle Dr.; 944–7766. Long a landmark in Chicago dining, Jovan's original restaurant was lost to a fire in 1982. Now the restaurant has returned at a new location. The ambience is a little more austere, but the quality is as high as ever. 5-course *prix fixe* dinners are featured as before, plus a Sunday brunch. Start off with your choice of more than a dozen appetizers and soups, including leek tartlet, paté selections, grilled rabbit sausage, snails, sweetbreads and goat cheese ravioli, and brie soup. Then choose your entrée. Perhaps rolled pheasant with pine nuts and cabbage, roast rack of lamb, or duck with black peppercorns and apples. Next comes an after-dinner salad and, for dessert, homemade ice creams, soufflé, and assorted tarts, cakes, and pastries. Finish up with coffee, espresso, or cappuccino. The restaurant's interior is contemporary in style with soft beige furnishings. AE, CB, DC, MC, V.

Truffles. Hyatt-Regency Chicago, 151 E. Wacker Dr.; 565–1000. The menu has a motto, "Prepare a few things perfectly," but there are more than a few: noisettes Tour Eiffel, canard rôti, selle d'agneau à la Reforme and truffle en croûte. Fresh vegetables are prepared at your table. Recent remodeling adds to the mood of contemporary elegance. AE, CB, DC, MC, V.

Expensive

Ambria. 2300 N. Lincoln Park West; 472–5959. This restaurant in the Belden-Stratford Hotel offers light, inventive nouvelle cuisine, with an emphasis on seafood. Every dish is beautifully garnished and presented. Sautéed fresh goose liver makes an excellent starter. Grilled fresh fish is consistently good. White chocolate mousse makes a delectable dessert. Or let the chef do his best by phoning ahead for a multicourse "degustation" dinner. Recorded classical music plays in the background. The service crew is young, but what it lacks in polish it makes up for in enthusiasm and friendliness. AE, CB, DC, MC, V.

La Cheminée. 1161 N. Dearborn; 642–6654. Located in an old townhouse, subdued lighting and a semirustic French country atmosphere produce a charming setting in which to enjoy fine cuisine and wine chosen from a list of 150. You'll find classic entrées such as steak au poivre, duck à l'orange, and veal Florentine, and appetizers such as quiche Lorraine and avocado stuffed with crabmeat. Gracious service is another plus. AE, MC, V.

Chez Paul. 660 N. Rush St.; 944–6680. Bill Contos has shown his interest in all that was fine in the Chicago of old. He's taken the Robert Hall McCormick mansion, remodeled it and furnished it with loving care. The cuisine follows suit, with a host of primarily French specialties. The menu is à la carte, starting with appetizers such as baked shrimp à la Paul, escargot, and baked crab. Then it's time for classic Gallic dishes such as cervelle de veau, sweetbreads, tripe, turbot, and canard rôti à l'orange. There's also a selection of beef dishes for the less venturesome. Brunch on Sunday. AE, CB, DC, MC, V.

L'Escargot. 701 N. Michigan Ave.; 337–1717. Ensconced in bright, attractive quarters within the Allerton Hotel, this country French restaurant features high ceilings, attractive posters, lots of greenery, and French pop music. White-washed walls serve as backdrops for large antique cabinets and breakfronts.

L'Escargot introduced cassoulet to Chicago and still features this tasty and very French peasant dish. But there are many other temptations as well. The changing array of dishes usually includes more than a dozen entrées plus innovative appetizers, soups, and desserts. Recommended are cream of watercress soup, rich with potato and leek flavor, roast duck, and for dessert, a buttery bread pudding. AE, CB, DC, MC, V.

Moderate

Bastille. 21 W. Superior; 787–2050. An appealing bistro-like approach to French food and service. The atmosphere is lowkey and casual, with butcher-paper tablecloths and a friendly informal service staff. A wine bar offers fine wines by the glass, a pleasant refinement—or you can order full bottles from a reasonably priced list. Most of the food offerings are of the grillade or rôtisserie school, but done with skill and imagination. Both meat and seafood preparations are featured (grilled sea bass is excellent, as are sweetbreads) with a changing array of daily specials, including cassoulet. The appetizer highlight: an assortment of pâtés. For special events such as Bastille Day (celebrated week-long), marquees spring up in the parking lot to house musicians, dancing, and other festivities. AE, MC, V.

Yvette. 1206 N. State Pkwy.; 280–1700. One of the hottest new spots in town (in America, according to one magazine!), this fashionable Art Deco spot in essence is 3 establishments in 1. There's a small sidewalk café in front, in warm weather the place to be "seen." This leads into a bistro and, in back of that, an informal dining room. 10 or more appetizer selections include oysters Provençcale and cream of mussel soup. Duck with cherry sauce and beef with a peppercorn sauce highlight the entrées. There's a plentiful supply of crusty French bread and sweet butter. Desserts feature a variety of tortes, tarts, and other pastries. There's piano entertainment during the evening. AE, MC, V.

Inexpensive

Le Bordeaux. 3 W. Madison St.; 372–2027. Just off the corner of State and Madison and down one flight, this little spot serves good French food at reasonable prices. It's a working partnership, with the owners handling the chef, bartender, and maître d' chores themselves. The changing handwritten menu offers dishes such as soft-shell crabs amandine, sweetbreads in white wine with artichokes, and caviar and veal sautéed with spinach in a cream sauce. This heart-of-the-Loop locale is crowded during lunch, quiet during dinner. AE, CB, DC, MC, V.

GERMAN

Deluxe

Golden Ox. 1578 N. Clyhourn Ave; 664–0780. The décor alone makes a visit worthwhile. There's an amazing collection of German paintings, woodcarvings, steins, and what-have-you displayed throughout the restaurant. Beamed ceilings, leaded windows, and handset tile floors add to the mood. The menu offers traditional German classics in enormous variety. Weiner rostbraten, tenderloin sautéed with red wine and onions, is the house specialty. Schnitzel aficionados may request the Holstein version (with fried egg, anchovies, and capers). AE, CB, DC, MC, V.

Moderate

Heidelberger Fass. 4300 N. Lincoln Ave.; 478–2486. Sauerbraten is a specialty here. Schnitzels also rank high, along with beef rouladen, smoky kasseler ribs, wienerrostbraten, and hearty sausage platters. Enjoy German draft beers, nonpareil liver dumpling soup, and hot apple strudel. Located in the heart of the old Germantown area, the restaurant has a décor reminiscent of an old European village, complete with homes and shops. Serves late. AE, CB, DC, MC, V.

Mirabell. 3454 W. Addison; 463–1962. An entire wing of this friendly, unpretentious Austrian spot is a beer garden that's open all year long. The trick is accomplished with glass-paned roof and walls that produce a room much like a hothouse. Heightening the effect is a profusion of live plants surrounding picnic-style tables and folding wooden chairs. In addition to a central area with a bar and a few tables and another wing that is a conventional dining room. One section of the menu offers 6 different versions of schnitzels (cutlets), including an excellent rahmschnitzel. AE, CB, DC, MC, V.

Schuliens. 2100 W. Irving Park Rd.; 478–2100. This gemutlichkeit German restaurant has been in business for 3 generations and was a speakeasy during Prohibition. Things are quieter now, but the Wiener schnitzel remains the same. Bartenders perform magic tricks and there are also guest magicians. AE, CB, DC, MC, V.

Inexpensive

Schwaben Stube. 3500 N. Lincoln Ave.; 348–8856. As German as its name implies. Hearty, tasty, home-style dishes that let you leave the table with a sated feeling. Food is served in 3 dining rooms that offer clean, attractive surroundings. Specialties are kasseler rippchen (smoked pork chop) with red cabbage, Weiner schnitzel, breaded pork tenderloin with apple sauce, veal chops, and deliciously prepared duck. For dessert, there's strudel—but check with the pleasant, efficient staff for specials. MC, V.

GREEK

Expensive

Taberna. 303 E. Ohio St.; 329–0262. If you time your arrival right, you'll see the chef preparing gyros, mounding chopped, seasoned lamb and large thin slices of meat on a spit that revolves slowly in front of an electric heater. As the outer crust of the meat turns to a rich, dark juicy brown, the chef carves off thin layers, which are served topped with chopped fresh onions. Other specialties are mousaka, dolmades, pastitsio, and chicken riganati. Split pea soup and egg-lemon soup are especially good. Located in the basement of the Time-Life building. AE, CB, DC, MC, V.

Moderate

The Courtyards of Plaka. 340 S. Halsted St.; 263–0767. Informality and hospitality are the charm of this unpretentious restaurant in the heart of Greek Town. All the usual Greek favorites are on the menu, along with some less familiar dishes like tzatziki, crisp slices of cucumber marinated in a thick garlic yogurt sauce, or cold octopus uniquely prepared in a special wine sauce. Moussaka is memorable, so is moschari stamnas, a flavorful Greek beef stew, tsipoura (sea bass) and sweet desserts like baklava and sokolatina. AE, CB, D, MC, V.

Greek Islands. 200 S. Halsted St.; 782–9855. Located in larger, more attractive quarters, this popular Greek Town spot continues to offer fine value. The grilled red snapper and sea bass are outstanding and the gyros excellent. Lamb is prepared in a host of styles. Octopus stewed in hearty tomato-wine sauce and deep-fried squid are specialties. As an appetizer, try taramosalata, a fish-roe spread delicious when slathered on crusty bread. If you're undecided, ask for a family-style combination dinner. Serves late. AE, CB, DC, MC, V.

Parthenon. 314 S. Halsted St.; 726–2407. Greek music blares from the juke box as flames leap high from saganaki (cheese spiked with brandy and lemon juice) appetizers. The front window provides clues to pleasures to be found within. Passerby can watch a whole lamb slowly spit-broiled to browned perfection. Tasty, crisp, outside cuts of lamb and beef barbecued in this manner are served along with onions and parsley as gyros. Seafood selections range from cod and sea bass to squid and octopus. Broiled snapper and sea bass are consistently good. Special family dinners (not on the menu) offer a good sampling of this traditional Greek kitchen. And, befitting a Greek restaurant, there are more than a dozen different lamb dishes. Serves late. AE, CB, DC, MC, V.

INDIA

Expensive

Bombay Palace. 50 E. Walton; 664–9323. A very chic atmosphere offering a menu so varied it is hard to choose. Some consider it the city's finest Indian restaurant. Murgh keema masala and lamb vindaloo are among favorites. Combination platters offer a chance to sample varied entrees. Modestly curried, but a helping of minted yogurt with cucumbers will cool the palate. Save room for mango ice cream and kulfi, a luscious combination containing rosewater and ground almonds. AE, CB, DC, MC, V.

Moderate

Standard India. 2546 W. Devon Ave.; 274–4175. This is definitely not the Taj Mahal, but a storefront restaurant where the emphasis is more on food than decor. Again, if not sure what to order, combination plates offer an opportunity to sample several dishes. Tandoori specialties here are rated above average. Curries of lamb, chicken, and vegetables are delicious and adventurously seasoned. AE, CB, DC, MC, V.

ITALIAN

Super Deluxe

Doro's. 871 N. Rush St.; 266–1414. Outstanding northern Italian cuisine, including many preparations rarely found on restaurant menus this side of the Atlantic, coupled with superior service. Extravagant Art Deco décor with crystal chandeliers, upholstered banquettes, and plush carpeting. Widely varied à la carte menu has dishes to please almost anyone, with an array of imaginative appetizers, soups, entrées, vegetables, and desserts. Veal dishes are a specialty. Homemade pastas include excellent fettuccine Alfredo, and an unusual ravioli filled with a combination of mild sausage and veal and complemented by a sauce of butter and sage. As a vegetable try baby artichokes dipped in egg batter and sautéed. AE, CB, DC, MC, V.

Deluxe

Gitanes. 2350 N. Clark St.; 929–5500. With white stucco walls, wooden ceilings and booths (some booths are curtained), this restaurant provides an intimate setting to enjoy well-prepared Northern Italian cuisine. Appetizers feature about half a dozen each of hot and cold selections—smoked seafood plate with salsa verde and mustard mayonnaise is representative of the latter, baked brie en croute of the former. Pastas include unusual combinations such as linguine with smoked salmon, cognac, prosciutto, and tomato. Entrées highlight a number of interesting veal preparations, plus such creative dishes as broiled, pancetta-wrapped filet with tomato, red wine, and rosemary, and grilled calf's liver with Lyon sausage, mushrooms, and red wine. Wines are served by the glass with dinner or at an attractive wine bar. AE, CB, DC, MC, V.

Pronto Ristorante. 200 E. Chestnut St.; 664–6181. With dash and style, the décor recreates the feel of a Bolognese trattoria. Sparkling white walls and crisp table linens provide a backdrop for a gleaming open kitchen, where a skilled crew prepares pasta by hand and cooks it to order. Seating is on a series of terraces that provide fine views of the kitchen activity. A rear section designed for more relaxed dining sports novel touches such as hanging lamps draped with chiffon scarfs. Menu emphasis is on northern Italian specialties, such as fettuccine Alfredo, sea scallops done with garlic and parsley, and veal in various preparations. Two unusual fettuccine variations are with seafood and curry sauce, or with cheese, butter, and smoked haddock. AE, CB, DC, MC, V.

Expensive

George's. 230 W. Kinzie. 644–2290. Successful Chicago restauranteur, George Badonsky (Tango, Bastille), has created a sophisticated, contemporary setting for this northern Italian restaurant. There are a dozen or so appetizers ranging from mussels with white wine and tomato to cold fettuccine with smoked meats and fresh oysters. Pastas are creative and unusual, such as penne made with either a 4-cheese combination or with a liver-and-tomato sauce. Entrées include scampi, shrimp, veal chops, lamb chops, and sole. Each day brings a supplementary menu with a handful of specials in all categories—

sometimes including abalone. For dessert try the white chocolate mousse. There's entertainment some evenings, often featuring modern jazz groups. AE, MC, V.

The Italian Village. 71 W. Monroe St.; 332–7005. 3 operations in 1, each on a separate floor and each with its own kitchen. On a subterranean level, you'll find La Contina, with a cozy setting for traditional Italian specialties, plus selections like steak Diane, flamed tableside, and squab with wild rice. Desserts also range from the Italian (zabaglione) to such choices as cherries jubilee and baked Alaska. Just off Monroe St. is the plushest of the facilities, the Florentine Room, where the emphasis is on northern Italian cookery and fine steaks. The décor is handsome, the staff efficient and courteous, and the tortellini first rate. Upstairs, the décor recreates an Italian village. There's a huge selection of reasonably priced dishes, including nearly 3 dozen pasta preparations. The balance of the menu ranges from pizza to saltimbocca. AE, MC, V.

Salvatore's. 525 W. Arlington Pl.; 528–1200. Northern Italian food develops an intimate kind of connoisseurdom of its own among its ardent advocates. In Salvatore's large, high-ceilinged dining room in an old hotel, you'll find a quorum of just such fans, drawn here for classic antipasti, conch salad, elegantly thin-sliced prosciutto with melon or figs, and zuppa di pesce, a fresh fish soup that becomes almost a ceremony. A whole fresh fish, maybe a small bass, cooked in its broth, is brought to the table, removed, and boned. Pastas par excellence include fettuccine in a creamy gorgonzola sauce, and spinach noodles with pine nuts, red peppers, fresh spinach and parmesan cheese. There is complete bar service and a fine wine list. Serves late. AE, CB, DC, MC, V.

Moderate

Armando's. 735 N. Rush St.; 337–7672. This restaurant has a long and proud history of pleasing out-of-towners and locals. Flocked wallpaper and framed oils create a pleasant setting for enjoying a wide array of well-prepared Italian dishes. Beef bracciole is a specialty, as are veal, chicken, and pasta preparations. Less venturesome patrons can select from an assortment of steaks and chops, plus several seafood listings. Ample portions, top-level service, and moderate prices add to the allure. AE, CB, DC, MC, V.

Febo. 2501 S. Western Ave.; 523–0839. Famous for nothing! The slogan of this southwest side family restaurant is intriguing but inaccurate. For years Febo's has been known for its good quality pasta—cooked al dente—veal, and other specialty dishes, all reasonably priced. Hard-line trenchermen go there for its well-known Fiesta specials (for 4 or more persons), sumptuous feasts that include doubles of pasta and entrée and much, much more. A long-time favorite at this sprawling, multiroomed corner restaurant in one of Chicago's Italian enclaves is garlicky chicken Vesuvio. Saltimbocca also is extremely good. Famous for just about everything, one might say! AE, CB, DC, MC, V.

Gennaro's. 1352 W. Taylor St.; 243–1035. The front door is locked, recalling days of old in speakeasy times. Push the buzzer and enter the good-eating world of Mrs. Gennaro. Fantastic homemade gnocchi, ravioli, and manicotti, piping hot and egg-noodle rich, with fresh tomatoes and genuine Parmesan in the aromatic sauces. The most tender and white veal for classic scallopini, also served with peppers. There is a full bar and adequate wine list. Reservations recommended. Casual and informal, take your appetite along; diners go away smiling. No cards.

Lawrence of Oregano. 662 W. Diversey; 871–1916. The punning name is reflected in a number of the offbeat menu listings, but the main culinary emphasis is on hearty portions of well-prepared, moderately priced, basically Italian-style dishes. Seasonings are designed for American tastes and tend toward less spiciness. Among the offerings you'll find chicken cacciatore, saltimbocca and bracciola, and a good assortment of soups, salads, egg dishes, sandwiches, and pasta preparations. Up front, a grocery store type of décor provides a display area for the kitchen crew's Italian creations and also houses an antipasto bar. Desserts include fresh strawberry pie. Serves late. AE, DC, MC, V.

Mama DeLuca's. 1612 N. Sedgwick; 337–2223. Gusty Sicilian-style food in a thoroughly informal setting. Pasquale and Mama take turns in the kitchen producing heady aromas and satisfying hearty appetites. When he's not cooking in the back, Pasquale doubles as a bartender and greeter. He's often to be found attired in an undershirt with a day or two's worth of stubble covering his face—it's that type of place. There are a number of small tables plus one large round one where everyone, including the cop on the beat, eats family-style. The special multicourse dinners are outstanding—particularly the vegetable dishes —but they must be ordered in advance. AE, CB, DC, MC, V.

Mama Mia! Pasta. 711 N. State St.; 787–5606. This counter-service restaurant 4 blocks west of Michigan Avenue's Magnificent Mile is to cafeterias what the Queen Elizabeth II is to river tugboats. A masterpiece of high-tech design, highlighting the Italian national colors of red and green, it has gleaming showcases loaded with ready-to-cook pastas and a reasonable selection of compatible Italian wines and imported beers. More than 20 different kinds of pasta are available, including whole wheat, tomato basil, beet, and spinach—all made fresh daily. There are 5 homemade sauces, plus daily specials such as walnut sauce and eggplant Parmesan. Desserts are freshly baked. Eat in (using plastic utensils), carry out, or buy pasta and sauce by the pound for parties and at-home dining. AE, MC, V.

Inexpensive

Villa Marconi. 2358 S. Oakley Ave.; 847–3168. A family operation, this old-time Italian restaurant exudes friendliness and good cheer. An attentive staff adds to the feeling of dining in someone's home rather than in a restaurant. Italian specialties are cooked to order. Pasta selections include tortellini, tiny rippled-edge dumplings filled with seasoned, finely ground meat; mostaccioli; gnocchi; ravioli; and spaghetti. Baked clams and grostini, crisp-toasted bread piled high with caper-and-anchovy-flavored chopped liver, make fine appetizers. House specialty is crisp, garlic-rich chicken Vesuvio. Finish with espresso or cappuccino. No cards.

JAPANESE

Deluxe

Benihana of Tokyo. 166 E. Superior St.; 664–9643. A floor show comes with your meal at the local branch of this successful Japanese steak house chain. It's provided by the colorfully neckerchiefed, white-garbed chef who displays his culinary talents as he cooks your food on a hot metal grill set right into the center of your table. He skillfully cuts steak, shrimp, and chicken into bite-size morsels to facilitate handling with chopsticks. As accompaniments there are mushrooms, onions, and bean sprouts grilled on the same surface as the meat. Seating is communal-style, with 8 to a table. If there are fewer in your party, you'll be seated with anyone else who happens along. AE, CB, DC, MC, V.

Hana East. 210 E. Ohio St.; 751–2100. A Japanese steak house and then some. Showmen-chefs put on a real performance right before your eyes as they prepare your meal on a teppan-yaki grill surface built into the center of your table. Their skill with knives, in particular, is fascinating. Steak, chicken, and shrimp are done in delicious style with flavorful sauces. Accompaniments include chicken soup with fresh sliced mushrooms, crisp salad with soy sauce-based dressing, and fresh vegetables done on the grill. The quality of both meats and vegetables is superior. AE, CB, DC, MC, V.

Hatsuhana Restaurant. 160 E. Ontario St.; 280–8287. Construction experts from Japan huddled with a creative young Chicago architect to fashion this open, airy, attractive setting for Japanese cuisine. Just the right Oriental touches create a welcoming, yet slightly exotic, feeling without sacrificing creature comforts. Customers dine either at handsome, unclothed butcher block tables or perch on stools at a long sushi bar. If you choose the latter, you'll be able to watch a fascinating show as nimble-fingered chefs create the various sushi specialties (raw fish slices on vinegared rice balls) to customers' orders. The sushi is also available for those seated at tables. Charts help you figure your way around ordering these raw delicacies. In addition, the menu offers regular entrées and dinners, with an emphasis on fin and shellfish. Shrimp and vegetable tempura, for instance, is particularly noteworthy. AE, CB, DC, MC, V.

Ron of Japan. 230 E. Ontario St.; 644–6500. Skilled cooks do their work at your table, as at Benihana, while a telescoping exhaust hood over the cooking surface wafts away the smoke and heat. Excellent beef is grilled teppan-yaki style, along with shrimp, mushrooms, onions, and bean sprouts. The shrimp, in particular—with a unique creamy topping concocted from eggs and butter—are worth a double order. Diners wear oversized aprons instead of using napkins, and eat with chopsticks from metal plates resting right on the cooking surface. The room is handsomely done with some remarkable decorative embellishments, including Japanese antiques. AE, CB, DC, MC, V.

Expensive

Hashikin. 2338 N. Clark St.; 935–6474. At the sushi bar up front, a skillful chef whips up tiny vinegared rice and fish delicacies before your eyes. You can sit at the counter here, at an assortment of tables and chairs, or dine in one of the tea houses in the rear and on the 2nd floor. There's a wide selection of seafood, chicken, and beef specialties. Reasonably priced complete dinners include soup, tempura, salad, teriyaki, or sukiyaki, and dessert. AE, CB, DC, MC, V.

Kiyo's. 2827 N. Clark St.; 935–0474. Luxurious digs and good value combine to make this place a favorite with Japanese–food fanciers. There is a whole series of comfortable "teahouses" where customers sit on the floor around low tables. A pit beneath each table provides a place for Occidentals to put their legs. Both the tempura (shrimp, squid, or whitefish) and sukiyaki are excellent. The appetizers alone are worth a visit; they include rarities such as shaved dried bonito fish and many versions of sashimi (raw fish). AE, CB, DC, MC, V.

Moderate

Kamehachi. 1617 N. Wells St.; 664–3663. A deft-fingered chef prepares vinegared rice balls topped with filets of various types of (usually raw) fish right before customers' eyes at the informal sushi bar ranged along one side of the restaurant. There's also table service in this scrupulously neat spot. Even from the tables, you can watch other chefs prepare tempura, yakitori, and a variety of Japanese specialties. AE, MC, V.

MEXICAN

Expensive

Cafe La Margarita. 868 N. Wabash Ave.; 751–3434. A little bit of Mexico just south of the bordering Rush St. nightclub belt, with lots of Mexican artwork and a cantina-like ambience. Caesar Dovininas, the owner, is interested in food and takes pleasure in discussing it with his guests. The bill of fare is extensive, offering traditional Mexican favorites, such as chicken in mole sauce and peppers stuffed with beef or cheese, plus more unusual items, such as calabacitas—squash stuffed with Mexican cheese. Good seafood selections, such as stuffed crabs with a mild cream sauce and melted cheese. Very good margaritas, as you would expect. AE, CB, DC, MC, V.

La Hacienda Del Sol. 1945 N. Sedgwick Ave.; 664–6812. A splashing fountain in the garden and handsome colonial appointments including crossed swords and equestrian gear. Host Alfredo Pizano built this fountain himself. He's justifiably proud both of it and of the food his kitchen crew turns out. All the usual tortilla-based dishes are available, including flautas, so called because of their long, thin, flute-like shape. Other choices are chiles rellenos, carne asada, and arroz con pollo. The menu is large enough to offer an interesting variety, and the staff is delighted to assist a guest whose Spanish fails him. AE, CB, DC, MC, V.

Su Casa. 49 E. Ontario St.; 943–4041. This converted coach house is now a charming 17th-century-style setting for the most elegant and handsome of the local Mexican restaurants. Chicken-filled enchiladas, cheese tacos, chiles rellenos, and other classic dishes highlight the menu. A number of more unusual Mexican dishes include shrimp Veracruz (served in the shell with a spicy sauce) and several steak preparations that use tender, good-quality meat. There's also a hearty Texas chili. Serves late. AE, CB, DC, MC, V.

Inexpensive

Mi Casa–Su Casa. 2524 N. Southport; 525–6323. It's well worth a trip off the beaten path to find this no-frills Mexican restaurant. Felix Gomez and his wife are warm, friendly hosts who make customers feel right at home. Prices are modest and the food top-notch. Fork-tender steak Milanesa is a specialty. It's sliced thin, covered with thick breading, and fried. Chiles rellenos, arroz con pollo, and combination plates of tacos, enchiladas, and tostadas are also good. AE, CB, DC, MC, V.

MIDEAST

Expensive

The Casbah. 514 W. Diversey; 935–7570. "Come with me to the Casbah" was Charles Boyer's line. Within recent years, more and more Chicagoans have been using it because of this fine establishment, which features Middle Eastern cuisine. You can start your meal with cheese borek, tissue-thin strudel leaves wrapped around a tasty filling, or kibbeh nayyee, a mixture of raw lamb and cracked wheat. Follow it with shish kebab in various forms or a puff-pastry envelope filled with Cornish game hen, almonds, and cinnamon. Or your choice can be sarma, a combination of ground meat and rice wrapped in grape leaves, or a fine preparation of lamb with cauliflower, pine nuts, and spiced rice. Serves late. AE, CB, DC, MC, V.

POLYNESIAN

Deluxe

Kon-Tiki Ports. 505 N. Michigan Ave.; 527–4286. 5 separate dining areas, plus cocktail lounge, each geared to a different port, taking patrons on a tour of Singapore, Saigon, Macao, Hawaii, and Tahiti. Among the more exotic entrées are beefsteak marinated in spices and coconut, then broiled and served with honey-baked oranges; chicken sautéed with tomatoes, fresh ginger, and spices; and roast duck coated with orange honey, crisped in peanut oil, garnished with shrimp chips, tomatoes, and pineapple fingers. Potables include a range of exotic drinks served in equally exotic receptacles. AE, CB, DC, MC, V.

The Kona Kai. Marriott O'Hare Hotel, 8535 W. Higgins Rd.; 693–4830. This is the largest of the South Seas restaurants in the Chicago area and features such delectable exotica as Konakai egg flower soup, shrimp stuffed with almonds, lobster or crab curry, and coconut-honey ice cream. The Royal Hawaiian is a meat-and-shellfish feast with Polynesian pork, shrimp and fresh vegetables served with Yang Chow fried rice and fresh pineapple. The adjoining lounge has a repertoire of 50 exotic drinks—the kind of rum-and-tropical-fruit-juice creations that are as good-looking as they are spirit raising. There is Polynesian entertainment every night. AE, CB, DC, MC, V.

Trader Vic's. 17 E. Monroe St.; 726–7500. Malayan tidbits (a combination of rumaki, curry puffs, and crab Rangoon) are a popular accessory for cocktails in this atmospheric restaurant in the venerable Palmer House. If there are at least 15 in your party and you have given a week's notice, you can have a whole barbecued pig fresh from the Chinese ovens. Indonesian roast lamb, several kinds of steak, squab, chicken, and chops are among the other meats prepared in the ovens. There is also a roster of curries, plus dozens of other selections, which are mostly Cantonese in origin. You also can order hard-to-find (in Chicago) abalone. Serves late. AE, CB, DC, MC, V.

SCANDINAVIAN

Inexpensive

Ann Sather's. 925 W. Belmont; 348–2378. No fuss. No frills. Just a very plain, clean, reliable establishment that seems to be a favorite of Scandinavian old-timers and family groups with lots of children. The menu is relatively limited, but the Swedish fare is top-notch. This is a popular breakfast spot (jammed on Sunday mornings) with thin pancakes served with tart lingonberry sauce and Swedish potato sausage—two popular items. Scandinavian handicrafts fill the attractively arranged window. If you like a cocktail before dinner, best stop off someplace else first. No liquor or wine is served, and customers are not encouraged to bring their own. Delicious fruit soup is usually available, as are Swedish meatballs, chicken, and a variety of desserts. No cards.

SOUTH AMERICAN

Expensive

El Inca. 6221 N. Broadway; 262–7077. Instead of a printed menu, Alberto Asturrizaga, owner of the restaurant, paints vivid oral pictures of the Peruvian food his wife Olinda has prepared. The choice varies from night to night. Among the unusual dishes may be duck prepared with wine and vegetables or lamb fried in oil with onions, oregano, and garlic, then steamed. AE, CB, DC, V.

Piqueo. 5427 N. Clark St.; 769–0455. Moises Asturrizaga and his staff lovingly prepare unusual and tasty food that is authentically Peruvian. So are the handicrafts displayed on the restaurant's walls. The selection isn't extensive, but there's a good variety of well-seasoned dishes that generally are not hotly spiced. Many of the ingredients are familiar ones, but the end results achieved with chicken, beef, and pork dishes are a new taste experience for most. Moises himself tells you what's available each evening. There's no printed menu. Among the dishes that turn up frequently are escabeche, a chicken dish; potatoes with a tasty cheese sauce; anticuchos, sort of a Peruvian mixed grill; and hearty soups. AE.

SPANISH

Expensive

La Paella. 2920 N. Clark St.; 528–0757. As you'd expect from the name, the featured dish at this small but attractive storefront restaurant is paella, a traditional Spanish stew-like dish. The delicious house version combines bits of meat, chicken, and seafood with saffron-seasoned-and-colored rice. Polite, attentive service makes customers feel welcome and relaxed as they enjoy the paella or other dishes, such as roast duck enhanced with mangoes and brandy sauce; chicken braised with wine, almonds, and garlic; marinated baked trout; and seafood casserole with lobster. Although this small, comfortable restaurant features Northern Spanish cuisine, daily specials highlight dishes from various regions of Spain. AE, CB, DC, MC, V.

Restaurant Toledo. 1935 N. Sedgwick Ave.; 266–2066. Start your meal with gazpacho or black bean soup. Then work your way through gambas à la plancha, fried shrimp in the shell, before moving on to a host of authentic Spanish entrées. House specialty is paella à la Valenciana with lobster, shrimp, scallops, mussels, ham, chicken, spicy sausage, asparagus, and other vegetables combined in a tasty mélange. Other Spanish dishes include duck prepared in a spiced sauce with green olives and orange slices and breast of capon stuffed with beef, ground almonds, grapes, and olives. If you fancy seafood, try zarzuelo de mariscos, which comes with a rich Spanish wine sauce. AE, CB, DC, MC, V.

NIGHT LIFE AND BARS. Mention Chicago's night life scene and many out-of-towners still have visions of a Capone-era beer truck delivering illicit booze to a back-alley speakeasy. That reputation has been hard to live down. Every time "The Untouchables" goes into television reruns, a whole new generation of viewers is introduced to Elliot Ness raiding some mob-associated watering hole. Despite what you may have seen on the late, late show, that image is truly a part of the past. Today Chicago's bar and night life scene is not unlike that in other major American cities. Obviously, the unique midwestern flavor of the city and the traditions of its ethnic neighborhoods continue to create a distinctive personality.

Currently, there are 6,300 liquor licenses in Chicago. These represent establishments as diverse as the city's population, ranging from sophisticated to sleazy. Some are issued to prestigious celebrity hotels, where the mood is subdued, low-key, genteel. Others, frequently changing, cover lively "in" spots considered trendy, fashionable, chic. These often come and go like a flash-in-the-pan performer, lasting only as long as the current craze, then reemerging under another name, with different decor, and a new personality. There are Mom-and-Pop grocery stores selling packaged goods across town from supermarket-sized liquor stores noted for carrying almost every drink produced worldwide.

The latest phenomenon is the sports bar, catering to enthusiastic followers of baseball, football, soccer, basketball, etc. Like-minded visitors would enjoy the camaraderie among fans in some of these; others are located in areas where one would not feel safe, even with Al Capone as a bodyguard! The greatest percentage of licenses is issued to family-operated, neighborhood bars.

A cross section of all these is covered in this section. Emphasis is on establishments in locations both easily accessible to visitors and of some special interest to them. It is particularly difficult to separate nightclubs by category, since one evening pop jazz may be the attraction, with a switch later in the week to punk rock. Some clubs are so diversified they really fit into several categories.

The areas covered include:

Downtown: The so-called heart of the city starts at the lakefront and moves west across the Loop. It stretches from the Chicago River on the north (about 600 North) to Congress Street on the south (600 South). The action here is often business-oriented, with a good choice of daytime and early evening favorites that quiet down when the after-work set heads back to the suburbs.

Off Downtown: Just north and west of the main business area, this section starts around the giant Merchandise Mart (housing NBC) and Apparel Center and extends out through a warehouse-factory area.

North Michigan Avenue: This is the elegant side of the city, the "Magnificent Mile" of pricey prestige shops, premiere hotels, and high-fashion lifestyles. It reaches north from the Chicago River (600 North) to Lake Shore Drive (950 North).

Rush Street: In its heyday this was the city's main night life district. Still bustling at night, but by day it looks rather like an old movie theater when the lights go on and patrons can see its shabbiness, with popcorn and gum sticking to the floors.

Old Town: Over a decade ago there was considerable renaissance and restoration in this neighborhood—imaginative boutiques, antique shops, popular bars. Now its character seems to ebb and flow like the tide. Although it has lost a lot of its original appeal, there are still some places worth a visit.

Lincoln Park: Chicago's trendy town house, condominium, and apartment dwellings set the restored Victorian mood of this area, which takes its name from sprawling, lakefront Lincoln Park. The area west of the park between Armitage Ave. (2000 North) and Diversey (2800 North) is full of popular new-wave establishments in rehabbed buildings.

The category *Potpourri* offers a sample of diverse neighborhoods.

A word of caution: Neighborhoods can change quickly in Chicago, as in most major cities. The most fashionable bar or nightclub in a high-rent district may be only one block from the fringes of a seedy, changing district. Walk in the wrong direction and it is not difficult to encounter trouble. It is always a wise precaution to ask your desk clerk or concierge about the safety of the area you intend to visit. They won't be offended, and will appreciate your common-sense approach, and may also have some up-to-the-minute suggestions on the newest "in" places. Be leery of taxi drivers steering you to so-called "hot spots."

There are places where it is safe to stroll day or night, like Michigan Avenue, which is the city's favorite promenade. There are others, like Rush Street's nightclub strip, where one can stroll but might get hustled along the way. Still other neighborhoods of interest to visitors are where it pays to take a cab and keep your eyes open. It is thus the world over. Don't let your common sense take a vacation just because you have.

NIGHT LIFE

Blues

Blues. 2519 N. Halsted; 528–1012. Live music seven nights a week in a clubhouse atmosphere. Small but internationally known among fans. Reasonable prices. Limited seating, so suggest arriving early.

The Checkerboard Lounge. 423 East 43rd St.; 373–5948. A no-frills, 100-seat hall in an out-of-the-way neighborhood on Chicago's South Side. Owner and legendary guitarist Buddy Guy attracts friends, followers, and anxious-to-learn musicians.

Kingston Mines. 2548 N. Halsted; 477–4646. A very funky club that alternates live music on dual stages seven nights a week. Like to play until the sun rises. Blues, Lilly's, and The Wise Fools are all nearby so blues enthusiasts can circulate between them. Cover, no minimum.

Lilly's. 2513 N. Lincoln; 525–2422. Big Time Sarah is one of the popular house acts in this cozy club where one can hear some of Chicago's old-time blues artists. No cover or minimum. Live entertainment Thursdays through Saturdays.

Theresa's. 607 E. 43rd St.; 285–2744. Heading toward its 40th year, this blues room is noted for hospitality. Theresa dishes up free chicken and potato salad during Monday night jam sessions, which often attract Junior Wells and Buddy Guy.

Uncle Steve's Blues Brothers Bar. 1446 N. Wells; 266–4978. The owner was a friend of the late John Belushi, whose "Blues Brothers" was filmed in Chicago. This speakeasy-like hideaway is just down the street from Second City.

The Wise Fools Pub. 2270 N. Lincoln Ave.; 929–1510. A cross between a college hangout and a nightclub. On busy weekends you may have a long wait in the bar before finding space in one of the music room's church pews. Cover and minimum.

Cabaret

Cabaret Gentry. 712 N. Rush St.; 664–1033. Back in the 1880s, this was the elegant home of one of Chicago's first society hostesses. Today the old mansion houses a basement bar, main-floor tavern, and an intimate showroom. Attracts a large gay clientele. No cover, no minimum. Often features pop pianists who favor audience requests.

Cellarachino. 1935 N. Sedgewick; 266–2066. A flamenco nightclub with performers from around the Latin world. Cover and minimum.

Crosscurrents. 3206 N. Wilton (north of Belmont at 900 W.) 472–7884. Locally noted for offering some of Chicago's most innovative bookings. An unusual blend of folk, rock, satire, jazz, and theater. Large lobby bar plus outdoor café and performance room, bakery, and assorted rehearsal rooms. Something offbeat is always happening.

Miomir's Serbian Club. 2255 W. Lawrence; 784–2111. Yugoslavian food is served to the accompaniment of Russian, Balkan, and Italian singers. Gypsy orchestra, violinists, and a rare cimbalon lure diners onto the dance floor. No cover or minimum.

Roxy. 1505 W. Fullerton; 839–1000. The mood of this popular spot survived a move and it continues to be home to a mind-boggling collection of movie memorabilia. High ceilings, airy ambiance, posters, caricatures. Actually wears three hats—a saloon, a restaurant, and a club.

Comedy

Chicago Comedy Showcase. 1013 W. Webster; 348–1101. The program is often a surprise at this bring-your-own-refreshments showcase.

Second City. 1616 N. Wells; 337–3992. The list of famous Second City graduates is longer than the credits for "Saturday Night Live" and includes Elaine May and the late John Belushi. Always innovative, it is a continual source of bright new talent. You can buy a ticket for the main show, then stay for the additional improvisational performance afterwards. Or come at about 10:30 P.M. and just see the improvisations without a ticket. Still a Chicago headliner after 20 years.

Zanies. 1548 N. Wells; 337–4027. Zanies is just down the street from famed Second City, their inspiration. A fun place that enjoys being outrageous. Two-drink minimum, plus cover charge.

Country

R & R Ranch. 56 W. Randolph; 263–8207. The Sundowners have been performing live country music in this unlikely location for 25 years. Old-time basement-level bar next door to the Woods Theatre is crowded with enough western memorabilia to fill a museum. Reward posters, animal skulls, and Indian rugs line walls along with valuable antique gun collection. Chili heads the menu.

Disco Dancing

Baby Doll Polka Club. 6102 S. Central; 582–9706. With the largest Polish population outside Warsaw, it seems natural that Chicago should have a first rate polka club. Ed Korosa plays a lively accordion and bouncy music keeps everyone moving. Music starts at 9:30 P.M. Fridays and Saturdays. Sunday radio show is broadcast at 5 P.M. No cover or minimum.

His 'n' Her's. 944 W. Addison; 935–1210. Although this club is a favorite video-rock-dance club with lesbians and gays, everyone is welcome.

BBC. 9 W. Division; 664–7012. Owned by former Chicago Bears linebacker Doug Buffone. There is a big screen for watching sports events and a large dance floor that attracts what is locally known as the Near North singles crowd. Open until 4 A.M.

Exit. 1653 N. Wells; 440–0535. One of the original video dance clubs. Sunken dance floor backed by a large movie screen mixes vintage films with new wave, heavy metal. Not for the timid.

Limelight. N. Dearborn and Ontario; 337–2985. Chicago's latest conversation-stopper is an eclectic, modernistic disco in the fortress-like former home of the Chicago Historical Society. Don't be surprised if guests and staff have hair colored like the rainbow. One local night-life critic labeled it "art deco gone tutti-frutti." Branch of London and New York Limelights.

Paradise/Chicago. 2848 N. Broadway; 871–1717. One of the city's trendy gay discos. Dramatic light show features heavy-duty music. Small restaurant includes Italian menu.

Snuggery. 15 W. Division; 337–4349. At the moment the Snuggery is considered one of the more fashionable singles bars. Lots of brass and antiques, with a cosmopolitan crowd.

Tania's. 2659 N. Milwaukee; 235–7120. Back again after remodeling. A center for Latin dancing seven nights a week, with the emphasis on Cuban dance music from the 40s to the 60s. Music starts at 8:30 P.M.

Folk/Pop/Rock

Biddy Mulligan's. 7644 N. Sheridan; 761–6532. This cozy room in a Rogers Park neighborhood plays so many kinds of music it is hard to categorize. Blues, rock, reggae, and big band jazz. Arrive early for good seat. Music starts at 9:30 P.M. featuring names like Lonnie Brooks, Buckwheat Zydeco, and the Piranha Bros.

Bob Gibson's Gourmet Chili Parlor & Music Emporium. 5101 N. Clark; 271–0400. This 70-seat music room has the feel of a suburban recreation room, relaxed and comfortable. Musician Gibson has been around a long time and knows almost any folk number requested. The outer restaurant and bar specializes in four types of chili and burgers.

FitzGeralds. 6615 W. Roosevelt Rd., Berwyn; 788–2118. Bill FitzGerald has re-created a big-city salute to old-time roadhouse memorabilia. It's all there, from deer heads on the wall to the down-home neighborliness of staff. Visiting musicians range from Cajun bands to Vanessa Davis.

Holsteins! 2464 N. Lincoln; 327–3331. Rated among the finest folk music clubs in the country. Bar is separate from 120-seat stage, so conversation does not interfere with some of the best in national, international, and local acts. Wise to call first since bookings change frequently and show times vary. Three Holstein brothers, well-known in folk circles, operate the club.

Irish Village. 6215 W. Diversey; 237–7555. Emphasis is on the ould sod with corned beef and cabbage the Tuesday night special, plus barbecued baby-back ribs, good ale, and folk singers. Live entertainment six nights a week. Showtime 8 P.M. Friday, Saturday 9 P.M.

Kilkenny Castle Inn. 3808 N. Central; 736–0709. This homey Irish pub is almost always crowded with friendly folk from Paddy's land. You don't need a brogue to order your Guinness on draught or Harp by the bottle, but nearly everyone has one. Music on Wednesdays, Thursdays, and Sundays starts at 8:30 P.M. and is free. Fridays and Saturdays, the entertainment starts at 9 P.M., with a $2 cover charge.

Minstrel's. 6465 N. Sheridan; 262–6230. A collegiate, neighborhood bar offering acts from reggae to rock in a Rogers Park setting near Loyola University. Moderately priced.

Orphan's. 2462 N. Lincoln; 929–2677. Three distinct environments: an outer room for drinking and conversation; a music room where jazz, rock, blues, and folk alternate, and the big band stage with room for dancing. Comfortable and casual.

Park West. 322 W. Armitage; 929–5959. Reconstructed movie theater has a seating capacity of over 700. Their Saturday night Video Dancestand is a multimedia attention-getter involving three screens and heavy music. Modeled after the Ritz in New York. Expensive.

Trammps. 622 N. Fairbanks Ct.; 944–0828. New and spacious with a high-tech look. Calls itself the Club of the 80s, features musical review and a jazz lunch. Formerly Dingbat's, the disco where Mr. T first started as a bouncer.

Wild Hare & Singing Armadillo Frog Sanctuary. 3530 N. Clark; 327–0800. Offers a touch of Jamaica as the city's most popular reggae club. Jamaican craftsmen set up shop outside, creating a mini-sidewalk market. Jamaican Red Stripe and Guinness Stout are the only beers served. Cover charge; moderate prices.

Hotel Lounges

Some of the city's most glamorous, sophisticated cocktail lounges are found in its prestige hotels. In recent years there has been a decided trend toward establishing traditional English-style hotels here—low-key, understated, very much in London's Knightsbridge tradition. These, added to Chicago's already existing luxury hotels, offer some worthy possibilities for an after-shopping cocktail, pre-dinner drink, or nightcap. It can be an interesting way to experience a hotel even if you aren't staying there. Here are only a few of some interesting possibilities:

Ambassador East. 1301 N. State Parkway; 266–0360. *The Pump Room* is the place where coast-to-coast celebrities detrained in the pre-jet age and headed for booth #1. Still elegant and especially popular with singles. *Byfields,* located in the same hotel, is a classic and classy cabaret presenting everything from folk to rock. A prestige place.

The Drake. 140 E. Walton at Michigan Ave.; 787–2200. There are several fine choices here. Sit around the fountain in the palmy, paneled, Edwardian elegance of the *Palm Court;* try the *Coq d'Or* as Queen Elizabeth did on her visit; or join the thousands who have carved their initials in the much acclaimed *Cape*

Cod Room's bar. No one can afford to build hotels in this grand baronial style today.

Hyatt Regency. 151 E. Wacker Dr.; 565–1234. Dramatic waterfall lobby is focal point for a variety of stylish bars.

Knickerbocker-Chicago. 163 E. Walton; 751–8100. *Limehouse Pub* and blond-oak paneled *Prince of Wales* bar are quiet and relaxing retreats.

Mayfair Regent. 181 E. Lake Shore Drive; 787–8500. Hand-painted Chinese murals of the large *Lobby Lounge* help make this one of the most attractive rooms in the city. Decor and mood are reminiscent of a town-house mansion.

Park Hyatt. 800 N. Michigan on Water Tower Square; 280–2222. This is a totally new concept in Hyatts—smaller, intimate, and quite wonderful. Drinks served in its lobby and in *La Tour's* very French restaurant bar.

Ritz Carlton. 160 E. Pearson just off Michigan Ave.; 266–1000. Take the elevator to the 12th floor and enter the garden-like *Greenhouse Bar* complete with large fountain, or opt for the plush, more nightclubby atmosphere of *The Bar of the Ritz.*

Tremont. 100 E. Chestnut. 751–1900. *Cricket's* is another of those low-key, high-class, club-like settings where celebrities like to relax.

The Whitehall. 105 E. Delaware; 944–6300. Their *Lobby Bar* exudes the quiet, traditional atmosphere so typical of an upper-class London hotel.

Westin. 909 N. Michigan; 943–7200. Bookshelves lining the walls give it a private den look. It features live jazz shows evenings after 8.

Jazz

Andy's. 11 E. Hubbard; 642–6805. Andy's is an informal, laid-back club that begins its day with jazz at noon Wednesday through Friday, serving food to 2:30 P.M. No cover for noon shows. Evening performances 5–8 P.M. The Rhythmmakers, Bobby Lewis' sterling trumpet, and the Swing Machine are among performers.

The Backroom. 1007 N. Rush; 751–2433. Although this is one of the city's smaller jazz rooms, it features first-rate talent. Don't be discouraged by appearances—it was once a horse barn now fancied up. Shows start around 9 P.M. Two-drink minimum.

Billy's. 936 N. Rush; 943–7080. The lounge bar of this nouvelle cuisine Italian restaurant has a cozy atmosphere with its own jazz trio. Moderately expensive, like much of Rush St. On the upper level.

Blondie's. 936½ N. Rush; 280–0963. A no-frills jazz club on the lower level of Billy's (see above).

Bulls. 1916 N. Lincoln Park West; 337–3000. Intimate cave-like cellar level features a number of jazz acts beginning at 10 P.M. weekdays, 9:30 P.M. weekends. This is an old-timer with emphasis on jazz vocalists.

The Dairy. 1936 W. Augusta; 252–4090. This unusual entertainment complex is in the immaculate refurbished Pure Farms Pioneer Dairy. There is ample space for dancing to music from the 20s, 30s, and 40s.

The Empire Room. Palmer House Hotel, State and Monroe; 726–7500. This gilded beauty looks like a transplant from Versailles and is a surprise setting for live jazz during noon lunch. One of the most beautiful rooms in Chicago.

George's. 230 W. Kinzie; 644–2290. A supper club with emphasis on northern Italian food. Curving back-lit glass brick bar is a conversation piece. Cover charge $8 to $10 with two-drink minimum.

Joe Segal's Jazz Showcase. Blackstone Hotel, 636 S. Michigan; 427–4300. Over 3 decades of quality jazz heard in an elegant setting reminiscent of café society. Attracts a dressy, classy audience every night at 9 and 11 P.M., and 1 A.M.

Leslee's. One American Plaza, Sherman at Grove, Evanston; 328–8304. Ultra-modern jazz club in basement of new office building. 20 kinds of imported beer. No cover or minimum. Live music Tuesdays through Saturdays, taped jazz Sundays and Mondays. Near Northwestern University.

Moosehead Bar & Grill. 163 W. Harrison; 922–3640. Large, friendly spot in the south Loop area. Crowded with everything from Mayor Daley posters to Coca Cola bric-a-brac. Noted for its jazz and good hamburgers.

The Raccoon Club. 812 N. Franklin; 943–1928. Very trendy, new art deco cabaret reminiscent of a classy supper club from a 30s film. Jazz-oriented entertainment. Beverages run from expresso and cappucino to eight types of bottled champagne. Elegant but affordable. Cover varies.

Rick's Café Americain. 644 N. Lake Shore Dr.; 943–9200. Humphrey Bogart's Club from *Casablanca* has been recreated on the first floor of an unusual Holiday Inn and become a great setting for some of the country's best jazz artists. Exceptional sound system, good service. Expensive.

Piano Bars

Eugene's. 1255 N. State; 944–1445. English country inn look complete with Hogarth etchings and leather wing chairs. Across from the classic Ambassador Hotel in the high-rent Gold Coast. Liquor list contains nearly 250 wines and more than 50 cognacs and armagnacs.

Manhattan. 1045 N. Rush; 751–2001. Deco-nouveau setting with New York flavor. Piano and vocalist to entertain you over drinks and appetizers. Dress code. Inexpensive. Cocktail hour 4 to 8 P.M.

Rendezvous. 1400 N. Lake Shore Drive; 280–8800. Settle into plush red velvet chairs and sip cognac, cordials, and sherries to the accompaniment of contemporary pop and light jazz. Lots of atmosphere, hard to believe this was once a hotel pharmacy.

Sage's. 1255 N. State; 944–1557. The ultimate in intimate—a nine-stool bar with two tables, fireplace, Hogarth etchings, dance floor. Classic, very Gold Coast.

Salvatore's. 525 W. Arlington Place; 528–1200. The place to go if you like to listen to a pianist with dramatic flair. A special and elegant locale in Lincoln Park.

Toulouse. 49 W. Division; 944–2606. This 65-seat restaurant also features a piano bar. Posh with French flair.

BARS

Sports Bars

Most major cities, particularly those with big-name sports franchises, have loyal sports fans. But Chicago, with professional football, basketball, soccer, hockey and baseball teams, tends to go off the deep end where sports are concerned. The result has been a whole new category of entertainment called the sports bar. These have been springing up not only near ballparks and stadiums, but also in the heart of night-life districts as well. Some are owned by local sports celebrities, others by sports enthusiasts.

Bernie's Tavern. 3664 N. Clark St.; 525–1898. In Chicago it is considered a badge of honor to be labeled a "bleacher bum." This is the place a lot of them congregate to commiserate about losses and to drink to victory.

Cubby Bear Lounge. 1059 W. Addison; 327–1662. One could describe this as a neighborhood bar with a split personality. Located directly across from Wrigley Field's front gates, it is packed wall-to-wall with boisterous, cheering, thirsty Chicago Cubs fans on game days. But since the "Cubbies" play only day games at Wrigley, the bar takes on a completely different mood at night. Then bands playing punk, new wave, and next wave rock try to see if they can make as much noise as the sports fans. Prides itself on being "aggressively entertaining." Inexpensive.

Hunt Club Taverne and Grill. Racine and Armitage; 549–3020. Bears' star Gary Fencik opened this new place and locals stop by hoping to see gridiron headliners. Noted for its popular outdoor area.

McCuddy's. 35th St. across from Comiskey Park, home of the Chicago White Sox. There are no phones, probably because the noise level on game days is so raucous no one would hear it ring.

Murphy's. Waveland and Sheffield Ave.; 281–5356. This is across from the bleachers entrance to Wrigley Field and a gathering spot for more Cubs followers who label themselves "bleacher bums."

Panzerotti's. 24 W. Elm. 266–0106. Has a three-hole putting green on its second level. Really buzzes on sports nights. Uniforms cover the walls.

She–Nannigans. 16 W. Division; 649–9093. Waitresses dressed as cheerleaders serve a singles crowd surrounded by paraphernalia ranging from Muhammad Ali's framed old workout clothes to a basketball backboard edged by walls of sports stars' autographs. 14 television monitors pick up games from across the country via satellite dish on the roof.

Ultimate Sports Bar and Grill. 356 W. Armitage; 477–4630. This was one of the first new-wave sports bars, complete with boxing ring and basketball hoop. Popular with Yuppie singles.

Z's Sports Tap. 1139 N. Dearborn; 337–3201. One of the old-timers where regulars insist it is sports and not the singles scene that attracts them.

There are many bars in Chicago that a visitor may want to explore and still stay within the area of his or her hotel. A selection of these, designated by area, follows.

Downtown

Most of the bars described in this section are the midday/early-evening variety catering to business types, but they are also worth a traveler's attention. Granddaddy of them all and on most lists of all-time favorites is **Berghoff's**, 17 W. Adams, which has been pleasing customers since 1898. This beautifully wood-paneled, traditional Old World restaurant looks like a transplant from Heidelberg or Munich. One of its many unique attractions is its turn-of-the-century stand-up bar serving the gemutlichkeit Berghoff family's own brands of whiskey and beer, plus a varied menu of sandwiches and salads. A tremendously popular spot with Chicagoans and tourists who enjoy the bar, and lunch and dinner in its exceptional dining rooms. This is one of Chicago's finest and a great dollar value.

Jesse Livermore's Champagne Cognac Bar, 401 S. LaSalle St., is in the Traders Building, originally built in 1914 as the Fort Dearborn Hotel. The beautifully restored property is now a historic landmark. Plush, green velvet sofas, rich Honduran mahogany, and a fireplace provide great atmosphere for sampling 14 diffferent kinds of cognac. **The Sign of the Trader** in the lobby of the Board of Trade, 141 W. Jackson, and **The Broker's Inn**, 323 S. LaSalle, is also popular with traders and brokers who begin arriving around 2 or 3 P.M.

Various professions tend to congregate at specific sites. **Bynion's**, 327 S. Plymouth Court, is a restaurant and bar frequented by U.S. attorneys who work in the nearby Federal Building. So is **Harry's Bar**, 18 W. Quincy. Commuters have their after-work gathering spots, too. One is **The Tiny Tap**, 112½ N. Clinton, west of the Northwestern Station. Another is **Cafe Bohemia** across from Amtrak's Union Station at 138 S. Clinton. **King Arthur's**, 212 N. Canal, is an English pub that's also been around for a long time. **Yesterday's Party**, 230 N. Michigan, is a popular homeward-bound stop with office workers in that area.

Slightly south is **Printers Row** at 550 S. Dearborn. This newly emerging south Loop district was once the city's printshop neighborhood and this restoration of an old printer's building dating to 1897 is typical of the area.

"Off" Downtown

This area begins just north of the Chicago River. When the giant Merchandise Mart and Apparel Center empty out at noon and 5 P.M., many occupants head for **Mad Anthony's** on the 15th floor of the Holiday Inn at the Apparel Center, 530 N. Orleans. For an even closer view of the river, there's **The Marina 300** in the bottom floor of Marina Tower, 300 N. State St. Ask to sit near one of its picture windows for a good view of the riverboat traffic and the lowering and raising of those giant bridges. At least once a year *The Medusa Challenger* comes through and works its jinx on bridges that go up and refuse to come down.

Many bars in this region tend to have an ethnic flavor. **O'Sullivan's Public House** at 495 N. Milwaukee is Chicago-Irish with the kind of turn-of-the-century bar that television fans remember from John Wayne movies. Just across the street is the **Como Inn**, 546 N. Milwaukee, a large, sprawling Italian restaurant decorated in Chicago-Italian baroque. Its bar and **Cafe Pappagallo** serve amaretto coffee and Italian wines to a large repeat business. One of the best deep-dish pizza restaurants in town is **Pizzeria Uno**, 29 E. Ohio, and celebrities who make the Chicago scene sing its praises. **Sogni Dorati** is an expensive nouvelle restaurant at 660 N. Wells, while **Little Joe's**, 1041 W. Taylor St. near the University of Illinois campus, is a folksy reminder of the city's Little Italy district.

One of Greek Town's liveliest restaurants is the **Greek Islands**, 200 S. Halsted, with a bar that favors ouzo, retsina wines, and the subtle aroma of moussaka, oregano, and feta cheese. The music may lure you down the block to the **Courtyards of Plaka**, 340 S. Halsted, and **The Parthenon**, 314 S. Halsted. It's almost like bar-hopping in Athens.

In a completely different mood, the **Baton Show Lounge**, 436 N. Clark, labels itself "home of the most lavish female impersonator shows in the world." Reservations 644–5269. Open 8 P.M. Wednesdays through Sundays.

North Michigan Avenue

There is a small section of Chicago "underground," just north and south of the Chicago River below Michigan Ave. and Wacker Dr., that actually has two levels, with duplicate streets above and below ground. The out-of-town visitor who stumbles onto it feels he has descended into a mysterious underground maze. Not surprisingly, some of the city's more conversation-stopping bars are located here. **Billy Goat Inn**, 430 N. Michigan, is one of them, reached by staircase from the upper level of Michigan Ave. It is a favorite haunt with newspaper employees who work only footsteps away (*The Chicago Tribune* is at 435 N. Michigan), and many a column has been hastily typed at one end of its bar. Also accessible from that lower level (as well as from the upper level) is **Riccardo's**, 437 N. Rush St., which caters to the same news clientele. Young, single professionals gravitate to the **Brassary**, 645 N. Michigan, while **Jerry's Deli & Pub**, 215 E. Grand, specializes in sandwiches and beverages to go.

Up on the main street level is **The Boul Mich**, 538 N. Michigan Ave. The **Gold Star Sardine Bar**, a few blocks east at 666 N. Lake Shore Dr., is locally acclaimed for its reheated White Castle hamburgers, a local taste phenomenon. **The Inkwell**, 226 E. Ontario, is across from the Museum of Contemporary Art, near CBS, and attracts the young media crowd.

Rush Street

Over the years Rush Street has gained the unenviable reputation as the place conventioneers go to for a night on the town. Their free-spending ways have attracted the expected number of B-girls, muggers, pickpockets, jackrollers, strip joints, porn shops, and other sleaze. Portions of it have, unfortunately, degenerated into something between the Bowery and the Barbary Coast. Other sections have interesting shops, restaurants, and very "in" bars.

Because Rush Street is the oldest nightclub section in town, adventure-seeking travelers still gravitate there. Do it with your eyes wide open and your hand on your wallet. It is pricey, crowded, and often rough and tough. Under no circumstances walk west. A public-housing project nearby has been the scene of many violent crimes.

Obviously what we're talking about here are the dives. There are also a number of trendy, fashionable nightspots like former Bear linebacker **Doug Buffone's Sweetwater**, 1028 N. Rush, which attracts sports figures and upscale singles. So does **Harry's Cafe**, at 1035, and **Jay's** at 1021 Rush. Other area notables are **Arnie's**, 1030 N. State; **Acorn** on Oak, 116 E. Oak St.; and **Hippopotamus**, 50 E. Oak.

Potpourri

Of the grand total of 6,300 liquor licenses it is hard to pick out all the headliners in this space. As neighborhoods change and evolve, new finds emerge almost overnight. But scattered close to the city, in such diverse locations as Old Town, Lincoln Park, and ethnic sections of town, are a number of establishments regularly mentioned by Chicagoans. Places like **Butch McGuire's**, 20 W. Division, who practically invented the singles scene. There's **The Old Town Alehouse**, 219 W. North, a colorful reminder of the Old Town area's glory days. **Geja's Cafe**, downstairs at 340 W. Armitage, manages to successfully combine flamenco guitarists with fondue. **John Barleycorn**, 658 W. Belden (2300 block of N. Lincoln), is another longtime survivor. Patrons like to sip their brew while listening to classical music and watching slides featuring the Art Institute's collection.

La Canasta, 3511 N. Clark, features pitchers of sangria and margaritas served on an enclosed patio, along with Mexican beer and exotic frozen drinks. The informal outdoor concept continues to grow in popularity. **Maple Tree Inn**, 10730 S. Western, features Cajun creole cooking and outdoor summer dining. Their bar serves a fiery Cajun martini and Dixie Beer in long-neck bottles. **Moody's Pub**, 5910 N. Broadway, also opens a lively outdoor beer garden in summer.

Those seeking traditional ethnic atmosphere will find it at places like **Zum Deutschen Eck**, 2924 N. Southport, in a large German restaurant reminiscent of a Rhineland inn. Costumed staff serve imported beverages. **Resi's Bierstube**, 2034 W. Irving Park, has Bavarian flavor, over 50 beers, and an impressive beer garden with grapes growing on trellises. **Schulein's**, 2100 W. Irving Park, features three generations' accumulation of memorabilia. One of their treasures is a copy of the Volstead Act, which was nailed on the front door by federal marshalls who closed it as a speakeasy back when mob beer trucks were trying to avoid Elliot Ness.

For more "finds," pick up a free copy of the *Reader*, which is distributed all over town and lists the latest entertainment happenings on the local scene.

If none of the above interests you, remember neighboring Evanston was the home of Frances Willard, and the gray board and batten house where she lived is still headquarters of the Women's Christian Temperance Union which she founded. It is open to visitors.

Take a travel expert along on your next trip...

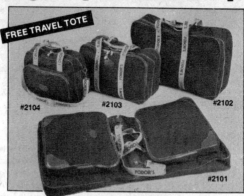

FREE TRAVEL TOTE

#2104   #2103   #2102

#2101

FODOR'S®
the travel experts.

When you spend fifty years in the travel business you're bound to learn a few things about quality luggage.

Basically you want it to be ruggedly made so it withstands the inevitable stresses of not-too-careful handling, and you want it to keep its good looks after many miles of hard use. Sounds simple. The problem is, luggage like that often costs a lot more than your whole vacation. **Not any more.**

Fodor's has found a line of luggage produced in the U.S.A. that meets our highest standards yet sells for a surprisingly reasonable price. We like it so much, in fact, that we've put our own name on it. We're sure you'll agree, this is truly a travel bargain.

100% cotton canvas treated for storm and water repelency, genuine saddle hide leather trim. Hand crafted made in U.S.A., durable extra strength cotton webbing, YKK nylon zippers.

Buy the complete set and save $50.00 plus you will receive a matching 18″ travel tote free. Retail value $20.

Special
Introductory
Offer: **$280** Complete Set

Also available as separate pieces:

Item 2101 —46″ Garment Bag with adjustable should strap, holds 4 suits or 6 dresses with many large compartments for all your accessories. Specially designed zipper closing creates an extra large storage compartment **$145**

Item 2102 —26″ Pullman Bag easily handles all your travel items **$65**

Item 2103 —21″ Triple zipper multipurpose carry on with convenient adjustable shoulder strap and special hanger fixture for one suit **$70**

Item 2104 —16″ Multi compartment tote with shoulder strap and multipurpose back pocket which will accommodate a tennis racket **$50**

All styles available in either brown or navy canvas with genuine saddle hide leather trim.
1 year guarantee against all damages with normal wear.

Order Now. Call 1-800-228-2028 Ext. 204

VISA **MasterCard** Charge it to your VISA or MASTER CARD
If lost or stolen you can reorder at a 10% discount.
We will gold stamp up to three initials free of charge.
Add $7.50 for shipping and handling. New Jersey residents add 6% sales tax.
Identification tags free with purchase. Allow 2-3 weeks for delivery.

INDEX